University Libraries

To __6/17/88_____ Date _____

From _____ Ext. _____

Melva

Scott wondered about cutter for this.

Thanks—

PH

Please give book back to Jan.

- ☐ review & comment
- ☐ per our conversation
- ☐ for your information
- ☐ at your request
- ☐ for your file
- ☐ forward to _____
- ☐ what should I reply?
- ☐ thank-you

DEVELOPMENT OF MASS MARKETING

The International
Conference on
Business
History **7**

DEVELOPMENT OF MASS MARKETING

The Automobile and Retailing Industries

Proceedings of the Fuji Conference

edited by
AKIO OKOCHI
KOICHI SHIMOKAWA

UNIVERSITY OF TOKYO PRESS

658.15
I61f
1980

UTP 3334–47173–5149
ISBN 0–86008–288–1

ORGANIZING COMMITTEE FOR THE SECOND SERIES INTERNATIONAL CONFERENCE ON BUSINESS HISTORY
1979–1983

Chairman:	Okochi, Akio	(University of Tokyo)
Treasurer:	Watanabe, Hisashi	(Kyoto University)
Secretary:	Yuzawa, Takeshi	(Gakushuin University)
	Daito, Eisuke	(Tohoku University)
	Hara, Terushi	(Waseda University)
	Ishikawa, Kenjiro	(Doshisha University)
	Kita, Masami	(Soka University)
	Miyamoto, Matao	(Osaka University)
	Udagawa, Masaru	(Hosei University)
Advisory Board:	Nakagawa, Keiichiro	(University of Tokyo)
	Kobayashi, Kesaji	(Ryukoku University)
	Morikawa, Hidemasa	(Hosei University)
	Yasuoka, Shigeaki	(Doshisha University)
	Yonekawa, Shin-ichi	(Hitotsubashi University)

Participants

Project Leader for the Second Meeting:
Shimokawa, Koichi (Hosei University)

Blaich, Fritz
(Universität Regensburg)
Church, Roy A.
(University of East Anglia)
Daito, Eisuke
(Tohoku University)
Fridenson, Patrick
(Université de Paris X
[Nanterre])
Hara, Terushi
(Waseda University)
Ishikawa, Kenjiro
(Doshisha University)
Lim, Jong Won
(Seoul National University
Livesay, Harold C.
(State University of New York)
Maeda, Kazunori
(Komazawa University)
McCallion, Stephen W.
(Ohio State University)

Miyamoto, Matao
(Osaka University)
Nakagawa, Keiichiro
(University of Tokyo)
Okochi, Akio
(University of Tokyo)
Toba, Kin'ichiro
(Waseda University)
Udagawa, Masaru
(Hosei University)
Watanabe, Hisashi
(Kyoto University)
Wilkins, Mira
(Florida International
University)
Yamada, Makiko
(Sangyonoritsu University)
Yamazaki, Kiyoshi
(Toyo University)
Yuzawa, Takeshi
(Gakushuin University)

CONTENTS

PREFACE

The second meeting of the Second Series International Conference on Business History was held January 5-8, 1980, at Fuji Education Center, Shizuoka, Japan, under the joint sponsorship of the Business History Society of Japan and the Taniguchi Foundation.

The Organizing Committee for the International Conference on Business History decided on the theme "Marketing in the Course of Industrialization and Internationalization" for the second meeting. Our initial aim was to trace the development of modern mass marketing and to describe the historical interactions between it and traditional systems of commerce. We hoped to do this through an international comparison of two branches of industry, in one of which a traditional system of commerce was dominant, and the other where a mass marketing system was utilized.

Accordingly, the Organizing Committee asked Professor Koichi Shimokawa, a leading specialist in the history of the automobile industry and marketing, to accept the role of Project Leader. Professor Shimokawa, in cooperation with the Board of the Organizing Committee, designed and organized the second meeting and, for the first time since the start of the series of Fuji Conferences on Business History, the number of papers solicited from abroad exceeded those from Japan.

The following Proceedings are a full record of the papers read at the meeting and relevant comments.

On behalf of the Board of the Organizing Committee, I would like to express my sincere thanks to Professor Shimokawa for his effort in editing these Proceedings and preparing a summary of the discussions. I would also like to thank the Taniguchi Foundation for its support of the meeting and publication of this book.

December 1980

Akio Okochi
General Editor and Chairman
of the Organizing Committee
for the International Conference on Business History

INTRODUCTION

To date, although many historical studies on traditional commerce and distribution have been made, little research has been done on marketing, despite its important role in industrialization. Modern marketing has been particularly neglected among the few works on the subject which are available.

Each country's historical development has affected, to some extent, the various aspects of its marketing growth. However, perhaps the rapid economic growth and industrialization during the 20th century has had the greatest impact. This is particularly true for the period from the 1920s and following World War II.

What are the main elements of modern marketing? An integration of mass production and mass distribution of consumer durable goods for a mass market will allow international marketing between countries and will inevitably have a modifying effect on the commercial and distributive ways of each country.

This book treats the subject of marketing in several countries from an historical standpoint, with particular reference to the automobile as a common denominator. Focusing on this typical consumer durable item, we can somewhat identify and compare the special historical and international features of modern marketing. We can also notice those NICS (New Industrialized Countries) where marketing has not yet become a factor to be considered and only matters of distribution are discussed.

The first eight papers contained in this book are primarily concerned with the origin and development of automobile marketing in five countries—Britain, France, Germany, Japan and the United States. They also refer, however, to the subject in an international

context from the end of the 19th century to the post-war period.
The last two papers deal with the history of distribution development in the retail field.

In the first article, Shimokawa, as project leader, compares the
special features of automobile marketing in the United States and
Japan. He also indicates points of discussion to be taken up by the
other participants. In the following paper Wilkins is concerned with
international auto marketing from an historical point of view. The
next article treats 19th century precursors to automobile marketing
in the United States by Livesay.

The succeeding four articles are concerned with the development
of the auto market, its demands, marketing techniques and distribution channels in developed countries. Church presents an
historical comparison of the marketing situation in Britain and
the United States before World War II, and Udagawa offers
details on the introductory period of auto marketing in Japan.
The article by Blaich analyzes the history of the distribution sector
of the German car industry, and the next treatise by Fridenson
sketches the complete story of the French automobile industry and
marketing from 1890 to 1979. Yamazaki's article is concerned
with the internationalization process of the Japanese industry in
its more recent history.

The last two papers offer contrasting analyses of the history of
the retail distribution sectors of two countries. Lim describes the
more recent history of Korea in which the development and evolution of retailing and distribution became the bridge toward modern
marketing, especially auto marketing. The paper by Maeda explains
the historical evolution of the retailing industry in Japan from
pre-war to post-war times.

In the summary chapter, a table lists various factors affecting
traditional commerce and modern marketing in both domestic and
international situations. Several points raised in participants' discussions are also noted, among them: special features of modern
marketing compared with traditional commerce and distribution,
domestic and international aspects of modern marketing, formation
of the mass market and the mature market, role of the automobile

franchise, auto distribution channels, sales financing, and special characteristics of auto sales as practiced in different countries.

Koichi Shimokawa

PART I

COMPARATIVE STUDY IN THE DEVELOPMENT OF MARKETING

Marketing History in the Automobile Industry: The United States and Japan

Koichi Shimokawa
Hosei University

Introduction

In an overview of the history of commerce and marketing, we can find, in each nation, specific features which reflect economic development, cultural patterns, commercial practices, distribution systems and particular market structures. As industrialization and mass production developed in the more advanced countries, and when mass consumption appeared in these nations, systematized marketing—which is different from traditional commerce and marketing—developed as modern marketing. This systematized marketing, based on a comprehensive managerial strategy whose objective was the actual creation of a market, involved, over time, an integrated program of market forecasting, production policy, pricing policy, market channeling and sales promotion. Historically, it was formed at a time when large-scale manufacturers, who were mass producing consumer durable goods, combined mass distribution and mass production for the mass market, and in so doing began to create a new market. Therefore, modern marketing means a comprehensive management system based on the combination of mass production and mass distribution. This does not eliminate the possibility of the creation of a modern marketing system by a mass retailer combining with a mass producer.

These modern marketing techniques emerged most quickly and in their purest form in the United States. It was here, where mass production originated, that consumer durable goods were produced and shipped to markets most rapidly. Two factors in particular

3

account for this. First, in order to increase labor efficiency and to introduce new technology in a situation where there was a structural shortage of skilled labor, producers developed product specialization and work standardization (typified by the American, or interchangeable parts system). This enabled the United States to pioneer mass production techniques. Second, as a relatively new nation the United States was little encumbered by traditional consumption habits, traditional commercial customs or traditional—and intricate—distribution structures. This meant, with the growth of industrialization, the rapid rise in urban population and the development of transportation and communication networks, a mass market which accepted mass-distributed standardized products could be created rapidly. These two factors interacted to lay the basis for modern marketing as a system of management which mass-sold mass-produced commodities for a mass market and which actively set out to create a new market.

We can see the origin of modern marketing most typically in late 19th century consumer durable goods industries—sewing machines, watches, agricultural equipment, cash registers, typewriters, and the like. But it is in the automobile industry that we can find the most typical advanced modern marketing in the area of consumer durable goods. Here, we can find a unified control of distribution and mass production processes by a large manufacturer, the achievement of mass sales and establishment of a management technique system for creating a new market with fair profit. The center of this structure consists in integrated product and sales policies based on market research, and a systematized integration of various organizational measures. To examine the development of automobile marketing, it will be best to look into its distinguishing characteristic—i.e., to focus on historical changes in dealer policy. By clarifying the methods automobile manufacturers used to establish mass sales systems in the process of creating a complete mass production system, we should be able in turn to understand the establishment and development of automobile marketing.

Therefore, we should first examine automobile marketing, the pattern of which is most firmly established. We need to examine the industry's introduction or establishment in industrialized countries, with particular attention to dealer policies and franchise systems. Then, we should clarify how it affected the distribution structure and the development of retailing industries in each country. By so doing, we can make clear the position and role of automobile marketing in the history of marketing development in each country. From this, an international comparison of automobile marketing might be possible. Furthermore, it is necessary to examine the role of international automobile marketing in transferring marketing techniques, and problems which have arisen in this regard in the respective countries.

At the same time, in discussing automobile marketing, we should discuss marketing in the New Industrialized Countries (NICS), where automobile marketing has not yet been completely developed. Here, we would like to analyze distribution structures and retailing in these nations, and clarify the present situation and future prospects with regard to introducing modern marketing. On this basis we can try to find points of agreement between NICS' marketing structures and those of the typical modern automobile industry.

On the basis of these points, I would like to discuss the formation and development of dealer policies and franchise systems in the United States automobile industry, where automobile marketing was first established, and then to relate this kind of automobile marketing to marketing history.

I. Automobile Marketing in the Early Period of the United States —Origin and Establishment of the Automobile Franchise System —

In viewing automobile marketing history in the United States, we can find two general tendencies. The first is that automobile marketing started as a sales organization-led marketing process and has been transformed into a manufacturer-led one. The second is that middleman-like sales organizations in the automobile marketing channels were gradually eliminated as modern automobile marketing techniques were established.

If we describe the general steps in the establishment of automobile marketing in the United States, we will be able to show the outline of each step of its history. At first, there was a variety of kinds of sales organization in automobile distribution channels. This was followed by a tendency toward the relative superiority of distributor and dealer. Next came the formation of the franchise system, and then a change from a free and open franchise system to an exclusive franchise system. This formation of an exclusive franchise system was combined with a situation where auto manufacturers were establishing mass production systems. Finally, systematized marketing based on sales planning and market forecasting came of age in the late 1920s. Between the 1930s and the 1950s, the most notable feature of automobile marketing in the United States was the modification of the exclusive franchise system by public policy regulation.

The general feature of automobile marketing is the establishment of the industry's base as a mass production industry. By establishment of mass production in the industry, the need for the formation of dealer systems and franchise systems, itself a response to this trend, was further strengthened. The industry had prior to this tried to solve the sales problem without an established dealer or franchise system, but the sales and distribution problem was quickly becoming critical in the industry because of the rapid rise of the mass production system. But this problem could not be solved by resorting to the established distribution system because there were too many problems in auto distribution to adopt it. The price of automobiles was very expensive compared with other consumer durable goods, and purchasing them through sales outlets required cash or advance payments. In addition, outlets were charged for promotional costs, had to carry seasonal inventories of automobiles and regular inventories of replacement parts, and also had to provide after-sales service. Consequently, the seller was required to make a working capital investment that could be greater than that of the automobile maker.[1] Under these circumstances, automobile makers depended on a wide range of channels, such as agents, department stores, mail order houses, and branch stores, because they themselves lacked credit arrangements and sufficient capital.[2] By so doing, they were released from the credit function in sales activity, and were able to secure parts on credit from suppliers and apply the deposits received as sales payments to these auto parts suppliers. This is the general pattern of automobile sales in the early automobile industry in the United States. Auto sales in this period, then, were profitable when business was good, but in general the business involved a good deal of risk. After all, the makers found their condition inadequate for the organization of specialized dealers or distributors, much less for sales financing.

From around 1907, by which time automobile production had made steady progress and the risk to makers had decreased, distributors with wealthy financial backing began to appear quickly. With an expanding market, the maker came to depend greatly on such well-financed distributors.[3] These distributors, however, provided more than just wholesaling and warehousing functions, and began direct selling activities. The development of specialized automobile dealers into a complete dealer organization, however, was impossible because of the remaining uncertainty and capital requirements.[4]

In addition to these two kinds of sales outlets, there was another outlet, the branch store. This branch store was a warehousing depot as well as a maker's direct sales outlet.[5] It functioned in the same way as the distributor, though there was some limit because of a shortage of capital and of managerial forces for selling; in this respect it differed from distributors, who invested large amounts of capital and took risks themselves. Until a maker-led dealer network appeared, however, the branch store took on some of its functions. It was generally established in areas without distributors, and its function in time changed from that of wholesale and retail to wholesale only.

It is difficult, they say, to clarify how the automobile dealer system emerged in the history of automobile marketing.[6] There was no clear-cut distinction between agent and dealer. Most dealer-like retailers handled carriages, bicycles, agricultural equipment, and furniture.[7] A considerable number of them became automobile dealers but they experienced financing difficulties at first. Large amounts of capital were needed for one to develop as an independent automobile dealer, but this financing problem made it impossible to complete a well-organized dealer network which was able to respond to the industry's requirements. Despite the difficulty involved in the development of a dealer organization, after 1907 the development of a dealership system by free entry was increasingly facilitated not only by the decline of risk but also by the improving profit potential of final automobile sales.

From 1907 to the beginning of mass production in the early 1910s, makers increasingly sought to establish their own marketing policies in response to the pressures generated by the mass production system. They also began to consider how to develop specialized dealerships and a sales and distribution network of their own. For example, during the 1908–1910 period, makers dropped the designation 'agency' from the franchise agreement and made provisions under which dealers were given "exclusive sales" rights; prior to this, contracts with agents or dealers were loosely written, without contractor responsibility.[8] But at this point, the purpose was more one of making the maker-dealer relationship equal than one in which the maker gained control over the dealer.[9]

As a result, when makers began to deal actively with sales problems, the status and function of the distributor was already well established. The distributor's activities allowed the maker to concentrate his efforts on production, while the distributor filled the gap, particularly the financial gap, between maker and dealer. He also provided the warehousing function needed because of the seasonality of sales and the serving of distant markets. Moreover, the distributor was better able to build up a dealer organization than was the maker. From his knowledge of the sales territories he served, the distributor was better able to identify competent dealers and conclude contracts with them.[10]

As mentioned above, the distributor's strengthened position reflected the relatively weakened positions of the maker and dealer; if the maker's position later strengthened, the distributor's would weaken or he would become a dealer.

In any case, as the distributor's function developed, the content of the franchise agreement which defined the relationship between makers and distributors or dealers was greatly changed. In the initial form, the agreement roughly set out the sales territory and gave the right or license for automobile sales in exchange for fixed compensation. In the new form the maker's position was elevated, especially with respect to terms of payment, which were now clearly defined.[11]

Even though the tendency was toward clarified terms in the franchise agreement in the 1910s, the situation was still confused by the large number of makers, each using its own form of franchise. Consequently, there were many forms coexisting in the sales and distribution systems and it was not unusual for a maker to use any number of sales and distribution systems concurrently. Until the early 1920s there were five types of sales and distribution systems. It is very interesting that the maker-dealer direct distribution system, which is most common today, was the type most rarely used.[12]

The situation later changed, to some extent as a result of the rapid decline in the function of the distributor with the coming of mass marketing of low-priced automobiles. The function of the branch store also declined somewhat later, as almost all large-scale auto makers went to a direct sales system with dealers. The strong position of the distributor was dependent upon: (1) the maker's volume remaining relatively low; (2) a large number of makers and types of automobiles; (3) makers and dealers having small financial resources; and (4) concentrated production centers with a broad market area.[13]

These four became less important with the start of the mass production of standard, popularly-priced cars, epitomized by the famous Model T Ford. The tendency for geographical decentralization of assembly plants rendered the role of the distributor at the center of the dealer network almost meaningless. Although the branch store's position rose temporarily just after the start of mass production, it soon lost its position because it could not develop effective sales management or adapt to the used car market. As the maker developed financial strength and as dealers likewise improved their financial status, it was possible to achieve the desired merchandising by retail dealers in direct contact with makers.[14]

As mentioned above, the transformation in automobile marketing in the 1910–1925 growth period was to channel-oriented marketing focused on new market cultivation stimulated by mass production. In this channel-oriented marketing policy the dealer's franchise stressed the equality of maker and dealer rather than the building of a competitive barrier to rival makers through exclusive dealership.

By the late 1920s direct distribution had strengthened and the content of the franchise agreement began to reflect the full development of the maker's marketing program. The establishment of the mass production system tended to lead to market saturation and the core of demand shifted from new demand to replacement demand. In addition, competition among the makers became more severe than before, and the maker strengthened his relationship with the retailer. The spread of direct distribution bypassed the distributor's wholesale function; makers now went through local assembly plants and local sales office operations. The storing and warehousing functions were divided between the maker and dealer.[15]

Accordingly, the development of a direct relationship between maker and dealer reflected close supervision, which made for more effective sales promotion and sales planning. Sales promotion and planning required sufficient parts inventories, uniformity of service procedures, reconditioning of used cars, and sound methods of merchandising. By building his own sales organization through direct distribution, the maker was able to integrate sales promotion and sales and production planning. The strengthened relationship with the dealer allowed the maker to include the dealer in his marketing system.[16]

With these developments, the franchise agreement went through major changes. From agreement over a principle of equality between maker and dealer the emphasis changed to exclusive dealing.[17] As a result, there was rapid collapse in the distribution mechanism that had a sharp division of functions between makers, distributors, and dealers. The content of the agreement came to spell out the inclusion and integration of the dealer in the maker's marketing system. In this situation the dealer's exclusive relationship with the maker was stressed. The merit of this relationship was in its total systematization of combined production and sales activity under a close relationship on both sides. This relationship also extended to parts distribution, maintenance service, and the used car distribution network.

With the intensification of competition among the big makers, each maker began to move into a marketing policy emphasizing differentiated product competition in the battle for a market share.

II. Development of Automobile Marketing in the United States —Sales Financing Support, Automobile Marketing Refining, and Changes in the Franchise System—

The introduction of a franchise system with stress on an exclusive clause for dealers was a natural development under the maker's marketing policy of differentiated product competition. Under these conditions, the dealer became a convenient and suitable extension of the maker as the vanguard of the maker's marketing, and yet was himself a risk-taker in the market.

The assumption of market risk by the dealer, as auto sales grew rapidly, and the development of mass production by the maker could not have been possible without the support of sales financing.

The history of installment sales in the United States began in the latter half of the 19th century in the furniture, sewing machine, piano, and harvester industries, among others. Sales financing in the automobile industry began after 1915, when the number of sales financing companies which began to regularly buy sales contracts from auto dealers increased rapidly. Specialized automobile financing companies were necessary from the start here because commercial banks were too conservative to create new credit arrangements for the discounting of installment notes. The sales financing company, as that financial intermediary, provided the service, and by transforming the notes of individual buyers into a form of commercial paper better adapted to bank operations, permitted a wider circulation of such paper through the banks. In addition, by pooling the notes of many buyers, the company provided a mechanism for a wider distribution of risks.[18] As a result, these rapidly developing automobile sales financing companies in time established a basic pattern of operations at two levels of finance, wholesale and retail.[19] In the field of wholesale financing, funds were made available to dealers upon the basis of their promissory notes or their acceptance of notes. In the field of retail financing, the dealer received a down payment of 30 to 50 percent from the buyer and the balance in the form of five to sixteen monthly installment payments, eight to ten installments being most common.[20]

Although commercial banks were hesitant about entering directly into automobile sales financing, the ultimate source of working capital required in sales financing companies was the commercial bank, because of its high interest rates.

The years 1921 to 1925 are regarded as a boom period in terms of organization and expansion of sales finance companies. In 1922, for example, there were about one thousand companies handling automobile promissory notes, and the number increased to about seventeen hundred in 1925. The installment credit balance of these companies was about $248 million in 1923. By 1926, however, the total had risen rapidly and was three times as much as in 1923—about $750 million.[21] In 1913, the number of installment sales as a percent of total automobile sales was zero; in 1925, however, installment sales of new and used cars was around 75 percent of the total.[22] What made possible this rapid increase in the number of sales finance companies was, of course, the rapid rise of automobile sales as part of the consumer durable goods boom. Yet the rapid increase in sales was also a result of the loosening of installment payment terms and changes in sales financing methods.

In the 1920s, three types of sales finance companies had emerged.[23] The first type was the pure independent who was small and engaged in financing other consumer durable goods besides automobiles. The second type specialized in automobile sales financing and, although financially independent from the makers, was usually related to a particular maker with respect to the kind of cars it financed. The third type was a subsidiary of a maker and handled only the maker's car models and the dealers selling those models. The leading example of this third type is the General Motors Acceptance Corporation (GMAC).

Of these three types, the second and third played active roles in the development of automobile marketing and sales financing. The first type was predominant in terms of numbers and its share of sales financing in the 1920s. Following further concentration among makers, however, the second and third types came to the forefront. Such second-type companies as Commercial Investment Trust and Commercial Credit Company, tied up with Ford and Chrysler, had their relationship strengthened to the point where they became third-type sales financing companies.[24]

GMAC was incorporated in 1919 with financial support from General Motors (GM). But it was not closely controlled by the latter, and bought notes on the sales of other makers' automobiles as well as other things.[25] After 1925 GM began to adopt a new franchise system that stressed exclusive dealership; this move was basic to the structural changes it had initiated. As a result, GMAC, controlled by GM, began to take a central role in this strategy by stressing exclusive control of dealers. Franchised dealers were restrained from selling non-GM cars, and were required to arrange all sales financing through GMAC. In time GM's control of its exclusive dealers through GMAC resulted in a smoothly operating system.

The expansion in installment credit by sales financing companies allowed capital-short dealers to push sales. Likewise, dealers were able to reduce their dependency on distributors and, by establishing the function of the dealer as superior to the branch store, provided conditions appropriate for the establishment of a direct sales system.[26]

The independent sales finance companies were the forerunners in setting up the credit arrangements described above. Later, the maker-related companies became the driving force behind the formation of the exclusive franchise system. Thus maker-related sales finance companies played the role of integrator in distribution and sales policy.[27]

As mentioned above, the equal relationship between maker and dealer, which involved distributors or branch stores as inter-mediaries, was replaced in the 1920s by the exclusive franchise system. Under this system, makers and dealers were directly con-nected; it was made possible by the growth of the big makers and the development of sales financing support. While called an exclusive franchise system, the new structure nonetheless varied with the individual maker's marketing techniques. This is apparent in a comparison of the marketing methods and dealer policies of General Motors and Ford.

In Ford's case, the remarkable success of the Model T from the 1910 meant that the company's market strategy tended to be governed by the production schedule for that car, on which the company's mass production system was based. This strategy, which aimed at market expansion and an increase in mass sales by concentrating only on the Model T, remained unchanged in the 1920s, even when the market began to be saturated. Ford compelled its dealers to make exclusive agreements with it although at the same time, in order to develop high-pressure marketing, it stressed their independence as business entities.

On the other hand, General Motors, under A. P. Sloan, had set up a new systematic business strategy and tried to challenge Ford in the 1920s, adopting different marketing and dealer policies. General Motors decentralized and adopted a policy of differentiated product marketing which included a coordinated, full-line product policy and the introduction of the popularly-priced Chevrolet as a direct challenge to the Model T.[28] Policy here was based on product differentiation, which in turn meant model changes, full-line market segmentation and the upgrading of the standard automobile. General Motors systematized demand forecasting and sales forecasting and, by scheduling production in accordance with information obtained thereby, established a uniform marketing system. Dealer policy was soon incorporated into this system. Prior to this, General Motors had had no general dealer policy since, having started as a holding company in combination with several medium-sized auto makers, there had been little uniformity in marketing policy among the different sectors of the organization.

General Motors carried out this organizational reform between 1921 and 1925. Its management strategy, as seen above, involved product differentiation and decentralization. The company also tried to keep fully informed about dealer stocks and to use this information, in combination with sales forecasts based on information received from the firm's general staff and from the operation division, to develop a systematic, coordinated production schedule.[29] Therefore, General Motors changed its traditional practice in which production schedules were set without reference to dealers' current sales volume, and considered that responsibility from the sales standpoint ceased with the delivery of the products to the dealer. This way of thinking persisted throughout most of the General Motors organization, except the Cadillac Division, until 1924.[30] By combining production schedules with sales forecasting and dealer inventory reports, General Motors was able to relate production to sales, and to profit thereby. At the same time, it recognized the need to form a well-organized dealer system and to understand the dealer business for the sake of higher sales efficiency on the part of the dealer. This meant that General Motors changed its earlier policy, which was to make as many cars as the factory could possibly turn out and then force dealers to take them, to a new policy where they would not require dealers to take cars in excess of what they could properly handle. The company thus enhanced the dealer's business efficiency, i.e., maker's business efficiency.[31]

In accordance with this new policy, General Motors substantially revised its franchise agreement in 1926. This revised agreement contained the following clauses:

1) A requirement that the dealer use the accounting system set up by General Motors.

2) A new "15 percent clause" whereby the dealer could not at any time be required to carry unsold cars in excess of 15 percent of his yearly allotment.

3) A requirement that the dealer contribute to the advertising fund and the used car disposal fund.

4) The prohibition on franchise agreement cancellation except on thirty days' notice.

5) A General Motors refund to the dealer with changes in new model prices.[32]

This new agreement clearly established the exclusive nature of the dealer's relationship with General Motors, but at the same time included features designed to help the dealer and to improve his position. The net effect was to systematize dealer policy by linking it to General Motors' overall marketing system. This meant not increased maker control over the dealer or maker domination through forced compliance with the terms of the agreement, but rather a promotion of dealer autonomy within the framework of General Motors' marketing policy and a coordination thereby of dealer activity with that policy.

Ford, on the other hand, pressured its dealers into exclusive contracts, stressed their function as sales organizations and kept them separate from the framework of company marketing policy. A typical example is Ford's 1929 franchise agreement: it allowed Ford to cancel franchises without prior notice and to change prices at any time without any obligation to make financial adjustments with dealers.[33] Ford deliberately rejected the idea of dealer participation in, and integration into, marketing policy, and continued to emphasize high-pressure marketing based on the production schedule. Its coordination of production policy with the production schedule amounted to an exclusive stress on production, and its policy stands in striking contrast to General Motors' coordination of dealer inventory reports and market and sales forecasts with its production schedule.

The basic elements of the marketing system and dealer policy which General Motors established in the 1920s were eventually adopted by Ford and Chrysler, and had a profound influence on automobile marketing in Europe and Japan. But even policy of the kind initiated by General Motors changed over time in response to new economic conditions and subsequent changes in strategy. The twin aspects of dealer policy—stress on the dealer's exclusive relationship with the maker and stress on the dealer's management autonomy—also changed with time.[34] The most important change came in the 1930s with the Great Depression and the resultant decline in auto sales and with the New Deal; the formation of a national dealers association (National Automobile Dealers Association) resulted in an increase in the power of dealers to bargain with makers for fair competition. Another related factor was the beginning of government regulation, with the establishment of the Federal Trade Commission and of anti-trust agencies. In the 1950s fierce oligopolistic competition between the "big three" and the frequent selection and dismissal of dealers intensified and the government responded with the newly enacted Good Faith Act and Truth-in-Labeling Law; this effectively meant the elimination of exclusive business clauses from franchise agreements.[35]

III. The Formation and Development of Automobile Marketing in Japan

Generally speaking, modern marketing began in Japan during the postwar period of rapid economic growth—i.e., from 1955, after the period of reconstruction. Both a mass production system for consumer durable goods and a mass consumption market were completely established during this period. The traditional distribution structure in Japan was extremely complex, divided as it was into many horizontal and vertical levels. This structure remained after the war, so that mass producers who rapidly emerged in the 1950s were not able to depend on traditional distribution channels or horizontal distributors, however large-scale their operations. Instead, they were forced to develop their own marketing system by forming their own distribution channels.

Modern marketing techniques existed in Japan to at least some degree even prior to World War II. Western influence had begun to affect consumption patterns, and new marketing techniques had been developed to handle some of the new, low-priced consumer goods (cosmetics, soap, western confectioneries, light bulbs, seasoning and the like). Department stores became increasingly common in the cities. But the mass market, such as it was, was one where production was limited to cheap goods and depended on a relatively small number of wealthy people in the cities.

The development of automobile marketing in Japan reflected the above situation. There was no systematic method of automobile marketing in Japan until after 1955, when mass production of passenger cars began. The system that developed was maker-led. Some marketing had, of course, been done in the prewar and immediate postwar periods, and this undoubtedly influenced subsequent developments in the field. The nature of automobile marketing in Japan prior to the 1950s was determined by the special nature of the nation's automobile market and production system. Before World War II, Western auto makers, Americans in particular, dominated the market for passenger cars. Customers were limited to the wealthy and the aristocracy, and to taxi drivers. Foreign domination of the market was possible because Japanese auto makers, while engaging in trial production, did not carry out mass production. Mass production depends on a balanced development of a wide range of production techniques—materials and engine production, dyecasting, stamping and the like—but there was no such balanced technological development in Japan at that time, and since Japan's military government required and fostered mass production only of trucks, this kind of development for passenger cars was not possible.

In any case, automobile techniques, the franchise system and dealer support mechanisms were introduced to Japan by General Motors and Ford when they began operating in Japan in the 1920s; once introduced, they underwent certain modifications in accordance with the nature of the market.

Toyota and Nissan, which emerged after the 1936 enactment of the Motor Vehicle Manufacture Law designed to protect domestic makers and shut out foreign competition, adopted and modified these techniques. Nissan led the way here with the production of the Datsun, the first mass-produced mini car, and establishment of a franchise system under the Nissan Motor Sales Company in which one dealership was set up in each prefecture. Nissan's innovation, carried out in the few years prior to the outbreak of the war, was the basis of the elimination of the dealer-led special agent system.

The most important marketing strategist in Japan at the time was Shōtarō Kamiya. Kamiya had served as sales manager for Japan GM, but resigned to take up the same position at Toyota Motors. Although he had acquired a grasp of GM's marketing techniques, at the same time he felt that the American franchise system, stressing as it did the contractual nature of the relationship between maker and dealer, was not appropriate to the Japanese context.[36] GM's franchise agreement required strict dealer observations of conditions related to the sales volume, method of sale and payment terms, among others; failure to follow the terms of the agreement to the letter resulted in an immediate cancellation of the franchise. This hardly made for good maker-dealer relations, and in addition failed to take into account the nature of traditional business relationships in Japan.

It was Kamiya's task to build a sales network for Toyota trucks at a time when the firm was in its infancy and product quality was uneven. His years with GM had enabled him to have contact with Japanese Chevrolet dealers; he was well aware of their dissatisfaction with the firm, and saw them as potential dealers for domestic cars. He persuaded Chevrolet dealers to become exclusive Toyota dealers and, with the help of regional capital investment, set up a dealer network.[37] In addition, he modified the franchise system model he had taken from GM, emphasizing a sense of corporate unity between maker and dealer and trying to humanize the relationship between the two parties.[38]

Wartime automobile distribution control and the difficulties of the immediate postwar period made it impossible for Kamiya to complete the market structure he envisioned; this was not done until after 1950, when Toyota Motor Sales (TMS) was separated from Toyota Motors. The separation of TMS came at a time of crisis brought on by a recession induced by the Dodge Plan and by a long strike; it was the result of the recommendation of a banking group that TMS be made a sales finance company along American lines. From the start, however, Toyota viewed TMS not simply as a sales financing organization, but as an instrument for the direction and development of its marketing system. In this way, the GM concept of market promotion could be made to fit the Japanese context, as Kamiya had planned before the war.[39]

As stated above, Kamiya had considered important the development of a relationship between maker and regional sources of capital that stressed group sentiment, but because of a low level of capital accumulation, regional capitalists were not always able to fund the dealer network fully. TMS supplied additional capital as needed to achieve the goal of one dealer per prefecture.[40]

TMS then borrowed from GM's dealer manual and introduced GM methods of financial management, credit management and inventory management, and standardized accounting procedures for dealers. It later adopted GM's information system, requiring dealers to submit reports on sales volume and sales terms every ten days.[41] The result was a change on the part of TMS from a production-oriented policy stressing the sale of as many cars as were produced, to a marketing-oriented policy stressing the production of as many cars as could be sold. Sales forecasting and planning were coordinated with production and project planning via close ties between Toyota Motors, TMS and the dealers.[42] The introduction of these marketing techniques came about as a result of TMS's active leadership and initiative, and reflected goals set by Toyota Motors. The system strengthened the corporate ties between maker and dealer and provided the basis for control of the dealer by the maker.

TMS also moved into providing installment credit as part of its marketing strategy. This was due at least in part to a lack of adequate credit facilities in Japan. The social prestige of distributors themselves was traditionally low and banks were not inclined to lend them money. On the maker's side, perennial capital shortages meant that there was no alternative but to turn to banks for financing; from the beginning, then, banks played a prominent role in providing funds to makers, who, in turn, made direct sales financing to dealers possible.[43] TMS became active in both wholesale and retail financing, establishing an installment sales system and, on the basis of its financial credibility, endorsing buyers' notes.[44]

In short, then, TMS carried out both distributing and sales financing functions; marketing in this case meant dealer management and operation of a franchise system together with sales financing. TMS's integrated marketing scheme had considerable influence on the development of marketing plans by other makers; Mitsubishi Motors and Daihatsu Motors, for example, patterned their systems after the one created by TMS. Exceptions to this rule were Nissan Motors and, later, Honda Motors, a relative newcomer that adopted a unique sales system quite different from those used by any of the other companies.

Nissan discontinued the operation of its Nissan Motor Sales Company after the war and began selling directly to dealers.[45] Prior to the war, Nissan dealers had been dealers for Japan Ford before working with Nissan, so that the influence on Nissan's marketing of the Ford system, with its franchise structure and stress on an exclusive franchise agreement, was considerable. Another factor was the dissolution of Nissan's main holding company as part of the occupation policy of breaking up the *zaibatsu*, which led to a considerable change in the top management personnel. New executives saw direct maker control over dealer as desirable, and the result was a system whereby Nissan exercised a good deal of control over the dealers, invested directly in them and oversaw dealers' sales financing. In terms of overall structure, then, Nissan resembled Ford; at least into the 1960s it was primarily technology oriented and, in a situation where sales presented no real problems as the market for passenger cars grew and as new lines were introduced, apparently saw no need to organize a sales finance company. But the acquisition of Prince Motors in 1966[46] and the rapid growth of car exports from about the same time, made Nissan modify its marketing system. After 1963 Nissan began setting up the Nissan Credit Company for consumer credit service.

Japanese automobile manufacturers differed, then, according to whether they distributed their product through motor sales companies or not, but most sold cars directly to dealers, one per prefecture set up by each maker. The stress therefore, was on a sense of group uniformity with emotional ties between maker and dealer, bolstered by capital investment and sales financing on the part of the maker, as well as other measures designed to help the dealer. All of this was, it could be said, at the expense of any sense of independence on the part of the dealer.

Honda Motors, on the other hand, set up regional offices and, through them, special sales agents.[47] Honda was the newest of the auto companies, having begun after the war as a manufacturer of motorcycles. Honda channeled its funds almost exclusively into equipment and technological development, and as a result had little room to invest in the construction of a sales network. First it organized a nationwide network of bicycle shops to sell its motorcycles and used them as the basis for developing special sales agents. These agents, such as they were, operated out of bicycle shops or, in some cases, farm equipment shops; there were many agents in each prefecture and no special territories or franchises. Agents operated freely; Honda imposed no sales quotas, although it held them strictly accountable for payments for the cycles they had ordered. To make the system effective and to assist agent activity Honda also set up a nationwide network of service centers (called the Honda Service Factory, or SF) for repair and maintenance of its motorcycles.[48] This relieved agents of the need to invest in such services and left them free to concentrate exclusively on sales. The system stressed agent independence rather than any financing obligation on Honda's part, and involved strict terms of payment and transaction. In this sense, it emphasized the ability of the individual agent and resembled American dealer policy. After Honda began automobile production, many agents reorganized as small-scale car dealers with the help of local funding, but Honda policy itself did not change.

Marketing by Japanese auto makers, then, differed with respect to organization and management, but all were characterized by a collective orientation based on a carefully established dealer network. In addition, they differed from systems where the maker dominated and where the exclusive, contractual nature of the relationship was stressed; rather, in Japan the reciprocal nature of the ties was stressed and profits were made through a marketing system based on cooperation and trust. This made possible for each maker the creation of an export strategy.

Conclusion

In this paper I have described the process by which the American automobile industry solved its marketing problems, an inseparable part of which was shown to be sales financing. The last section of the paper examined how automobile marketing was introduced into Japan from the United States, and how it underwent modification in accordance with the nature of the country's distribution system and social structure.

Automobile marketing, above all, requires a systematized, firmly established modern marketing structure—more so than consumer durable goods. Automobiles are expensive and their replacement demand is high; mass production is impossible here without the integration of sales forecasting, product policy, production schedules, sales promotion and dealer policy—without, in other words, a total marketing system. No such modern marketing system existed when automobiles first began to be produced, nor could it exist until there was high demand for automobiles and until automobile makers found themselves having to compete fiercely for a share of the market. This point was reached in the United States in the 1920s, and it was during this period that General Motors, under A. P. Sloan, established an automobile marketing policy that was to become the pattern for modern marketing systems. Until GM's policy was laid down, dealer policy and franchise system formation underwent a series of complicated changes over time. In chronological order, these changes were as follows: first, a period of multiple distribution channels dominated by retailers; second, a period of producer-retailer equality and of growth of distributors; third, a period of producer domination based on mass production and of establishment of an exclusive franchise system; and fourth, a period of assistance to dealers within the structure of the franchise system and of organization of dealers as one element of the maker's marketing structure. In the course of this transition, sales financing was carried out first by independent finance companies, then by maker-affiliated finance companies as well and, finally, by commercial banks; this further accelerated the development of automobile marketing.

An examination of the development of automobile marketing which focuses on dealer policy in terms of franchise agreements highlights the dual nature of the relationship between maker and dealer: on the one hand the maker stresses the dealer's role as one part of a unified marketing system, while on the other hand the maker insists that the dealer is an independent business entity, not an agent contractor, and regards him as a distribution safety valve. Dealer policy has tended to shift between these two attitudes according to circumstances, so that makers sometimes stress dealer's ties to its structure and at other times stress dealer autonomy, sometimes stress the exclusive nature of the franchise and at other times assist and otherwise conciliate dealers. Public policy with regard to franchise agreements can be viewed as an attempt to regulate the conflicting interests that arise as a result of this relationship between maker and dealer.

At first, Japanese auto makers adopted the marketing techniques developed in the United States, especially those of General Motors and Ford, without change; but as they were applied in Japan, the techniques were substantially altered. Franchise agreements and dealer assistance policies resembled those in the United States to a certain degree, but the tight group uniformity and close, cooperative relationship between maker and dealer were major departures from techniques common in the United States.

Japanese auto makers thus integrated the distributing and sales financing functions; from the beginning of the introduction of the franchise system the maker formed a special group of dealers. Consequently, a group management system was established, based on a sense of common sentiment among the members, even though the maker played the leading role in introducing sales financing and inventory service policies, among other things. The continued survival of a dealer was assured by his membership in a dealer group, and he was able to enjoy success in the expanding automobile market by fully adopting policies recommended by the maker.[49] As a result, dealers have very rarely changed to other makers in Japan.

Automobile marketing in Japan is characterized by an extremely low dealer turnover, a sales volume per dealer ten to twenty times the average in the United States because of the large size of many dealers in each prefecture, and a canvassing sales system employing mostly college graduates, rather than a showroom sales system as in the United States. Under the guidance of the maker, dealers establish repair shops and provide complete maintenance and technical service. The maker also provides careful training for salesmen, technical service personnel and customer service personnel employed by the dealer. Finally, the maker also sends management personnel as required by the dealers, and helps dealers with the employment of new personnel.

As a result, Japanese automobile marketing, with its strong maker-dealer ties and sales financing support system, is clearly different from its American counterpart. Of course there are some variations: some, such as Toyota, have their own motor sales company, and some do not; some invest in dealers and some prefer that dealers rely on local capital. These differences reflect some difference in marketing strategy, but all are characterized by the above ties, and this has been critical for the development of automobile marketing in Japan. It reflects specifically Japanese cultural patterns and social customs which attach importance to sentimental ties. There is, in effect, no American-style one-sided franchise system with formal contracts. Rather, Japan's systematic, integrated marketing system is based on close interrelationships and interdependence, which are in turn made possible by the sense of group teamwork felt by both maker and dealer.

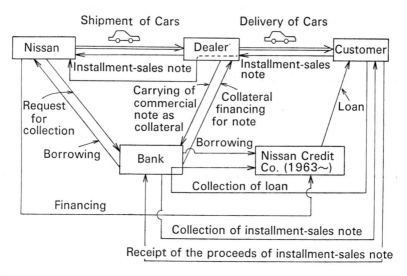

FIG. 1   Sales Financing Procedure Followed by Nissan Motors.

TABLE 1 (a)   Credit Financing Amount by Maker for its Group Company.

	year	1965	1966	1967	1968
	Automobile (Total)	1,077	1,672	2,671	3,884
	Corporate loan	—	430	598	891
Total credit	Group financing system	1,077	1,242	2,073	2,993
	Electric appliance (Total)	1,296	1,431	1,801	2,468
	Corporate loan	26	58	176	522
	Group financing system	1,270	1,373	1,625	1,946
	Automobile (Total)	714	947	1,520	2,120
	Corporate loan	230	389	587	773
The balance of	Group financing system	484	558	933	1,347
credit at the	Electric appliance (Total)	870	965	1,242	1,773
end of the year	Corporate loan	23	50	159	476
	Group financing system	847	915	1,083	1,297

Source: MITI (ed.), Japan Installment Association, *Consumer Credit Statistics,*

TABLE 1 (b)   The Balance of Collateral Financing for Auto Installment Sales

year	1965	1966	1967	1968	1969	1970
Total	389,761	485,626	581,194	670,059	766,974	841,007
National Banks	318,888	400,648	471,283	554,883	625,112	682,968
City Banks	148,080	173,861	192,310	230,182	279,596	302,125
Local Banks	121,181	156,252	192,605	229,838	243,710	272,377
Mutual Banks	70,873	84,978	109,911	115,176	141,864	158,039

Source: Nippon Bank, *Annual Report of Economic Statistics.*

(One hundred million yen)

1969	1970	1971	1972	1973	1974	1975	1976	1977
6,300	8,175	9,398	11,777	13,156	12,984	16,595	17,564	17,763
1,336	1,590	1,563	1,863	2,183	1,189	1,790	2,254	2,469
4,964	6,585	7,835	9,914	10,973	11,795	14,805	15,310	15,294
3,669	4,533	4,992	5,720	6,819	7,885	8,512	9,597	11,303
1,524	2,262	2,369	2,053	1,968	2,135	2,398	2,010	1,893
2,145	2,271	2,623	3,667	4,851	5,750	6,114	7,587	9,410
3,414	4,389	4,986	5,992	6,893	6,546	8,088	8,831	9,234
1,180	1,426	1,460	1,531	1,955	1,238	1,426	1,941	2,352
2,234	2,963	3,526	4,461	4,938	5,308	6,662	6,890	6,882
2,758	3,535	3,949	4,422	5,042	5,772	6,192	6,886	8,071
1,328	2,021	2,200	1,977	1,808	1,939	2,116	1,834	1,798
1,430	1,514	1,749	2,445	3,234	3,833	4,076	5,052	6,273

pp. 4–5, 1978.

notes. (One million yen)

1971	1972	1973	1974	1975	1976	1977
921,706	1,042,557	1,118,498	1,113,289	1,247,697	1,338,793	1,458,274
744,167	858,712	912,768	900,247	1,010,810	1,094,261	1,185,617
317,630	357,997	373,334	361,844	418,931	431,631	459,977
305,740	360,201	393,006	395,001	435,275	184,756	524,089
177,539	183,845	205,730	213,042	236,887	244,532	272,657

TABLE 2   Number of Dealers by Company in Japan (Members of Japan

Company	year	1952	53	54	55	56	57	58	59	1960	61	62	63
Isuzu		37	37	39	40	42	56	50	60	75	76	78	81
Toyota		50	50	50	64	102	109	110	108	109	147	171	176
Nissan[1]		47	48	49	48	60	64	87	99	101	102	102	100
Nissan Diesel										58	58	58	58
Hino									38	43	47	45	49
Mitsubishi		41	59	64	47	46	75	94	91	88	73		118
Fuji (Subaru)										36	40	42	43
Daihatsu						67	68	69	90		93	95	95
Matsuda (Mazda)						46	46	46	47	90	92	90	90
Honda													
Suzuki													

Note: The second, third, and fourth lines under Nissan give the figures for

NOTES

1. Koichi Shimokawa, "Marketing and Sales Financing in the Automobile Industry: U.S. and Japan." *Proceedings of the Third Fuji Conference*, Edited by Keiichiro Nakagawa (Tokyo: University of Tokyo
   Press, 1978), p. 122.
2. Charles M. Hewitt, *The Development of Automobile Franchises* (Bloom-
   ington, Ind.: University of Indiana Press, 1960), p. 9.
3. Richard M. Clewett, *Marketing Channels* (Homewood, Ill.: Richard
   D. Irwin, 1954), p. 92.
4. Shimokawa, *op. cit.*, p. 123.
5. Clewett, *op. cit.*, p. 85.
6. Hewitt, *op. cit.*, p. 10.
7. *Ibid.*, p. 10.
8. Charles M. Hewitt, *Automobile Franchise Agreements* (Homewood, Ill.:
   Richard D. Irwin, 1956), p. 41.
9. Shimokawa, *op. cit.*, p. 124.
10. Clewett, *op. cit.*, pp. 94–95.
11. Shimokawa, *op. cit.*, p. 124.

Automobile Dealers' Association).

64	65	66	67	68	69	1970	71	72	73	74	75	76	77	78	79
89	86	79	80	80	78	79	77	78	79	82	81	84	86	92	103
181	188	199	225	240	265	267	267	276	278	281	284	285	290	291	251
103	105	104	102	104	104	104	106	106	107	106	104	101	101	100	101
		91	90	69	64	62	62	60	61	60	60	60	60	60	59
		59	62	75	75	72	72	73	72	73	72	72	71	68	
											62	59	59	58	42
58	58	58	61	61	65	67	68	37	37	37	39	40	40	40	51
50	49	50	44	43	44	48	50	51	51	51	51	52	53	53	56
134	119	123	132	136	134	129	130	135	142	142	136	138	282	324	322
45	46	46	49	51	52	55	55	57	59	61	64	64	64	63	63
81	75	73	72	67	65	66	65	70	68	68	68	66	68	68	63
91	91	94	105		99	109	110	109	122	125	127	127	124	123	123	121
										154	250	259	250	272	198
										94	87	88	85	84	45

Prince dealers, Nissan Sunny dealers, and Nissan Cherry dealers, respectively.

12. Ralph C. Epstein, *The Automobile Industry* (New York, 1928), p. 133.
13. Clewett, *op. cit.*, p. 95.
14. *Ibid.*, p. 99.
15. Shimokawa, *op. cit.*, p. 127.
16. Clewett, *op. cit.*, pp. 102–103.
17. Tsutomu Furo, *A Criticism of Marketing Channel Behavior* (Tokyo, 1968), p. 81.
18. Yasuo Yajima, *Credit and Consumers* (Tokyo, 1971), p. 60.
19. Lawrence H. Seltzer, *A Financial History of the American Automobile Industry* (New York, 1928), pp. 54–55.
20. Epstein, *op. cit.*, p. 116.
21. Japan Association of Machine Industry (JAMI), *The Reality of Sales Finance Companies in America* (Tokyo, 1963), p. 44.
22. Epstein, *op. cit.*, p. 116.
    Seltzer, *op. cit.*, p. 55.
23. Shimokawa, *op. cit.*, p. 133.
24. *Ibid.*, p. 133.
25. Yajima, *op. cit.*, p. 62.
26. Shimokawa, *op. cit.*, pp. 134–135.

27. *Ibid.*, p. 135.
28. Alfred P. Sloan, *My Years with General Motors* (New York, 1964), pp. 62–69.
29. *Ibid.*, p. 119.
30. *Ibid.*, p. 132.
31. *Ibid.*, pp. 283–284.
32. Hewitt, *Automobile Franchise*, *op. cit.*, pp. 86–87.
33. *Ibid.*, p. 88.
34. Koichi Shimokawa, *A Study of the Business History of the U.S. Automobile Industry* (Tokyo, 1977), p. 184.
35. *Ibid.*, pp. 209–212.
36. Shōtarō Kamiya, *My Life with Toyota* (Tokyo, 1976), p. 31.
37. Toyota Motor Sales Co., *Our Years with Motorization* (Tokyo, 1970), pp. 40–41.
38. Hiromichi Osuga, "Historical Analysis of the Japanese Automobile Distribution Mechanism—on the Background of Group Specialization and Scale Enlargement." *Jidosha to sono sekai* (September, 1975), p. 6.
39. Toyota Motor Sales Co., *op. cit.*, pp. 77–78.
40. Shimokawa, "Marketing and Sales Financing," *op. cit.*, p. 136.
41. *Ibid.*, p. 137.
42. Toyota Motor Sales Co., *op. cit.*, pp. 114–117.
43. Shimokawa, "Marketing and Sales Financing," *op. cit.*, p. 137.
44. Toyota Motor Sales, *op. cit.*, pp. 120–123.
45. Yonosuke Miki, *Challenge of Nissan* (Tokyo, 1967), p. 137.
46. Prince Motor Sales Company's organization is still in existence.
47. Honda Motors, *The History of Honda* (Tokyo, 1975), pp. 64–65.
48. *Ibid.*
49. Shimokawa, "Marketing and Sales Financing," *op. cit.*, p. 139.

COMMENTS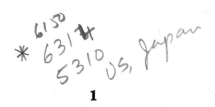

1

Harold C. Livesay
State University of New York

I found Professor Shimokawa's paper both fascinating and tantalizing: fascinating in the story it tells, tantalizing because it raises many questions, each of which could serve as a subject for a conference like this one. In addition, this paper certainly provides a solid justification for the theme we are considering here, for it underlines the indispensable role of mass distribution in the development of mass production. Certainly we need to know more about the methods used by Japanese manufacturers in their rise to global scope. From the perspective of an American consumer, as well as an American scholar of business, I have always regarded the success of Japanese automobiles in the United States as more a triumph of marketing than of engineering.

Professor Shimokawa's research discloses a significant example of one of my own favorite themes, continuity in history, by showing how much Toyota and Nissan drew on the marketing strategies of General Motors and Ford. This leads him to yet another of my own particular fascinations, the degree to which cultural differences necessitate the adaptation of "universal" methods to local conditions. At the same time, one is struck by the fact that within various industrial societies there are tendencies toward convergence in production technologies, as well as in the products themselves, as witness the drive toward "worldwide cars," originally ignited by Henry Ford, now practiced with consummate skill by German and Japanese manufacturers, and latterly adopted as a strategy even by General Motors, historically an aggressive proponent of product diversity.

In order to maximize the utility of my comments within the context of this conference, however, I would like to focus briefly on one specific difference between American and Japanese automobile marketing depicted by Professor Shimokawa; that is, the tendency of Japanese dealers to develop close ties to their manufacturers, striving toward an organic harmony of purpose, while American dealers and producers developed and retained an antagonistic outlook.

This difference, I would argue, is symptomatic of not only cultural, but also geographic differences between the two countries, and points to factors in the United States that are commonly underestimated or overlooked by American scholars as well as their counterparts abroad.

There is a tendency, for example, to put too much stock in the term "national market." If national market is used to mean one in which a high level of purchasing power rose far and wide, and one in which improvements in transportation and communication made it possible for some types of manufacturers to market their products everywhere, it can be accepted although major reservations must be attached. Commonly, however, it suggests a kind of homogeneous emporium into which manufacturers could pour goods through an increasingly centralized distribution system, a notion that overlooks the residual power of localism in American society, still a force so potent at the time of the automobile's introduction that no manufacturer, no matter how vigorous, could afford to overlook it.

The United States at the time of the automobile's introduction and rise to the status of consumer durable was a largely rural country; moreover, it was a country in which much of the disposable income was rural. The golden age of the Model T was coterminous in its early years with some of the most prosperous years American farmers had ever known. It was, after all, these rural, small-town folk, whom Henry Ford knew from his own experience, that formed in his mind the primary market for mass-produced automobiles. The sense of local community in the United States was strong and often ethnically based. As late as 1920, over half the American population had been born abroad, or were the children of foreign parents.

Manufacturers, therefore, were selling to strangers—not just people unknown to them personally, but people who lacked the common cultural traditions of a society as old as Japan's. National manufacturers, therefore, needed to establish a local identity and did so by appointing as dealers men who were pillars of the local community. The dealers themselves scrupulously retained their identity as local figures and avoided becoming identified as puppets of distant, powerful manufacturers. In this connection, it should be remembered that Americans since before the Revolution regarded the centralization of power in locations far removed as potential sources of tyranny, whether political or economic. By the late nineteenth and early twentieth century, many Americans regarded the concentration of power in the hands of industrial corporations as one of the principal threats to cherished American virtues of competition and self-reliance.

In these circumstances, then, it is unsurprising that dealers in the United States clung to their independence and presented a fractious, rather than a harmonious, partnership to the manufacturers who had no choice but to rely upon them.

I hope these comments may add a small dimension of further understanding to Professor Shimokawa's excellent work.

2

Eisuke Daito
Tohoku University

By the middle of the 1920s, the period of initial growth in the American automobile industry came to an end. Although several changes such as growth of per capita income and population, product improvements, and cultivation of export markets, might increase demand for new cars, success and failure of automobile manufacturers began to depend more on shrewd marketing than before. In these circumstances, there emerged an exclusive franchise system which integrated dealers into a new marketing strategy by the big manufacturers. As is well known, this innovation was introduced by General Motors. It seems to me that the major theme of Professor Shimokawa's paper is to examine the nature of this innovation and its impact on other American and Japanese firms. I would like, therefore, to make some comments on this topic and some others which are closely related to it.

Professor Shimokawa writes on page 14 as follows: "Policy here was based on product differentiation, which in turn meant model changes, full-line market segmentation and the upgrading of the standard automobile....Dealer policy was soon incorporated into this system." What I can learn from this is that the essence of the innovation is the integration of many tactical elements into a unified grand marketing strategy. I also find, however, one element left untouched in this paper. It is the *pricing policy*. Was the elasticity of demand so low that the price was no longer a major means of competition? Isn't it natural to think that some changes were needed in pricing practices in the 1920s when a considerable portion of new purchases began to involve trade-ins?

My second request is for Professor Shimokawa to expand further his statement that "by combining production schedule with sales forecasting and dealer inventory report, General Motors was able to relate production to sales, and to profit thereby" (p. 15). While the new policy was based on sales forecasting, the traditional one was to "make as many cars as the factory could produce," and "force" dealers to take them. By the traditional policy, production schedules could be determined rather easily, but at the expense of dealers' profits. Theoretically speaking, by the new policy every change in sales forecasting demanded a corresponding change in production schedule and product mix. This would sometimes mean a lower operating rate in the factories as well as an excessive inventory of parts. What scheme was developed by General Motors in order to cope with these difficulties and to find a mutually acceptable level of inventory and rate of operation?

Lastly, it is very interesting to learn that the franchise system in Japan was designed after that of American firms but developed its own unique features. Professor Shimokawa attributes this uniqueness to "Japanese cultural patterns and social customs which attach importance to sentimental ties" (p. 25). It is quite natural for the cultural pattern to exert a strong influence on the relationship between dealers and manufacturers, but it could be argued that there is another important difference between the U. S. and Japan, based on the facts which Professor Shimokawa shows us: that is, while mass production started much earlier than fully-developed marketing management in the U.S., systematic marketing management had already been adopted, at least on a small scale, when mass production started in Japan. It is sometimes pointed out that when the price of a new car declines to the level of 1.4 times per-capita income, markets for cars enter into a stage of rapid growth. This level was reached in the middle of the 1960s in Japan. By that time, big manufacturers had already established their nationwide franchise system. Dealers as well as manufacturers could therefore enjoy lasting prosperity. I think that the friendly relationship between them in Japan can be explained, at least to some extent, by this lasting prosperity.

PART II

DEVELOPMENT OF AUTOMOBILE MARKETING

Nineteenth Century Precursors to Automobile Marketing in the United States

Harold C. Livesay
State University of New York

My purpose here is to discuss the evolution of marketing in the United States during the nineteenth century, and to relate this evolution to the marketing strategies ultimately adopted by American automobile manufacturers. Superficially this is a story of institutional change that begins in the hardware bins of the all-purpose merchants who dominated all forms of distribution at the beginning of the nineteenth century and ends in the showrooms, parts departments, and repair shops of the modern, franchised automobile dealership.

The story deserves, indeed requires, a more detailed accounting, however, for its broad outline manifests deep-seated changes within the fabric of American society, changes that, by requiring shifting strategies of marketing, generated irresistible dynamics of institutional change. Among the welter of forces at work in nineteenth century America, two seem to have been most significant in their impact on marketing. The first was technology; the second, and by all odds the more important, was the changing nature of the market itself, for while the nineteenth century United States shared the advancing technology common to many western nations, it experienced an explosion of population, geographic area, urban concentration, and consumer buying power that remains, in combination, unique in history. In this swiftly changing environment, success in manufacturing absolutely demanded the development of marketing systems that not only took into account the characteristics of the products themselves, but also accommodated themselves to the realities of a market that rapidly became larger, more potent, and, paradoxically, both more concentrated and more diffuse simultaneously.

The marketing task proved so difficult and so essential that, as Glenn Porter and I have argued in detail elsewhere, the giant integrated corporations that rose to dominate the American industrial economy by the end of the nineteenth century resulted more from the vexing perplexities of mass distribution than from the exigencies of mass production.[1] Since the process of industrialization and market expansion occupied the entire nineteenth century, the automobile industry, emerging only at the end of the period, had a large, existing body of techniques to draw on, and drew on them freely. Enjoying this advantage of the latecomer in an already highly developed market economy, successful car manufacturers borrowed marketing methods from the whole range of existing industries—producers' and consumers', durable and perishable.

Indeed, the most striking thing about the resulting combination was the fact that only the combination itself was novel; about the techniques themselves there was little new at all. Even today this industry, the most important manufacturing component of the American economy, markets its products through channels embracing a curious juxtaposition of ultramodern and pre-industrial techniques. In its computerized translations of product orders into parts manufacture, inventory, shipment, assembly, and, finally, delivery of finished vehicles, producers rely on the most sophisticated electronic data processing available. This intricate chain, however, begins and ends in the franchised dealership, an institution with ownership structure and sales methods much like those of the traditional mercantile house. This fact, recognized by companies and customers alike, often crops up in modern advertising campaigns such as one in which the Ford Motor Company urges customers to "go to [their] neighborhood Ford dealer's store." A major element, then, of American automobile marketing thus antedates not just the automobile industry and American industrialization, but is in fact older than the United States itself. The development of automobile marketing is thus another example of historical continuity, as evident in business history as it is in political, cultural, or diplomatic history.

One line along which this continuity can be seen clearly is the history of marketing. In its simplest terms in the United States, this involved manufacturers turning to the existing, preindustrial network of mercantile houses as outlets for their products. When, for one reason or another, the existing agencies proved unwilling or unable to adapt, inadequate or uneconomical merchants or manufacturers, or sometimes the two in concert, adapted the old ways to fit the new needs, retaining as much of the old as was practicable.

Thanks to the labor of many historians in the United States and elsewhere, we know a great deal about these traditional, all-purpose merchants, both those resident in the coastal cities of the American colonies, and their brethren in the hinterlands.[2] Buying and selling at wholesale and retail, arranging all the supporting functions of commerce such as shipping, insurance, advertising, and perhaps most important, finance, these were the preeminent men of American business prior to industrialization. Tied together by familial connections, common religious affiliation, or business associations that often went back generations, these merchants formed networks through which flowed not only the products of America and Europe, but also the information about credit standing, prices, crop and market conditions necessary to viable commerce. Fundamental to success in mercantile trade was an intimate knowledge of local conditions, including a thoroughgoing understanding of where prospective customers lay, and which of them could be relied upon to pay their bills. This knowledge of the local market, part of the merchant's lore since time immemorial, proved to be something that no nineteenth-century manufacturer of consumer durable goods could afford to be without, no matter how large, rich, and powerful his firm might be.

The monumental process of change brought on by the industrial revolution overtook the mercantile community in the United States shortly after the country was formed in 1789. In the first instance, the change resulted from an industrial revolution once removed, that is, the industrial revolution in Great Britain. The insatiable appetite of the British cotton textile industry, Eli Whitney's invention of the cotton gin, the peculiar suitability of conditions in the southern United States to plantation cotton agriculture soon combined to flood many American merchants with an unprecedented volume of business. The result (and this, too, is well documented) bore out Adam Smith's observation that the degree of speculation is limited by the size of the market, for many American merchants, reacting to the expanding market for cotton in Britain and manufactured goods in the United States, turned to specialization in either services or products. Some, abandoning actual trade in goods altogether, formed shipping lines, banks, or insurance companies. Others followed the course of New York merchant Anson Phelps who, in less than thirty years, sold his ships, quit retail trade, and concentrated solely on the exportation of cotton and the importation of copper and tin plate.[3]

In other sectors we find the merchants' role diminished by the actions of a manufacturer. In producers' goods, the swiftly ramifying technical complexity of products such as locomotives led manufacturers like Matthias Baldwin of Philadelphia to bypass merchants by selling to railroads directly, a change facilitated by the fact that while the value of each unit produced was large, the number of customers was relatively small. In consumers' perishables such as ice and fresh meat, entrepreneurs like Frederick Tudor and Gustavus Swift had to establish their own network of refrigerated facilities because existing merchants could not or would not get the job done. As consumers' durables such as the sewing machine and typewriter appeared in mass-produced quantities, the need for parts, service, finance, advertising, and instruction in the use of the machines forced manufacturers to supercede untrained and undercapitalized independent local merchants as outlets for their products.[4]

In each of these instances, however, the adaptation was a gradual one, occurring first in the largest, most concentrated market areas. In many cases, the actual transition involved the conversion of an independent local merchant into a full-time company employee, with staff, facilities, and activities bolstered by infusions of capital and training arranged by the manufacturer.

The automobile industry, however, patterned its marketing system most closely after that developed by Cyrus Hall McCormick to distribute his mechanical reaper, first marketed in the early 1840s. McCormick, too, turned to the existing mercantile network, found it inadequate, and modified it to suit his peculiar needs.[5] Curiously enough, he began his marketing network not by relying on any of the specialized wholesale houses that had resulted from the work of his manufacturing contemporaries, but rather by enlisting the aid of the local retail merchants in small-town, rural America, a few of them specialized dealers in grain or livestock, but most of them unspecialized keepers of "general stores."

Plenty of these retailers still existed in the 1840s and in fact survived well into the twentieth century as the dominant agencies in retail distribution of non-perishable foods, shoes, clothing, dry goods, and notions, in short, the whole range of products that ultimately became the domain of the department store, supermarket, and the dime store. These storekeepers survived because of the diffuse character of the market they served, the relatively undifferentiated nature and technological simplicity of the goods they sold, and their knowledge of local conditions, particularly their intimate acquaintance with the credit-worthiness of their customers.

Many of these customers were, of course, farmers, the chief income producers in the overwhelmingly rural America of the 1840s. Cyrus McCormick, himself the son of a farmer in the Shenandoah Valley of Virginia, knew first-hand of the critical role that storekeepers played in local commerce, and they soon came to play an equally critical part in the fulfillment of his ambitions. From the first reaper, handcrafted in his father's farm workshop in the 1830s, McCormick fashioned a dream of an industrial empire in which the far-flung grain fields of America would become a domain patrolled by his scarlet chariots with their flashing knives.

Converting this dream to reality meant mass production based on interchangeable parts. By the late 1840s this legacy of Eli Whitney and his successors was an available technology that McCormick could and did quickly adapt. Reading the trends of settlement correctly, McCormick moved from Virginia to Chicago in 1848, placing himself at the commercial nexus of the emerging American grain belt by opening a factory that could produce hundreds of machines. Mass production, however, demanded volume distribution to customers scattered over the broad expanses of the American midwest, a region with which McCormick himself was largely unfamiliar and where he personally was unknown to the inhabitants. From the early days in Virginia, sales problems had claimed much of McCormick's time. In the new location it became his foremost concern as he sought to tap the new market presented by the rise of large-scale commercial agriculture.

McCormick faced a market made up of thousands of independent farmers. Tough customers in every sense of the term, they refused to buy reapers sight unseen. They demanded demonstrations, especially ones where manufacturers pitted their products against one another. Success at such competitions demanded the presence of an expert at the reap-off to adjust the machines to local conditions and to make running repairs. In the early days, McCormick himself attended many exhibitions. As the search for markets and sub-manufacturers took up more of his time, he dragooned his brothers into service. Relying on family members or on old, trusted acquaintances was traditional in preindustrial America, as it had been for centuries before in Europe. But mass markets made such nepotistic methods obsolete. No one had a family that large. For manufacturers who, like McCormick, produced volume goods for diffuse markets, mass distribution presented greater problems than mass production and forced the manufacturers to create organizations to handle sales as well as manufacturing.

Marketing the reaper involved more than competitions and displays at county fairs. After the move to Chicago in 1848, McCormick participated in fewer such events because the outcome was often uncertain. Sometimes his machine lost; sometimes the local judges turned out to be biased in favor of a competitor's product. The McCormick reaper did win its share of medals, prizes, and certificates of merit, which the company proudly displayed. But competitors did the same, and farmers, facing conflicting claims, often believed none. In addition, farmers found that results of hard daily usage fell suspiciously short of those of the staged competitions. The result, as the editor of the *Farmers' Register* observed, was grave injury inflicted on deserving inventors themselves, as well as on the public by the *puffing system*. Every new invention . . . whatever may be its . . . merit or demerit, is ushered forth with puffs upon puffs. Dupes are made, and knaves who puff, and sell, profit at the expense of the fools who believe and buy . . . . The more discreet . . . who know the working of the puffing system, stand aloof, and trust [neither] true statements [nor] false.

Since reaper marketing demanded extensive personal contact, McCormick gradually relied more on a far-flung network of salesmen, on his company's reputation, and on his factory's ability to outproduce any competitor's, than on showboating before increasingly skeptical audiences at bucolic gatherings.

The reaper was for its time a delicate and complicated machine. In fact, nothing so complex had ever been widely marketed before. Few customers, moreover, could claim much mechanical expertise; unlike the manufacturers of railway equipment, McCormick sold to a nonexpert clientele. From the outset McCormick salesmen had to instruct farmers in the use and care of the machine. Even the mules and horses that pulled it had to be broken to the task; otherwise they had a tendency to bolt across the fields, trying to escape the rattling contraption that pursued them.

In the 1840s, when sales were numbered in the dozens, McCormick often urged his brothers to handle deliveries personally: "William or Leander could attend to . . . putting together, explaining, and having printed directions [for the machine]." Later, printed instructions accompanied every machine, explaining its operation, adjustment, the need for lubrication, the best technique for sharpening the cutting knives, and the replacement of broken parts.

Printed instructions or not, the machines often broke down, requiring repairs or adjustments that the farmers would not or could not perform. The early reapers acquired a reputation for fragility that constituted one of the major sales obstacles to be overcome. This reputation survived long after the reaper passed from the experimental stage. In the 1850s, for example, one farm journalist wrote that all reapers, even McCormick's, were of little value unless there was "a blacksmith shop at each corner of the field."

Breakdowns often resulted from farmers' attitudes toward maintenance, an attitude similar to one once encountered by an automobile service manager friend of mine. A furious customer confronted him with a car that rattled, shook, and belched smoke. A quick check showed that the car had sixty-four thousand miles on the odometer and no oil in the crankcase. "Did you ever change the oil?" my friend asked. "Change the oil! Why the hell should I change the oil?" the customer demanded heatedly. "I paid eight thousand dollars for this car. What the hell was wrong with the oil they put in it? I'll never buy this make again." Like this frustrated motorist, many farmers felt that a machine that cost so much should run by itself and forever. One weary reaper repairman commented, "I am sorry I enlisted [for this job] but there is no use. I shall go through with the job if I live . . . . The machines are in the worst plight imaginable. I have found them outdoors and frozen down. Just where they used them last." But even the most bull-headed characters had to be accommodated, as McCormick knew, lest they become enemies. In the early years the factory supplied the farmers with the name of a nearby mechanic, in addition to the printed instructions. "I think it would be well to refer persons in the vicinity of Richmond to Mr. Parker for repairs," one of McCormick's agents wrote in 1845. "It is desirable to give satisfaction to all if possible, for now in the infancy of the reaper's existence a few dissatisfied persons might do you serious injury." But such casual arrangements with people who owed no particular allegiance to the company proved unsatisfactory. The need to provide reliable service over a widespread area contributed to the development of a network of company agents.

The company also had to supply spare parts. After the first few years the parts were interchangeable, but the fact that the reaper was frequently redesigned meant that parts for one year's model often would not fit another's. The company tried to meet this difficulty by furnishing a set of spares with each machine. When this proved unsatisfactory, a parts department was established at the Chicago factory. Farmers could send a defective part to the plant, where it was matched against a collection of all the machines the company had ever built. Once identified, the drawings could be pulled from the files and the part duplicated in the company shop. This method proved slow, expensive, and unsatisfactory. The machines broke down during the harvest, when they were most needed, and few farmers could wait for the factory to duplicate the defective component and return it. Parts stockpiles had to be established so that they could be got quickly when needed.

Finally, the reaper cost a lot of money—an average of $130 before the Civil War. Few farmers had that kind of cash, and banks, which had no interest in consumer finance, would rarely lend it to them. The company, therefore, had to interpose itself as a credit intermediary, selling machines on the installment plan and using its own superior credit to borrow operating funds until farmers paid up. Obviously the company couldn't restrict credit sales to members of the McCormick family, its friends, and their acquaintances; in effect, McCormick had to pawn his firm's resources and lend the proceeds to thousands of strangers scattered across the prairie outback. No small sum was involved: by 1858 farmers owed McCormick half a million dollars; two years later this had grown to a million dollars.

To survive in this kind of risky business, the firm needed reliable credit information before the sale and aggressive debt collection after it. In the East, formal credit rating services, the forerunners of Dun & Bradstreet, appeared in the 1840s and 1850s, but these agencies supplied no information on the probity of midwestern farmers.

Some structure thus had to be devised to demonstrate the machines, sell and repair them, supply spare parts, evaluate credit, and make collections. During the Virginia years, McCormick had relied on a motley troop consisting of himself, other family members, newspaper editors (thought useful because of their potential value as publicists), and blacksmiths. These catch-as-catch-can arrangements worked badly enough in Virginia, but broke down entirely after the company moved to Chicago and began mass production. Searching for a solution to this combination of marketing problems, McCormick found himself in unexplored territory, for no manufacturer had yet encountered similar vexations. What McCormick had to have was a widespread network of dependable agents, loyal to the Chicago factory and its products but familiar with local business conditions, farming practices, and, above all, the credit-worthiness of prospective customers. No prototype of such a network existed; however, distribution of general merchandise, much of it sold on credit, had long since been perfected in small-town, rural America. It was the province of merchants and storekeepers in the towns and peddlers in the countryside.

On this existing foundation, McCormick found he could build. Successful merchants, though he could know but few of them personally, at least belonged to a trustworthy category and had long experience with credit sales. Beginning with an adaptation of the merchant-peddler system of the 1850s, the company developed a sales and service system that evolved from a loose-knit assortment of agents and subagents (whose functions corresponded roughly to those of merchants and peddlers, respectively) into a highly structured, closely regulated network of franchised dealerships. These marketing problems, ultimately encountered by all mass producers of goods with similar inherent problems of sales, service, and finance, thus contributed to the shift from personalized to bureaucratic business methods that invariably accompanied industrialization.

McCormick's new sales methods roused the ire of his farmer customers, who regarded dealers as unwelcome intruders that disrupted the farmer's direct relationship with the company and had the gall to charge for the depersonalization. Responding to these attacks, denying that its agents were "parasitic middlemen," the firm used examples it thought its rustic critics could comprehend. His agents, McCormick argued, were as necessary to him "as clerks were to the owner of a store." After all, the company asked, "Would you, a farmer, sell a horse on credit to the first stranger who came along?" In the 1870s and '80s this plan evolved into a network of franchised dealerships. Copied and expanded to national scale by wagon and carriage manufacturers, it became the prototype for modern dealerships that sell automobiles and other consumer durables requiring demonstrations, service, and financing.

The success of this system of sales and service, the first of its kind, and not simply the productivity of his factory carried Mc-Cormick to the top of the farm machinery industry and kept him there despite fierce competition and the expiration of his patents.

In the beginning the company's agents and subagents restricted themselves largely to sales and credit functions, leaving mechanical problems to the factory's parts and repairs departments, or to company mechanics sent out from Chicago after the season's production was finished. As the years passed, the agents assumed these responsibilities as well. The company expected its agents not only to provide showrooms to display the machines, "travel thoroughly ... through the wheat growing portions" of a specific district, sell to "responsible and trustworthy farmers only," hire "efficient assistant agents," deliver machines, "devote themselves actively to putting up, starting and setting to work the ... reapers," and make collections, but also to stock spare parts and make repairs. Eventually the company got out of the repair business altogether, telling its agents that the factory "should not be made a graveyard for broken down or imperfect machines....Our rule ... is that every general shall take care of his own wounded and bury his own dead." This ukase meant that dealers also had to repair and resell trade-ins, although in practice the overhauls were often limited to whatever a paintbrush could accomplish.

Dealers also had to perform auxiliary services, such as stocking twine for the binders (machines that tied the wheat in bundles as it was cut) that came on the market after the Civil War, and negotiating with railroads for rebates on shipments to their territories.

Originally, the company made year-to-year arrangements with its representatives. Soon, however, the principal agents became permanent company employees, working on a salary rather than a commission basis, restricted to the sale of McCormick products, and held responsible for hiring and supervising subagents. The agent's lot was not always a happy one. When the factory overproduced, he came under great pressure to push the machines into the market. This often led to sales to farmers who could ill afford further debts. McCormick thus engaged in a forerunner of the modern technique of restoring the market's vital signs by injections

of consumer-credit adrenalin, a method that reflected traditional
American confidence in the better days to come.

When factory output fell short of demand, angry customers
swarmed about the agent like hornets. Most burdensome of all,
the company hounded its dealers to collect from the farmers, many
of whom could not pay, and some of whom felt that old man Mc-
Cormick with all his money could, like the dentist, wait.

Obviously a successful agent had to be an aggressive character
indeed. The company exhorted its representatives to have "spunk,"
"grit," and "sand," to "spit on your fists," "make it hot for them,"
and "to keep on top of the heap." When the competition got hot,
apparently something more was required. One home office representative, commenting on the failure of a Minnesota agent, wrote,
"Edgar [has] trouble all over his dis[trict] .... The only reason
I can assign is that he has too many *churchmen* for [sub-] agts. I
believe in religion & temperance but it ain't worth a 'cuss' to run the
Reaper trade on in Minnesota: it requires cheek & muscle and
I am sorry to say some 'evasions' from the truth to successfully sell
McCormick harvesters with the opposition we have....You have
got to fight the Devil with fire and it is no use trying to fool him
on sweetened water."

As the field organizations expanded, the company offices in
Chicago underwent an evolution of their own. A subdivision of labor
soon separated the manufacturing function from the others. By
1859, the company's office had specialists who dealt exclusively
with one particular aspect of business outside the factory, including
agent supervision, collections, purchasing, shipping, repairs and
spare parts, and accounting. In time each of these individuals
metamorphosed into a department with an office and field staff.
A printing department published a company newspaper called
The Farmers' Advance that reached a circulation of 350,000 in the
early 1880s. The company also published 800,000 thirty-page pamphlets annually, printed in five or six different languages, some
8,000 colored show cards, and repair catalogs listing spare parts
and their prices.

From his first days in business, McCormick had pioneered in

widespread advertising. As sales expanded, the policy continued with unabated vigor and soon boasted a specialized staff of its own. "Trying to do business without advertising," the company declared in *The Farmers' Advance*, "is like winking at a pretty girl through a pair of green goggles. You may know what you are doing, but no one else does." Advertising not only reached the market, but, as the company found, expanded it as well, persuading many a farmer to buy machines he neither needed nor could afford.

Development of the field sales force and the office staff began under Orloff M. Dorman, a Chicago merchant and quondam partner of Cyrus McCormick, who joined the firm in 1848. Orloff worked in tandem with William McCormick, who soon took sole charge. When William died in 1865, control of the field and office forces passed to professional managers, another milestone on the road from family to bureaucratic management.

By fair means or foul, the whirlwind activities of the sales organization successfully connected the McCormick works to its widely dispersed customers, creating a forced draft that kept the factory's boilers at full steam. From 1500 machines in 1849, production rose to 15,000 annually in 1880. Not until thirty years later did the Ford Motor Company, the United States' largest producer, attain such volume.

Clearly, then, Cyrus McCormick's firm, building from the base of a preexisting, largely traditional mercantile network, perfected sales methods that met the distribution problems presented by mass production of complex, expensive units that required providing demonstrations, instruction, customer finance, parts, and service to buyers scattered far and wide across the American expanses. The similarity between the problems confronted by McCormick in 1850 and by automobile manufacturers half a century later, and the solutions adopted by both need no elaboration here. It is worth noting, however, that throughout the course of American economic development, newly arriving industries had the advantage of preexisting structures that could be adapted to their needs. The automobile industry presents a particularly salient case of this prevailing historical continuity.

Notes

1. Glenn Porter and Harold C. Livesay, *Merchants and Manufacturers: Studies in the Changing Structure of Nineteenth Century Marketing* (Baltimore, 1971).
2. See, for example, Bernard Bailyn, *The New England Merchants in the Seventeenth Century* (Cambridge, Mass., 1955); William T. Baxter, *The House of Hancock: Business in Boston, 1724–1775* (Cambridge, Mass., 1945); Stuart Bruchey, *Robert Oliver, Merchant of Baltimore, 1783–1815* (Baltimore, 1956). This list could be extended to cover a dozen or more volumes elaborating the merchants' role throughout preindustrial America. The picture, however, remains consistent in them all.
3. The classic study of the emergence of merchant specialization remains Robert G. Albion, *The Rise of New York Port* (New York, 1939) and is expanded to broader coverage geographically, chronologically, and in terms of industries in Porter and Livesay, *Merchants and Manufacturers*.
4. Livesay and Porter, *Merchants and Manufacturers* details these cases and has extended references to merchants' papers and scholarly case studies on which the argument rests.
5. The basic source for McCormick is William T. Hutchinson, *Cyrus Hall McCormick* (New York, 1930 and 1935), 2 vols. I have developed the thesis that incorporated local storekeepers into the dealer network that became the automobile industry's prototype in *American Made: Men Who Shaped the American Economy* (Boston, 1979), especially chap. 4.

COMMENTS

1

Kin'ichiro Toba
Waseda University

I found Professor Livesay's paper interesting, although it does not deal directly with automobile marketing. It makes clear the characteristic features of American social and economic conditions in the latter half of the nineteenth century when the original pattern of the mass marketing system first emerged. When it is necessary to interpret a phenomenon, historians have to look back to the past for its causes. Professor Livesay's beautiful descriptions of Cyrus Hall McCormick's efforts to build up distribution channels is a task of this kind.

I was also interested in the way he showed that marketing success mainly depends on the effective utilization of traditional distribution channels. This is quite true because, if all existing channels rejected a new product, no producer could force its distribution. He showed his entrepreneurial ability in his effective reorganization of these old channels to fit his new product. His marketing efforts succeeded in widely distributing his reaper, which had been produced by modern mass production technology. Many business historians attach too much importance to the creation of a new marketing system, but successful adaptations as McCormick's should not be ignored.

This paper clearly explains how McCormick created the modern distribution system while effectively utilizing the traditional distribution channels. It was half a century before American automobile manufacturers organized their franchise dealer system. As Professor Livesay points out, McCormick was really a forerunner of modern American marketing because the automobile manufacturers were able to run on the rails laid down by him.

However a further question remains to be considered: Who were the real innovaters in the field of mass marketing? The answer would be that the modern American mass marketing system was created by such business geniuses as McCormick, Ford and Sloan (of General Motors), but this has to be seen in the context of the social and economic environment of the United States. I would say that the American social and economic environment provided a really fertile soil from which many types of modern marketing systems developed. The franchise system, dealer system, chain system and such other retailing systems as the supermarket, discount house and mail-order house were all American born.

The social and economic environment of the United States was very different from that of countries in Europe in terms of size, population, egalitarian tendencies in the society, equality of income distribution, nonexistence of time-honored, traditional distribution channels and so on. All of these conditions contributed greatly to the development of the modern marketing systems. What happened in automobile marketing was only one aspect of the phenomenon. In the case of the automobile, it was an international product from the beginning because of its high price and position as a status symbol, and also because it needed repairing, requiring a good supply of parts and regular service. It needed a big market and it was only in the United States that such a big market existed in the first half of the twentieth century. As seen in the papers by Professor Church and Professor Blaich, there were no favorable conditions in Britain and Germany comparable with those seen in the U.S. This might be one reason why modern marketing systems didn't develop in either country apart from those brought by American manufacturers.

The above discussion leads to my first question for Professor Livesay. He puts stress on the continuous development of the modern marketing system as seen in the case of the United States. If so, why have Volkswagen and Toyota, instead of American automobile manufacturers' subsidiaries in Europe, achieved a big success in international automobile marketing?

Professor Livesay describes in his paper that Cyrus Hall Mc-

Cormick was a forerunner of Ford and General Motors as a modern
marketing organizer. Is there any evidence that Ford or General
Motors imitated the marketing system of McCormick? Are there
any historical documents about it? This is my second question.

The Ford Company started tractor production in 1917 and was
very successful in competing with International Harvester's tractor
during the 1920s. In 1929 its production well exceeded 100,000.
Besides its excellent technology, Ford's success was achieved by
effectively using its distribution channels for automobiles. But
Ford suddenly stopped production and withdrew completely from
this field. Why did this happen? This is my third and last question.

2

Makiko Yamada
Sangyonoritsu University

In this paper, Professor Livesay tries to prove the following two
arguments: (1) The giant corporations that rose to dominate the
American industrial economy by the end of the nineteenth century
resulted more from the vexing perplexities of mass distribution
than from the exigencies of mass production. (2) There is a
historical continuity throughout the course of American economic
development—that is, newly emerging industries took advantage
of preexisting industrial and economic structures. In order to
demonstrate these arguments, he discusses comprehensively the
evolution of mass marketing in the United States during the nineteenth century using the case of Cyrus McCormick's firm as an
example. However, I would like to make two comments on this
paper.

1) Since there is a lack of analysis and demonstration of how
McCormick's marketing methods and distribution system acted
as precursors to automobile marketing in the United States, it is

difficult for me to see precisely the logical sequence of McCormick's marketing innovations in the marketing system adopted by American automobile manufacturers. Of course, from his argument, I can imagine or see that the automobile which, as a product, had some similarities to the reaper, could take advantage of preexisting structure—that is, sales methods perfected by Cyrus McCormick.

The reaper, like the automobile, was for its time a delicate and complicated machine and an expensive durable item, so McCormick encountered several problems. First, at the time, nothing so complex had ever been widely marketed before except railway equipment; McCormick had to sell to nonexpert clientele, since his customers were farmers who could not claim much mechanical expertise. Second, because the reaper was an expensive machine and farmers did not have stable and constant earnings, he had to sell the machine on credit so that he faced problems of credit rating and debt collection. He solved these problems by an adaptation of the merchant-peddler system of the 1850s. The company gradually developed this sales and service system into a highly structured, closely regulated network of franchised dealerships and expanded it to a national network of such dealerships in the 1870s and '80s. According to Professor Livesay, these franchised dealerships became the prototype for modern dealerships that sell automobiles and other consumer durables requiring demonstration, service, and financing. Although I agree with his argument that McCormick's marketing system was a precursor to U.S. automobile marketing, I wish that Professor Livesay had shown precisely and in detail how the automobile manufacturers adopted this preexisting marketing structure.

2) It seems to me that Professor Livesay ignores the fact that the mass production system became the core of the business system in the nineteenth century. Without the innovation of the mass production system, there would never have been the evolution of a mass marketing and distribution system. Throughout the course of American economic development, the mass production system based on the concept of interchangeable parts was a unique invention which made the American business system different from those of other advanced countries in the nineteenth century.

Moreover, it made American industry the forerunner of the modern business system which has been diffused all over the world and has improved the world economy.

When McCormick had a dream of an industrial empire, he converted his dream to reality by adapting mass production. Then he encountered the problem of volume distribution to customers scattered over the broad expanse of the American midwest, and consequently he developed the mass marketing system including demonstrations, service, and financing. The idea of interchangeable parts had not yet enveloped the automobile industry when a few dozen men experimented with motor cars in the United States and European countries. Even Ford's early automobiles were custom-made. Moreover, most of the forerunners of the automobile industry on both sides of the Atlantic viewed self-propelled vehicles as a luxury to be built and priced for the rich. Leyland, who had been a master machinist in the post-Whitney firearms industry, introduced the concept of interchangeability of parts to American automobile manufacturers as well as British. But Ford was the first manufacturer who absorbed Leyland's doctrine by mass-producing the Model T (even though Ransom Olds and Billy Durant had considered the motor car's potential as a consumer product). After the mass-produced car became a consumer product, the American automobile manufacturer took advantage of preexisting marketing methods and enjoyed the benefit of the latecomer in an already highly developed market economy.

So, when we consider the historical continuity throughout American economic development, we should not neglect the effect of the mass production process invented by Eli Whitney.

The Marketing of Automobiles in Britain and the United States before 1939

Roy Church
University of East Anglia

Many of the differences to be found in the evolution of the marketing of automobiles in Britain and the United States are explicable in terms of either the chronological development of the industry or of the contrasting characteristics of markets. We shall consider in turn, therefore, the perception and creation of a market for automobiles, national market characteristics, the phase of initial demand, the maturation of the market, the structure and organization of distribution for automobiles and parts, marketing methods, and policies on overseas sales.

I. Market Creation and National Characteristics

There is little need for speculation in explaining the early rapid growth of the American automobile industry in a country of great distances with a large population and high per capita incomes. But in addition to higher income levels, possibly a more even income distribution in the United States encouraged the emergence of a market which was not only potentially larger than those facing European entrepreneurs but also more egalitarian in character. These possibilities received reinforcement from the social history of American consumption, in which the purchase of consumer durables of some complexity was already a fact well before the introduction of the automobile. This feature of American consumption owed much to the precocious development of mass production techniques applied to the production of fairly sophisticated machinery, from agricultural equipment to typewriters and sewing machines.

The availability of an established engineering industry in which entrepreneurs were familiar with the concepts of manufacturing standardized interchangeable components and parts for assembly, enabling low-cost production of complex finished goods, was another important element influencing entrepreneurs' perception of the possibilities for automotive production and, equally important, in conceptualizing the market potential for this new product.[1] It has been argued, by contrast, that the approach to the market, rather than its sheer overall size, was probably critical in explaining the weakness of the early automobile industry in Britain.[2]

Not until 1913 did W.R. Morris, later Lord Nuffield, become the first British producer to assemble relatively low-cost light cars, but by that time Henry Ford had already demonstrated quite conclusively that even in Britain a market for relatively low-cost automobiles did exist. It is significant that it was Morris, with experience in selling cars from his garage and agency, rather than the engineer entrepreneurs, who led the movement towards volume production by a British company.[3] In 1913 W.R. Morris had found that it was possible to obtain components from British firms, at a price, so long as the numbers involved were not large, which raises the question why a components industry based on volume production for several firms had not developed before 1913. The reasons are not clear, but there were certainly social influences at work which contributed to a perception of the British market as substantially dissimilar from that which emerged in the United States, where even in the 1890s numerous engineers had begun to build prototypes and to publicize the merits and possibilities of a type of automobile with design and weight characteristics markedly different from those being built in Europe.[4]

The introduction of the automobile in Britain, however, depended less on free translation of the handsome French models than on more exact imitation of the vehicles imported into Britain, which initially set the standard and fashion. A handful of engineers responsible for the earliest experiments in Britain—Simms, Lanchester, Austin and Napier—sought to produce British models comparable with the French, but a more successful group in influencing market formation was the importing agents. Unlike would-be American purchasers of French automobiles, hampered by a 45 percent *ad valorem* duty on cars of medium price until 1913, British agents could import into an unprotected market, and it is not surprising that French automotive exports to Britain dwarfed those shipped to the United States.[5] Another factor which reinforced French dominance in the British automobile market was the influence of the several Anglo-French companies formed in these early years, helping the sale of French cars in Britain.

From the very beginning, some of the American pioneers experimented with the low-cost production of motor cars which were sturdy, though not carriage-like, relatively cheap and suitable for rough country usage over long distances, whereas the handbuilt, individually constructed vehicles made in Europe for a mainly urban clientele for use on European roads were more suited both to potential British purchasers and to the even more superior road surfaces in that country. But European cars were expensive to buy and maintain, in comparison with the American models built in volume on the basis of parts and components assembly. The image projected for the early cars imported to Britain was thus determined initially by the character of supply.

The initiative in defining the market was taken by a handful of mostly wealthy men who, having imported motor cars mainly from France, proceeded to promote their ownership in Britain, though the commercial momentum owed much to Harry J. Lawson, a flamboyant company promoter of dubious reputation but possessing a remarkable flair for publicity. With the interests of his motor car companies in mind, in 1895 he spearheaded the campaign to secure the lifting of the speed limit of 5 miles per hour and publicized the cause, which was vital for the trade, by organizing exhibitions and banquets to which he invited members of the aristocracy and other public figures of influence, including Members of Parliament. Afraid that Lawson's association with the motoring movement might be hindering the car's acceptance by the public, Simms and others established a breakaway Automobile Club, the aims of which included the achievement of a respectable image for the motor car. Demonstration tours and trials followed, in much the same way as they did in the United States, and a motoring press sprang into being simultaneously in both countries to foster the growing interest in motoring.[6] In 1903 the speed limit on British roads was raised from 12 to 20 miles per hour, one tangible symbol of acceptance, despite continued condemnation by those who criticized the pollution and danger caused by the motor car.

By 1905 the industry's output had increased to a level enabling some manufacturers to produce enough on a regular basis to cease direct selling to the consumer and to appoint agents, though frequently the initiative came from independent agents whose business had been established originally on the basis of imported vehicles. The origins of the early agents, and indeed of the early distribution arrangements for the sale of cars, owed much to the practices developed by those in the bicycle trade. By the 1890s cycling was a well organized sport and pastime; national and local associations and clubs arranged races and trials, and the enthusiasm of cyclists was shared by the many repair shops established by mechanics in many towns throughout the country. As the cycle industry grew, manufacturers appointed authorized agents to handle sales, parts supplies and repairs, and when some of the leading companies, such as Humber, Rover, Singer and Triumph, began to make motor cars too a distribution system already existed.[7]

Others took the initiative by approaching car makers whose models they wished to sell, allowing the cycle trade to decline as they gained a foothold in the sale of cars. This was the pattern adopted by a handful of leading independent motor agents, including S.F. Edge, Charles Friswell, Harvey du Cros and George Heath, and Watts & Brandish, who contributed much to the popularization of French, Belgian and German motor cars between 1895 and 1910. Other leading agents were C.S. Rolls, third son of Lord Llangattock, G.N.C. Mann (electrical engineer) and H.W. Egerton, and David Carlaw (instrument maker). In each case, and in others, the impetus towards car dealing often came as much from the sporting enthusiasm for cycling or motoring as from the economic background and rational investment considerations, though active participation in the sport and a sensitivity to the commercial prospects for the sale of the motor cars went together in the formative years of the trade. The cycle agent was typically a prominent member of the local cycling community and the same was true of the early motor agents, who no doubt recognized the opportunities for arranging a similar conjunction of social and sporting activity with commercial penetration.[8]

A key role in the formation of the early market for motor cars was played by the independent importing agents, notably Edge, Friswell, Rolls, Letts, Jarrott and Mann Egerton, whose activities suggest that all were in agreement in the conception of the market they were aiming at by regarding the car as an expensive luxury item for the pleasure of the rich at sport or play. Lawson succeeded in attracting the interest of the Prince of Wales in 1896; Friswell, on behalf of the Standard Motor Company, secured the contract to supply cars to transport King George V and Queen Mary on a state visit to India in 1912; Napier published the names and titles of the distinguished aristocratic purchasers, British and foreign, and it was not the only company to do so[9]. Not surprisingly, in 1907 the *Economist* described the market which had been created, in which the motor car had become the substitute for the carriage and pair, adding that until it could compete with the horse and trap it would not come into general use.[10]

There is some evidence that agents occasionally frustrated the efforts made by manufacturers to introduce cheaper standardized vehicles; this suggests that they too should share the blame hitherto laid on the shoulders of British engineers,[11] for a preoccupation with individuality and highest-quality, high-cost motor cars which inhibited the extension of car ownership. A turning point in the development of the British market occurred in 1907, when Percival Perry assumed control of the agency in which he had been involved since 1904, selling Ford cars in England. Until that time the national character of the market, underlined in the publicity generated by British agents and in the trade press, had resisted the "cheap and nasty" American automobiles. The report on the new Ford Model N which appeared in *The Car* significantly referred to the designers' having devoted care "to the actual working parts rather than to the attainment of a fine finish," and it was the lowest-priced four-cylinder car on the market.[12]

Despite the continuing prejudice against American cars, Perry's conviction that there was a market for low-cost motor cars remained, as did his personal admiration for Ford, whom he had met on a visit to the United States. When he was invited to become the head of a Ford branch in England in 1909 he accepted immediately. The agency had lacked sufficient financial resources or commitment from his partners, but in his new position he was able to demonstrate the validity of his convictions. By 1913 Ford sold more cars made in England than the five largest British companies —Wolseley, Austin, Singer, Rover and Morris. Nearly 29 per cent of total production in England were Model T Fords.[13] The Ford's relative success in the British market is explicable entirely in terms of its low price, for it was the only American car to secure sizeable sales in Britain, and it was heavily criticized for making only a single concession to the British market, namely the positioning of the steering wheel to give a right-hand drive.

This underlines the national character of markets for automobiles in the formative years. Whereas in the United States the long straight roads of uneven quality favored the large-engined, high-powered vehicles, which could sustain high speeds over long distances and required infrequent gear changes, it was the small-bore engines with long stroke which were more suited to British and European road conditions. This difference was to receive powerful reinforcement from the tax on motor vehicles introduced in 1921. Assessed on horsepower, which was calculated by means of a formula based on the piston diameter multiplied by the number of cylinders in the engine, the horsepower tax thus put an artificial premium on small-bore engines with long stroke and penalized the American type of large, high-powered cars.[14]

Levels of real income were important determinants of the size and structure of the market for cars, while for the sales of a particular company relative prices were often critical, especially in the 1920s. All cars were subject to tax, which was a sizeable component of real motoring costs, including petrol duties, and in aggregate these elements were heavier in Britain than in most countries, mainly due to the horsepower tax of 1921. From the mid-1920s, France and Germany had introduced their versions of a horsepower tax, but the formulas differed from those adopted in Britain, which continued to exhibit higher motoring costs than other countries.[15] In 1939 calculations made by the Society of Motor Manufacturers and Traders (S.M.M.T.) suggest that the total amount payable on a 1500-cc car travelling 8,000 miles a year, in the form of direct taxes, taxes on fuel and compulsory insurance, might have totalled £26 in the United Kingdom, compared with £6.50 in the United States (£19 in France, £15 in Germany).[16] To the extent that it is probable that the overall weight of taxation reduced the level of demand below what it would otherwise have been, government hindered the growth of the domestic market. But at the same time, the intended effect of the horsepower tax was to penalize American-style cars, and to that extent the government was indirectly responsible for adding to the degree of protection already affecting the British market which, since 1915, with only a brief experiment in free trade in 1924–25, developed behind a 33 1/3 percent import duty.

Manufacturers and traders have ignored these national characteristics only at their peril and to their loss. A striking illustration of this can be found in the history of the Ford Motor Company in Britain between 1919 and 1928, the period when the direction of the company was removed from the hands of the experienced Percival Perry. It was in that period when cars produced by Morris, Austin and Singer succeeded in ending Ford's dominance within the low-price cluster.[17] When Perry was recalled in 1928 he was successful in pressing the introduction of policies which had hitherto been rejected in Detroit, including a new model specially designed to meet the specific road and taxation conditions, and the anglicization of the Ford Company's public image in Britain by the formation of the Ford Motor Company Ltd., with 40 percent of the shares available to British investors.[18]

The characteristics of automobile marketing are related to the characteristics of the market for motor cars; consequently it is relevant to record briefly the chronology and dynamics of the demand for motor cars. It is convenient to distinguish two phases of the early growth of the motor industry, namely those dependent upon *initial* demand and upon the more characteristic long-term factors of changes in real income and costs. By initial demand is meant simply that which is attributable to the purchases made by those consumers who could afford to buy motor vehicles as soon as they learned of the existence of motor vehicles and realized their utility and desirability. In this phase, elasticities of income and price (or rather motoring costs collectively) are likely to be less important, at least directly, than what might be called the elasticity of product improvement; the propensity to reallocate *existing* income towards cars as their reliability improves and real motoring costs fall. This elasticity of product improvement was gradually superseded over time by those of income and price, and the resulting situation has been called a "mature" or "fully developed" market,[19] in which the dominance of second-hand cars quickly becomes a feature.

II. From Initial Demand to Market Maturity

The 1920s brought a widening of the British market beyond the aristocracy but little further than the upper middle class, the wealthy, professional and business communities. This relative lack of social depth provides a further contrast with the evolution of the market for automobiles in the United States. Indeed, even in 1939 car ownership in Britain was still predominantly middle class, for at least 50 percent of all car owners fell within the AB categories.[20] In the United States it is reckoned that by the late 1920s factors *other* than those arising from the demand for a new product, as reflected in the relationship between first-time and other buyers, exercised the greatest influence on the overall demand for vehicles.[21] In Britain the transition to a mature market occurred in the mid-1930s after the Slump, but the transitional phase was lengthy, as witnessed by the relative stagnation of home sales for nearly a decade after 1925, and by views widely expressed by contemporaries, both within and outside the trade, that saturation had been reached in the market for motor cars at home.[22]

The period of initial demand falls roughly into two phases from the marketing standpoint. In the earliest phase product improvement concentrated on evolving a basic design which could function reliably; in the second, after 1913 until the mid-1920s, a series of technical innovations were introduced which, because they were not visible to potential purchasers, needed to be publicized. These consisted of four-wheel braking systems, low pressure pneumatic tires, valves and valve gears, air cleaners and oil purifiers, oil cooling radiators, hydraulic brakes, etc., all of which enhanced performance enormously. The most effective method of publicizing these otherwise invisible features was through competition in reliability trials, and stunts, all of which continued to be important in the 1920s.[23] This was also the period in Britain of competitive price cutting on a scale which pushed down the real costs of motor purchase, and this stimulant to sales was reinforced by the widespread adoption of installment buying (a practice already familiar to the purchasers of pianos, another semi-luxury status symbol). By 1927 installment buying accounted for 60 percent of car sales in Britain, compared with 75 percent of all sales of motor vehicles, new and used, in the United States in 1925.[24]

The fact that real price reductions continued in the late 1920s and early 1930s without stimulating further significant new owner sales, whereas the absence of such price falls in the later 1930s coincided with huge increases in car ownership, underlines the powerlessness of marketing methods to overcome barriers to purchase when they take the form of inadequate levels of real income. This is partly explicable by the fact that vehicle replacement can be postponed. An investigation coordinated by the S.M.M.T. suggested that the average "expectation of life" was just over eight years during the 1930s.[25] Another lesson learned from the stagnation of the late 1920s, however, was the capacity of the small cars of less than 12 h.p. to survive the diminution in sales and to increase penetration, both at home and overseas, as car purchasers traded down.[26] This led to a proliferation of small car models, as Austin was joined by Morris, Rootes, Standard and Ford, in the seven to ten horsepower range. Furthermore, as the basic technical design of motor cars throughout the range more or less stabilized,[27] two important technical innovations—the displacement of paint and varnishes by cellulose sprays and the introduction of stamped steel bodies—contributed to an increasing emphasis upon styling and accessories. In the late 1920s the trend in motor car design and construction was described by *Autocar* reporters at the Motor Show as showing new consideration for the "owner-driver" by attention to closed saloons, easy access to engine and simpler maintenance, and concern to provide greater comfort for the driver—who could no longer be presumed to be a chauffeur. Thus the phase of mature demand, when it emerged after the Slump, was characterized by a different type of model-price competition, in which model proliferation and product differentiation was the strategy adopted by car producers and stressed by the distributors. Given the technology of volume production achieved in Britain in the early 1930s, and given the minimal scope for price competition, success depended more than ever upon modifications in design, styling and effective overall marketing in the search for hitherto unidentified market segments. A condition for survival by the small specialist producers was a similarly marketing-oriented strategy to discover niches within those market segments. The other major feature of the mature market for motor cars was the dominance of replacement demand, which by 1930 exceeded 50 percent of all new car purchases. They rose well above that figure in the Slump, and returned to about the 50 percent level in the mid-1930s. This development in the market increased the importance to manufacturers of cultivating brand loyalty even more than previously.[28]

In the fully developed market of the United States by the late 1920s, manufacturers sought to persuade motorists to replace old cars with new ones by introducing new models every few years, to accentuate the old-fashioned appearance of previous models. During the intermediate years, models received cosmetic attention in order to make one year's model distinguishable from the last. The intention was to accelerate replacement, and the success of such a policy kept up the level of demand. Similar forces were at work in the British market in the 1930s, when replacement purchases became the main feature of new car sales.[29] Models were changed every few years—if with reluctance by such veterans of the trade as Sir Herbert Austin—and "face-lifts" in the interim were designed to stimulate more rapid replacements. At the same time, first in the United States and then in Britain it was recognized that in a mature market absolute minimum price assumed diminishing relative importance to consumers, compared with improved quality or appearance.[30] This became apparent even in the economy car classes, as the experience of Ford and Morris demonstrated. When the Morris Minor was offered to the market as the first £100 car, it was the sales of the slightly modified version, costing around £110, which boomed. As Sir Miles Thomas, Morris's sales manager, later remarked: "No one wants to keep down with the Jones's." A similar lesson could be learned from Ford's attempt to capture the market dominated in the mid-1930s by the Morris Minor, by slashing the price of the 8-horsepower Ford Popular by 20 percent. The price cut secured an immediate impact in the market and sales rose, but still the cheap Ford cars were outsold by dearer cars which offered more comfort, performance and sometimes individuality.[31]

These events reflect the peculiar nature of demand for motor cars, which in the mature phase derives from the need for replacement and their high visibility. The result is that unlike bicycles, which were inexpensive items, or stoves, which were both inexpensive and of limited social visibility, motor cars acquired a special disfunctional utility, as objects of status. For all of these reasons, and because of a relatively low price elasticity of demand for motor cars in the mature phase, the stress on price competition among manufacturers largely disappeared in Britain in the 1930s and was replaced by model/price competition and product differentiation on lines not dissimilar to those which had already emerged in the United States. Within the distributive system, however, concealed price competition was more difficult to eliminate.

III. Distributive Structure, Organization and Policies

The evolution of the distributive structure was similar in many respects in the early stages of the trade in the United States and Britain. In the United States cars were frequently sold direct from the factory, or else marketed through regional distributors who were free to create their own local agencies in their territories. There were also independent dealers doing business directly with the manufacturers.[32] However, whereas in the United States dealers were held to contracts which required them to trade exclusively in the cars produced by one particular manufacturer, dealers in Britain normally retained their freedom to represent several manufacturers, receiving commission through trade discount. The British Motor Trade Association (B.M.T.A.) was formed in 1910 to regularize trading practices and to enforce retail prices and trade margins set independently and published by the manufacturers. At such an early stage in the development of the motor trade this proved to be a difficult task and not surprisingly, by 1914 some of the larger British manufacturers had appointed main distributors, though chosen dealers received supplies of cars from a particular manufacturer. The extension of this practice explains the introduction of a standardized discount in the trade by the M.T.A.[33]

The franchise system, as the American system was called, was introduced to Britain by Ford in 1919. All contracts involving almost one thousand dealers and wholesalers handling Ford cars were canceled, wholesale distribution was abolished, and agents were offered contracts directly by the company. The British trade press, manufacturers and traders condemned the policy: "Ford Knifes Bunch of British Agents" was a headline in one of the journals.

Under the new arrangements, Ford dealers were to be allocated a fixed sales quota, their turnover was expected to increase and they were to be required to carry increasingly larger stocks of cars and parts, paid for on delivery irrespective of whether they resulted from the dealer's order. Of the 1,200 Ford dealers in existence in 1919, only 400 renewed their contracts, though more drifted back later. Coinciding as it did with the unwillingness of Ford managers to provide a model to suit the British market, and to compete with Morris and Austin in the early 1920s, this radical alteration of Ford's distributive arrangements seriously damaged the company's position in Britain. These developments occurred at a time when dealers were flocking to William Morris, asking for a sole agency for Morris cars. Morris dealers increased from 400 in 1923 to 1,750 by 1927. The former British manager of Ford, Percival Perry, might have revealed bias in his assessment of his American successor's commercial policy, which he reckoned had "ruined the marketing system," not least because Anderson "quarrelled with all the best motor agents in England." Not until 1928 were relationships improved, when Perry re-introduced a more flexible dealer policy, though it also accompanied the introduction of new Ford models adapted more to British needs, which was almost certainly the more significant factor in the recovery.[34]

As price competition intensified in the 1920s, both Morris and Austin sought to establish exclusive dealing, but with only partial success; some became 100 percent Austin or Morris dealers, but the most important distributors continued to handle up to eight or ten different makes of car. Small dealers, especially, handled several makes in the more remote parts of the country. In 1924 William Morris offered some insights into the relationships between Britain's largest car maker and his dealers, and his attitude towards them. In the United States distributor's credit was often employed as the basis for an enlarged expansion of showroom stocks, whereas the custom in Britain was for dealers to pay on delivery, "cash on the cylinder head." In 1921 Morris's distributors conceded some part of the dealer's margin in order to enable Morris to introduce his spectacular price cut, which meant that the distributors and dealers had to be prepared to expand business as fast as the growth of Morris Motors. Such a policy called for a degree of confidence in, and commitment to, Morris, his cars and his policies, which justifies attributing to them an important role in the commercial and manufacturing success of Morris Motors in the 1920s.[35]

In 1924 Morris explained the difficulty he had faced in persuading dealers to alter their habit of thinking of car sales in small numbers, whereas his own aim was to sell cars in large numbers: "We get our own profit; we keep the dealers' profit reasonable, simply in order that we may sell cars in quantity. Having educated the dealer to this point of view, the next trouble of the sales manager is to train him to the idea of personal expansion. For instance, if one of our dealers sold a hundred cars last year, he was probably extremely pleased with the result. He thinks his showrooms, his sales staff and everything else is superb—and good for another ten years. What our sales department wants, however, is a sale of 200 cars next year and not a repetition of the previous feat."[36]

Austin adopted a different approach to distributors to challenge Morris's lead and shortly after World War I arranged favorable

credit terms with Industrial Corporation Ltd. in order to enable
distributors to hold a stock of Austin's models. In 1928, when the
company's financial strength had returned, the Austin Finance
Company was formed for the purpose of selling cars to agents on
bills, a measure designed to bring agents now earning slimmer
unit profits greater discounts to encourage larger stocks, and to
secure for the car-making enterprise an improved cash flow. The
company's bankers loaned £0.5 m. to the Austin Finance Company
to finance this venture, enabling agents to pay only 25 percent
down in cash.[37]

Merchandising automotive vehicles in Britain was extensive and
well developed, differing from American practice more in degree
of advancement than in principle.[38] So far as cars manufactured by
British firms were concerned the distributive structure by the mid-
1920s was two-tiered. Distributors were appointed at various
locations throughout the country and allocated a closed territory
in which to conduct wholesale business. Distributors appointed
agents, or dealers, and subdealers (none of whom was restricted as
to territorial sales), and it was the responsibility of distributors to
ensure that the retailers within their territory offered proper service
facilities for the vehicles handled. Contracts between distributors
and manufacturers and between dealers and distributors usually
ran for a year, from one motor show to the next, and prescribed the
terms and conditions on which the representation was based,
together with an estimate of the number of cars which might be
sold in the territory during the period. But in many instances competition prompted manufacturers to stock distributors or dealers
on a consignment basis.

The agents' or distributors' commission was between 12 1/2 and
20 percent, usually in the neighborhood of 15 percent of the
selling price of the car. Distributors who contracted to take a large
number of vehicles each year, and who pressed the claims of their
principal by keeping cars for show and demonstration and large
supplies of spares, could receive higher percentages. In cases where
the total commission was 15 percent, the dealer would commonly
take 12 1/2 percent, the distributor 2 1/2 percent. There is no
evidence of differential discounts for large and small cars, but the

potential drop in aggregate discounts on sales of small rather than large cars was offset by rebates on volume sales granted by manufacturers.[39]

In the mid-1930s the structure was similar though the distinction was clearer between sub-dealers, or retail dealers who differed from dealers or distributors in that they were not permitted to sell at trade terms to other dealers but could only sell retail to the customer. Casual dealers, large in number but responsible for a very small proportion of total sales, were under no obligation to stock new cars, though normally they provided some service facilities and they sold direct to the consumer only. Approximately one-third of all distributors' sales were made to consumers, the remainder to the trade at special terms. Dealers sold about three-quarters of the new cars they handled to the consumer. The number of sales outlets in 1927 exceeded those run by the estimated 13,000 members of the M.T.A., whereas the estimate for outlets in 1938 was 13,000. Between 900 to 1,000 were distributors or main dealers, approximately 2,500 were dealers, 3,500 retail dealers and the remainder were casual traders.[40]

The M.T.A. could act as arbiter in breach of contract cases, but in fact manufacturers and "concessionaires" (representing suppliers of foreign cars) rarely took measures against dealers. Dealer members each possessed showrooms or garages, and were suitably equipped to act as dealers in accordance with the requirements of the Association. One thousand more described themselves as automotive dealers, but failed to satisfy the qualification. These were in a position to cut prices without fear of sanction from the M.T.A., but even members of the Association were found on occasion to split commissions as a way of competing with others on price in what was ostensibly a fixed price system.[41] William Morris described his own method of handling one of the major sales problems in the 1920s—price cutting by Morris dealers:

"Wherever we find that the price of a car has been cut below our standard rates, we hold the direct dealer who controls the territory in which the price cut was given absolutely responsible. The sales department takes the utmost trouble to discover precisely by whom the sale was carried through. When we have traced down the dealer responsible, we insist on the payment of the difference between the price at which the car was sold and the list price. Practically every week we have a cheque in as a result of an illicit sale which we have tracked."[42]

The emergence of a substantial market for second-hand cars from the mid-1920s compounded the price maintenance policies of Morris and other manufacturers acting through the M.T.A., to the consternation of those dealers and manufacturers hostile to cut-throat competition. Increasingly from the late 1920s dealers had to learn to buy used cars profitably, as well as to sell new cars, as the proportion of trade-ins to new sales increased, for until agents learned to gauge the probable selling values of used cars money was lost and capital locked up in second-hand cars for which no profitable outlet could be found, due to the excessive allowance given to the original owner. This, of course, was a direct reflection of the "maturation" of the car market.

In an attempt to eliminate this practice, the M.T.A. printed a list of used car prices from time to time, beginning in 1927 and published in the *Motor Trader*. So anxious was the M.T.A. to secure effective control of trading practices that, prompted by dealers' pressure on manufacturers to increase margins in order to offset the squeeze on dealers' own margins caused by competitive increases in the discounts they allowed on used cars, the "Nemesis" scheme was introduced in 1933. The principal feature of the scheme was to encourage local traders to inform M.T.A. head office of price-cutting practices on the understanding that the M.T.A. would conceal the informant's identity and deal with the offender. Sir Miles Thomas, a former member of the M.T.A. Committee, recalled that *agents provocateurs* were used to uncover what was deemed to be unfair price competition.[43]

The high financial mortality among dealers was the aspect of the used car problem which eventually prompted manufacturers to join with traders in the formation of a joint Committee of Manufacturers and Retailers which issued a report in 1934. The major recommendation was a reconstitution of the M.T.A. so as to provide for a two-thirds manufacturer majority on its council and all committees. The turning point in the campaign to solve the used car problem proved to be the *manufacturers'* acceptance of responsibility for the implementation of the M.T.A. rules as a code of conduct, each manufacturer henceforward incorporating a clause in its respective contract with all distributors and dealers requiring membership in the M.T.A. The task of enforcement was tackled by the appointment of independent legally qualified chairmen to disciplinary tribunals and the employment of a lawyer as chief executive. The Joint Committee also recommended the annual publication of a National Used Car Price Book which laid down the maximum allowance that might be given for a used vehicle when accepted in partial exchange.[44] From 1935 any dealers found to be exceeding the maximum price, or giving discounts larger than those permitted by the manufacturers and printed in the National Used Car Price Book, were threatened with temporary exclusion from trading by cutting off the supply of new automobiles.[45] Attempts to control retail prices achieved only partial success, mainly because of the requirement that the committee should be unanimous in cases where exclusion was considered, but the growth in the stock of used cars was always an important factor threatening the complete collapse of price maintenance. Nonetheless, evidence presented by manufacturers to a subcommittee of M.T.A. in 1938 revealed a unanimous view that, despite the difficulties of control, the M.T.A.'s price protection scheme had been "of marked benefit to the industry,"[46] a cautious assessment which probably concealed a lack of control of the casual traders and smaller dealers, but reasonable satisfaction with the behavior of the more important retailers.

The relative, though tardy, success in controlling price competition between dealers in Britain contrasts with the attempt which had been mounted by the American government in 1933 to introduce a code of fair competition and price control. This occurred as part of President Roosevelt's New Deal program, and consisted of regulations for dealing with partial exchange by including maximum discounts. The declaration by the Supreme Court in 1935 that the entire program was unconstitutional threatened to destroy this attempt at control completely, but some states promptly introduced a license law intended to eliminate

excessive price competition by regulating allowances on used cars.
In several other states dealers themselves began to operate used
car price plans through local dealer organizations.[47]

The existence of a used car market had minimal effects upon the
market for parts and accessories, which in Britain was supplied
increasingly by British manufacturers by the mid-1920s.[48] Not until
after 1918 had clear distribution patterns of tire and electrical
accessories emerged, but until then garages typically received
supplies from manufacturers on a sale or return basis. With the
growth in trade in the 1920s and especially the policy, introduced
first by William Morris in 1914 and followed by Austin and others in
1918, of incorporating electrical equipment as standard fittings,
distributive arrangements became more uniform. Again, as in the
export of vehicles, American manufacturers of mechanical components, accessories, and ignition and electrical spare parts and
batteries appointed local agents who used the channels available
to British manufacturers. Between 65 and 75 percent of these
items, in value terms, were sold by manufacturers through an
intermediary to a retailer, though the figure was higher for ignition
and electrical equipment. The remainder were sold from manufacturer direct to retailer.[49]

In the tire trade between 55 and 65 percent of sales passed from
manufacturers direct to a tire house or dealer, the remainder
involving a wholesaling intermediary in addition.[50] The dealer sold
direct to the customer. Although tire houses dealt almost exclusively
in tires, dealers—including distributors such as garages and motor
agents who sold components, parts and electrical equipment—also
sold tires. Important changes occurred in the late 1920s in response
to a context of growing competition. One was the introduction of
a 33 1/3 percent duty on tire imports, which led to the American
tire-selling companies in Britain—Firestone and Goodyear—almost
immediately converting to manufacturing. The other was the formation in 1929 of the Tire Manufacturers Conference (T.M.C.) and in
1930 of the Motor Factors Association (M.F.A.). The policy which
was introduced by T.M.C. and upheld by the M.F.A., in conjunction with the B.M.T.A., was retail price maintenance, and while

initially the principle was accepted that, as in the vehicle trade, manufacturers were free to fix their own prices, a common price level for first-line tires soon emerged. Uniform procedures for dealing with price changes on a trade-wide basis were agreed upon in 1935. In fact, however, implementation was considerably less than effective, especially as the largest proportion of tire sales was replacements. Price competition, though tempered by collusion, was not eliminated and in almost all cases resale prices of second-and third-line tires were free of control in the late 1930s.[51]

In the electrical accessory market contracts were negotiated direct with vehicle producers, with Lucus leading the market from the mid-1920s based on its ability to offer entire sets of equipment. Otherwise, except for spark plugs, the replacement trade was conducted through vehicle distributors or electrical specialists appointed by suppliers as service agents, rather than directly through general motor factories, but the distinction between wholesaling and retailing in this branch of the parts trade was not at all rigid. As for price maintenance, there was little need for the Motor Agents Association to enforce it as the manufacture of the various items was monopolized even before Lucus acquired virtually all of the suppliers by 1930.[52]

IV.　Marketing Methods at Home and Overseas

It may seem surprising that despite the lag in the development of a mature market for motor cars and the even longer delay before relatively low-income earners became car owners, British marketing methods and selling techniques were similar to those employed in the United States, though until World War I they were aimed at a luxury market. From the early 1920s, when Morris unlocked the volume car market in Britain, inter-firm competition in that section of the market depended much upon the efforts of sales managers in the car making firms stimulating concentrated sales campaigns to sell their models. Writing in 1924, William Morris remarked that commercial managers had to convince dealers that the worry and trouble of expansion was worthwhile. They must talk to the dealer "about better showrooms, about the cubic space arrangement for the sale of larger numbers of cars, of the art of selling and advertising, of the number of staff per sale and so on."[53]

Some British manufacturers were not far behind their American counterparts in promoting the professionalization of salespeople. In response to initiatives taken by the Institute of Motor Salesmanship, Austin established a Sales Training Centre at Longbridge in 1932, offering a month's extension course of intensive training to salespeople employed by Austin agents, following a three months' course at the Institute's London headquarters. The company also arranged for lecturers to visit dealers' territories to lecture and advise on improving sales methods, particularly in relation to Austin motor cars.[54] Like American manufacturers, during the 1920s British manufacturers paid increasing attention to improving after-sales service, though Ford was the first to introduce a standardized scale of charges for the repair of Ford cars in Britain in 1919. Austin followed immediately, the first British manufacturer to do so, and Morris introduced a similar policy in 1923.[55] In 1924 William Morris emphasized the importance of persuading dealers to hold a sufficient stock of spares: "It will be realized that most of the work attached to dealing with complaints falls under the same heading—the giving of services to the man who had once bought the car. The satisfied owner is one of the best selling media in this trade. . . . Only by service after purchase can you keep the owner satisfied—and get his selling force behind your product."[56] Manufacturers also set up service schools offering courses aimed at familiarizing sales staff with car repair and service,[57] reinforcing the American acknowledgement that by the mid-1920s the rapidly expanding garage and service facilities in Britain revealed ample recognition that adequate servicing had become "as potent a factor in increasing automotive sales as advertising, price, or other consideration."[58]

By the mid-1920s American manufacturers received expert advice from the United States Bureau of Domestic and Foreign Commerce that "modern and intensive selling methods" currently employed in Britain were essential for American manufacturers seeking to break into the market for automobiles: "the science of advertising has made great strides in Great Britain. . . . all modern mediums are available to the automotive industry." The same American observer was impressed by a cooperative advertising campaign at that time being conducted in the press by British car manufacturers as part of a nationwide campaign to persuade the public to buy British products.[59] But while this approach was novel it proved to be an infrequent occurrence, even though the letterheads of some individual manufacturers and occasional independent advertisements continued to appeal to patriotic instincts. Lord Nuffield and Sir Herbert Austin, for example, continued to emphasize that their cars were providing employment for British workers, a claim of course which Ford could—and did— also stress in the mid-1920s.[60] Such "nationalistic" publicity seems to have been the only clearly "indigenous" sales technique. Indeed, it is virtually impossible to distinguish between indigenous and imported marketing methods, apart from that consequent upon the exclusive dealer structure which gave Americans such tight control over the retail trade, but which remained only an aspiration among the large British companies and was never fully achieved.

The trade press, national and local newspapers, posters and circulars carried the bulk of all advertising copy, and by the 1930s the largest British firms had followed the Americans by venturing into film. American advertising, typically handled by specialist agencies, tended to be more verbose and fanciful in content, compared with the rather more pedestrian appeal to be found in British advertisements. The difference is likely to be explained more by cultural differences than by the competence of publicity personnel, who in the case of the larger companies were typically recruited from the trade press. It is worth noting that when the Rover company's new manager adopted extravagant prose and employed semi-military metaphors the dealers revolted against what they considered to be a style more characteristic of American flamboyance and inappropriate for British car makers in general and for Rover—specializing in the medium-quality models—in particular.[61] At the annual meeting of Austin dealers, however, the assembled company joined together to sing the Austin Unity Song, specially composed in 1930 by leading music hall artists of the day. Sir

Herbert Austin (surprisingly), and his dealers apparently accepted an element of razzmatazz at the annual banquet not normally associated with British business behavior.[62]

With regard to availability of credit for installment purchase, British dealers were able to offer more favorable terms than did their American counterparts in the 1920s, reflecting general credit conditions and the flexibility of British financial institutions. Thus when William Morris decided to introduce a "hire purchase" scheme his reluctance to lock up his company's capital in such an enterprise led him to reach an agreement with the United Dominions Trust. Partly financed by advances from Morris Motors, who had to approve the contracts with the owners, the Trust bore the major financial commitment. Morris considered the advantage of such an arrangement to be the company's ability to inform potential customers of the terms of hire purchase, without ambiguity.[63] Other, less financially strong, car firms were assisted in their hire purchase sales by a handful of separate finance companies. A few of the largest London dealers typically required 25 percent deposit, with the balance payable in monthly installments over one or two years. Added to the more favorable credit terms available to British purchasers, a further contrast was the very low proportion of agreement violations in Britain compared with the United States.[64] In other respects practices were similar, for a survey of advertising in the 1930s showed the proportions of dealers' resources spent on distribution, including advertising, was not very different from that in the United States, estimated producers' distribution costs as a percentage of producers' sales revenue accounting for between 5 and 10 percent. In both countries the amount spent specifically on advertising automobiles was about 4 percent of the estimated net value of sales, and did not fall within the category of "substantially advertised goods." Expenditure on certain parts and accessories, however, was substantial, notably tires and tubes, brake linings and spark plugs, where product differentiation was almost impossible to achieve without advertising.[65]

Small in value, early British automobile exports were sold through independent distributors, though some of the leading firms had arranged foreign dealerships well before 1914. In 1909 Austin, for example, set up dealerships in France, Scandinavia, India and Japan. After World War I the major firms, Morris and Austin, extended to local traders exclusive rights to distribute their cars within a particular territory and encouraged them to develop a network of dealers. Intermediate between the manufacturer suppliers and the overseas distributors were the merchant houses who performed the same role for automobile exporters as for other exporters, packaging, forwarding, extending credit and bearing the financial risks in dealing with customers. As the volume of trade increased, the merchants' role diminished, concentrating upon providing financial and shipping services, as manufacturers developed closer relationships with their distributors and took a detailed interest in their sales performance. The logic of this trend was for the large companies to create special responsibilities for the exporting function within the organization, both for cars and spare parts. Thus Austin appointed one of his independent distributors as export director in 1922 and Morris set up a special export department in 1924, initially concerned with sales promotion but subsequently expanding to include shipping arrangements too. This trend towards closer control over, and integration of, exporting was shared by other firms, though final prices charged overseas were never completely under the control of the head office.[66]

Before Ford had introduced his assembly plant at Manchester in 1909, American exports in Britain were handled by agents in much the same way as the rest of international trade. Many of them continued with this policy after World War I. American manufacturers granted concessions to agents in Britain who were responsible entirely for the conduct of trade in the British market, the final selling price usually being left to the local agent's discretion. Otherwise, the "concessionaires" for American cars conducted business through identical channels to those used by domestic manufacturers.[67] The reasons explaining the relative lack of success of this arrangement are obvious, for the 33 1/3 percent import duty in operation from 1915 rendered even more expensive the more heavily taxed large-engined American cars of the type which American producers continued to offer to British purchasers. Success was only achieved by those companies, especially Ford and later General Motors, which adopted local assembly, at least saving expenses in duty and freight, and making it easier to modify vehicles to accord more with the demands of the British market.[68] The aforementioned advantage, of course, was only potential, and Ford failed to exploit it between 1919 and 1928.

Nonetheless, local assembly or manufacture was central to the advice offered to American manufacturers by government officials in the 1927 report, two years after General Motors had acquired Vauxhall as its bridgehead in the U.K. Indeed, the highly detailed informative surveys of overseas markets for motor vehicles issued by the Bureau, from the first in 1912,[69] are indicative both in their scope and succinct presentation of the importance attached to commercial intelligence. Compared with the American reports, the survey carried out by British officials in 1925[70] contains excessive detail, dense and ill organized to the point of indigestion—even for the curious and persistent academic! The American reports are models of clarity including unambiguous and specific recommendations.

Comparing net imports with exports after 1921, British car manufacturers may be seen to have succeeded in selling the distinctive low-cost, low-horsepowered cars, especially during the slump of the early 1930s, and sustaining that momentum thereafter. The growth in exports of chassis only from the mid-1930s reveals that belatedly British firms were beginning to adopt a strategy of local assembly in increasingly protected overseas markets, though the movement in this direction was both slow and limited.

While local assembly was the preferred alternative for competition in protected overseas markets, British firms were slow to adopt a similar strategy even though the position of British companies was eroded by the reduction or removal of preferential treatment by Dominion governments and rising import restrictions in Europe. Morris was eventually drawn to try this policy after the failure of his Societé Française des Automobiles Morris, formed in 1924 with indigenous connections, to overcome an apparent sales resistance to Morris cars. William Morris promptly resolved "to have a crack at the French" by acquiring the manufacturing facilities of the Léon Bollée at Le Mans. Between 1924 and 1928 a combination of poor location, unreliable suppliers, ineffective management and what William Morris interpreted as a perverse, if admirable, patriotic aversion to the purchase of foreign cars, produced a loss of £150,000, and the company was dismantled in 1931.[71] In the 1930s both Morris and Standard began to experiment with local assembly on a modest scale in Australasia, but without much success, for to render economic the long-range overseas stock-holding of components a substantially larger global sales volume was required than was achieved before 1939.

Conclusions

Before 1914 the national character of markets explains the differences between the kinds of vehicles which were most popular in the United States, compared with the type of best-selling models in Britain and Continental Europe. Thereafter, a modified version of the low-cost "utility" American car, designed to suit British and European road conditions and tastes, was sold by methods not dissimilar from those introduced by American manufacturers, though their use was less intensive in application and a little later to receive widespread acceptance in Britain. Aggressive selling methods, marketing techniques and the employment of hire purchase, or time payments, were common features in both countries, especially after 1920. The evolution of distributive structures and organization were also similar and even after 1920 differed more in degree, with regard to exclusive dealing, than in kind or intent. A notable contrast, however, was the degree of belated success achieved by British motor traders and manufacturers to control the prices of new cars and to stabilize the used car market by enforcing an agreed set of discounts. Finally, the American consular service provided a marketing intelligence of a superior quality compared with that available to the British motor trade.

Notes

1. H. J. Habakkuk, *American and British Technology in the Nineteenth Century* (Cambridge, 1962), pp. 203–204.
2. S. B. Saul, "The Motor Industry in Britain in 1914," *Business History*, V (1962), pp. 42–43.
3. P. W. J. Andrews and Elizabeth Brunner, *The Life of Lord Nuffield* (Oxford, 1955), pp. 71–76.
4. John B. Rae, *The American Automobile* (Chicago, 1965), pp. 8–19. On cars priced at less than $2,000 the duty was 30 percent, and above that price 45 percent. The duties were reduced in 1922 to 25 percent.
5. James M. Laux, *In First Gear* (Liverpool, 1976), pp. 98–99.
6. H. G. Castle, *Britain's Motor Industry* (London, 1951), pp. 45–51.
7. Kenneth Richardson, *The British Motor Industry 1896–1939* (London, 1976), pp. 211–212.
8. *Ibid.*, pp. 211–213, 216–217, 219.
9. Charles Wilson and William Reader, *Men and Machines, A History of D. Napier and Sons, Engineers Ltd., 1808–1958* (London, 1958), pp. 87, 89; J. R. Davy, *The Standard Car, 1903–1963* (London, 1963), pp. 17–18.
10. W. E. Plowden, *The Motor Car and Politics* (London, 1971), pp. 36, 39.
11. S. B. Saul, "The Motor Industry," *op. cit.*, p. 43.
12. Mira Wilkins and Frank Ernest Hill, *American Business Abroad* (Detroit, 1964), pp. 23–25.
13. *Ibid.*, pp. 5, 36–38.
14. E. A. Rouch, "The Overseas Automobile Market," *PIEA*, XVIII (1923–4); Maurice Platt, "The Effects of National Conditions on the Auto Design in Great Britain," *PIAE*, XXXII (1937–8), pp. 258–336; F. A. Stepney Acres, "The Requirements of the Colonial Market," *PIAE*, XVIII (1923–4), pp. 628–644.
15. U. S. Department of Commerce, *Motor Vehicle Taxation in Foreign Countries* (1927), pp. 24–27.
16. George Maxcy and Aubrey Silberston, *The Motor Industry* (London, 1959) p. 48.
17. Roy Church and Michael Miller, "The Big Three." *Essays in Business History*, Edited by Barry Supple (Oxford, 1977), pp. 172–175.

18. Mira Wilkins and Frank Ernest Hill, *op. cit.*, pp. 142–144, 155, 187–194.
19. George Maxcy and Aubrey Silberston, *op. cit.*, pp. 38–39.
20. Automobile Association, *The Motorist Today* (London, 1966), no pagination.
21. George Maxcy and Aubrey Silberston, *op. cit.*, pp. 38–39.
22. Michael Miller and Roy Church, "Growth and Instability in the British Motor Industry between the Wars." *Instability and Industrial Development 1919–1939*, Edited by Neil Buxton and D. H. Aldcroft (London, 1979), p. 189.
23. H. G. Castle, *op. cit.*, p. 161.
24. Cyril Ehrlich, *The Piano, A History* (London, 1976), pp. 98–104; United States, Bureau of Domestic and Foreign Commerce, *Installment Selling of Vehicles in Europe* (1928).
25. Political and Economic Planning, *Motor Vehicles* (London, 1950), p. 62.
26. Michael Miller and Roy Church, "Growth and Instability," *op. cit.*, pp. 192, 199.
27. Maurice Platt, "The Effect of National Conditions," *op. cit.*, pp. 272–278.
28. Political and Economic Planning, *Motor Vehicles* (London, 1950), pp. 61–62.
29. George Maxcy and Aubrey Silberston, *op. cit.*, pp. 136–138.
30. Sir Miles Thomas, *Out on a Wing* (London, 1964), p. 168.
31. *Ibid.*
32. J. B. Rae, *op. cit.*, p. 18.
33. H. G. Castle, *op. cit.*, p. 149; P. W. S. Andrews and Elizabeth Brunner, *op. cit.*, pp. 116–117; K. C. Johnson-Davies, *The Practice of Price Maintenance* (London, 1955), pp. 1–4.
34. St. John Stevas, unpublished typescript history of the Ford Motor Company in Britain, pp. 116–119; Mira Wilkins, *op. cit.*, p. 100; P.W.S. Andrews and Elizabeth Brunner, *op. cit.*, pp. 116–117.
35. P. W. S. Andrews and Elizabeth Brunner, *op. cit.*, p. 116.
When Austin, advised by his dealers to introduce a smaller, popular car, requested their financial support they declined, but Austin's future financial viability was in serious doubt at the time.
Roy Church, *Herbert Austin: The British Motor Car Industry to 1941* (London, 1979), pp. 71–72.
36. Quoted in P. W. S. Andrews and Elizabeth Brunner, *op. cit.*, pp. 122–123.

37. Roy Church, *op. cit.*, pp. 90–91.
38. United States, Bureau of Domestic and Foreign Commerce, *Automotive Industry and Trade of Great Britain* (1928), p. 18.
39. G. C. Allen, "The British Motor Industry." London and Cambridge Economic Service, *Special Memorandum No. 18* (1926), p. 14; Committee on Industry and Trade, *Further Factors in Industrial and Commercial Efficiency*, Part II (1928), pp. 110–111.
40. James B. Jeffreys, *The Distribution of Consumer Goods* (Cambridge, 1950), pp. 350–351.
41. United States Bureau of Domestic and Foreign Commerce, *Automotive Industry, op. cit.*, pp. 18–20.
42. Quoted in P. W. S. Andrews and Elizabeth Brunner, *op. cit.*, p. 122.
43. Sir Miles Thomas, *op. cit.*, p. 185.
44. Political and Economic Planning, *op. cit.*, p. 44; K. C. Johnson-Davies, *op. cit.*, pp. 5–8.
45. K. C. Johnson-Davies, *op. cit.*, p. 7.
46. *Ibid.*
47. *Ibid.*, pp. 111–112.
48. United States, Bureau of Domestic and Foreign Commerce, *Automotive Industry, op. cip.*, p. 28.
49. J. B. Jeffreys, *op. cit.*, pp. 353–354.
50. *Ibid.*, p. 356.
51. Monopolies and Restrictive Practices Commission, *Report on the Supply and Export of Pneumatic Tyres* (1955), pp. 15–49.
52. Roy Church, "Innovation, Monopoly and the Supply of Vehicle Components in Britain, 1880–1930." *Business History Review*, LII (1978), pp. 226–249.
53. Quoted in P. W. S. Andrews and Elizabeth Brunner, *op. cit.*, p. 122.
54. Roy Church, *op. cit.*, (1979), p. 50.
55. *Ibid.*, p. 91; R. J. Overy, *William Morris, Viscount Nuffield* (1976), p. 78; U. S. Bureau of Domestic and Foreign Commerce, *Automotive Industry, op. cit.*, p. 22.
56. P. W. S. Andrews and Elizabeth Brunner, *op. cit.*, p. 123.
57. *The Times*, October 29, 1930.
58. U. S. Bureau of Domestic and Foreign Commerce, *Automotive Industry, op. cit.*, p. 22.
59. U. S. Bureau of Domestic and Foreign Commerce, *Automotive Industry, op. cit.*, pp. 18, 44.
60. R. J. Overy, *op. cit.*, pp. 76–77; *Ford Times*, September 1925, p. 617.
61. George Oliver, *The Rover* (London, 1971), pp. 100–102.

62. Roy Church, *Herbert Austin, op. cit.*, pp. 151–152.
63. P. W. S. Andrews and Elizabeth Brunner, *op. cit.*, pp. 118–119.
64. United States, Bureau of Domestic and Foreign Commerce, *Automotive Industry, op. cit.*, pp. 20–21; P. W. S. Andrews and Elizabeth Brunner, *op. cit.*, p. 118.
65. Nicholas Kaldor and Rodney Silverman, *A Statistical Analysis of Advertising Expenditures and of the Revenue of the Press* (Cambridge, 1948), pp. 31–32, 147.
66. P. W. S. Andrews and Elizabeth Brunner, *op. cit.*, pp. 200–203; Roy Church, (1979), *op. cit.*, p. 93.
67. United States, Bureau of Domestic and Foreign Commerce, *Automotive Industry, op. cit.*, p. 19.
68. *Ibid.*, p. 15.
69. United States, Bureau of Domestic and Foreign Commerce, *Foreign Markets for Motor Vehicles* (1912).
70. Committee on Industry and Trade, *Survey of Metal Industries*, IV (1928).
71. P. W. S. Andrews and Elizabeth Brunner, *op. cit.*, pp. 157–159, 207.

p. 59

COMMENTS

Patrick Fridenson
Université de Paris X—Nanterre

The British historian Peter Mathias wondered in a recent article whether the British industrialization process was unique. Let us apply the same type of question to the marketing of automobiles in Great Britain and study its specificity.

An important point which comes out of Professor Church's paper is how much Britain was an importer in the initial stage of the automobile industry, up to 1914 and even to 1919: an importer of foreign cars (mostly French, then American), of foreign parts (mostly American—remember Morris's difficulties in 1913—or German, with Bosch), of foreign capital (mostly French, then American), of foreign technology (the French sold licensing rights to British firms and they had an assembly plant in Britain, and in 1911 came Ford, of course), of foreign marketing procedures (e.g., the translation of French designs, the part played by the dealers importing French cars, and in 1919 the introduction by Ford in England of the exclusive dealership). This was certainly not so only because Britain had a low tariff; the U.S.'s higher tariff did not protect it entirely from European influence, at least until the success of the Model T. Could we not go further, and ask ourselves the following questions: Were not all countries importers in the initial stage of the automobile industry? Has it not something to do with the convergence theory we discussed earlier? Is the position of the British automobile industry comparable to that of other new British industries? How does the import of foreign procedures augment the strength of national distribution channels and of national culture?

A second point calling for comment is Professor Church's distinction between Austin the production man and Morris the marketing man. It is clearly not specific to Britain: one could draw parallels with Toyota and Nissan for Japan, with Renault and Citroën for France (in the interwar period and, in a reversed position, since World War II), and to some extent with Ford and Sloan's General Motors. It looks as if there was some kind of division of labor in major firms competing in their home market—reminding us of the tensions between marketing men and production men inside the firms themselves. What is Professor Church's explanation of this dual pattern which, after all, was observed in Europe and Japan even after Sloan's victory over Henry Ford? To which market needs or necessities does this double type of strategy answer?

A third point would be to try and see Britain's major marketing specificities so far as the automobile industry is concerned. No doubt a strong one is that Britain was able to solve before 1939 most of the used-car problems, and apparently without resorting to the law. We would like to know from Professor Church why Britain succeeded where other countries failed, and to what extent this success may be linked with (a) discounts for dealers and (b) pricing policies. A second specificity, when we compare Britain with the continental European nations, is the quick success of installment buying: 60 percent of car sales in Britain as early as 1927, compared with 75 percent in the U.S. in 1925. This is all the more striking as car makers established their own credit companies later than did their French counterparts; Morris established the first one only in 1929. Then, my question is: How far did credit sales rest on a national tradition? What was the part played by local dealers (the initiative being taken already in 1903 by Charles Rolls in London) and local financial institutions? What made British customers so eager to buy on time in the 1920s?

Finally, I wish to bring a quick qualification to Professor Church's opinion that the American car was largely determined by America's inferior road surfaces. Of course, road surfaces do matter considerably in the selection of the automobile products preferred by a nation's market, but I am not totally convinced that this factor was so important in American manufacturers' and engineers' early thinking. As long as they thought of the urban, luxury market, they would import not only French and other European cars, but also what has been called the French design. The trend toward a relatively cheap and light car seems to me much more connected with the growing perception of the potential market among America's rural population.

p, 59: comments

2   90 - 2

* 6150
041 21
044 1   6314
5310,   UK, US

Takeshi Yuzawa
Gakushuin University

Professor Church has presented an excellent paper which will raise considerable discussion among us. He considers the comparative history of the automobile industry between Britain and the United States, focusing his attention mainly upon marketing. His paper clearly analyzes characteristics represented in both countries, making use of such tools as an idea of developmental stages. I think his paper will be much appreciated in this conference.

The British and American automobile industries both started just a little later than the French and German ones. The American automobile industry made rapid progress, led especially by Henry Ford. The British automobile industry also progressed remarkably from the 1910s, but was partly assisted by an American car maker, Ford Motor Company of Britain. Comparing the productive ability of car manufacturers in the two countries, I think it mostly depends on the introduction of mass production and mass marketing systems, because Ford had taken a leading role in both countries by the latter half of the 1920s. Therefore I am especially interested in the way Ford moved into the British car industry and how the Ford "system" was partly transformed in its adaptation to British society. In order to investigate this point further, we would need Professor Church to expand more fully on the words "social influences" (page 60).

Similarly, in marketing, it seems a very serious problem to me how British dealers coped with the American marketing system. Indeed, Perry was fired on account of the dealer policy enforced by the Detroit head office (though he was able to recover his position after 1928). I would like to know the differences between the dealer policies advocated by Perry and the American head office and especially the way in which Perry formulated his dealer policy after his return. I am immediately reminded of Kamiya's dealer policy with respect to Toyota, for Kamiya was trained under Japan General Motors. As Professor Udagawa's paper shows, Kamiya tried his best to modify GM's dealer policy so that it could be easily adopted in Japan. The paper states that Kamiya stressed an "at-home" sales method in which "human factors such as mutual understanding and the spirit of cooperation should be taken into consideration when administering dealers." Therefore I am very interested in the influences exerted on Perry by the Detroit head office and his transformation of that policy in adapting to the British dealer system. Of course, Professor Church touched on this point on page 65, but I would like to know more details concerning Perry's role in the development of British motor marketing.

Professor Church categorizes two stages of demand for motor cars, initial demand and a mature market. I think this idea is very useful to our topic. He also emphasizes that the shift from initial demand to a mature market occurred in the 1930s. As Maxcy & Silberston stressed, a new form of competition, "model-pricing" competition, began in the 1930s with the appearance of new models (*The Motor Industry*, p. 106). The 1930s were one of the turning points in the development of automobile marketing, but I suppose this developmental pattern would be applied more properly to the American automobile industry. In America, Ford's Model T drastically declined in its share of total car sales, especially from 1927, and GM's full-line policy made its appearance in full readiness; in Britain, comparatively high-middle-class cars dominated the car market from the beginning to the mid-1920s except for

light cars made by the English Ford Co. In other words, I think
initial demand did not appear so purely in Britain as in the U.S.,
and thus many companies kept making different kinds of cars. It
seems to me that there existed a fully developed market in Britain
from the start.

In relation to this point, we have to consider the role of GM in
Britain through its control of Vauxhall. Whereas GM had a dominant position in the American car market, it could not play such
a positive role in Britain. Probably the existence of a fully developed
market prevented GM from introducing its full-line policy into
Britain, for many car makers had already supplied many kinds of
cars. But I have no materials to prove this point. I ask Professor
Church to explain GM's weak position in Britain as compared
with its strong position in the United States from the latter part
of the 1920s. At the same time we would like to know the relation
between GM and Vauxhall from 1928 and the dealer policy forced
upon Vauxhall by GM.

Generally speaking, British dealers had a stronger position in car
sales than American dealers, and kept it through the 1930s. According to Professor Shimokawa, an exclusive franchise system
was introduced in America in the 1920s with a mass production
system, and Ford pressured its dealers into exclusive contracts,
stressing their function in the sales organization and keeping them
separate from the framework of company marketing policy. On
the other hand, GM pursued a dealer policy which included
coordination of dealer inventory reports and of market and sales
forecasts with its production schedule. There was a striking contrast in dealer policy between the two companies. I wonder if
these different policies affected the British market system separately,
and if traditionally independent British dealers could maintain their
power in spite of foreign pressure. What was the main reason why
British car makers succeeded only partially in establishing exclusive
dealing, notwithstanding Morris's and Austin's attempts?

The Development of the Distribution Sector in the German Car Industry

6150
0441
6314
5310
♯ Germany

Fritz Blaich
Universität Regensburg

I.

The distribution sector, by which I mean the marketing organization and customer service, played only a subordinate role in the German automobile industry until the middle of the 1920s. The many firms which began production of the automobile after the turn of the century delivered to mostly a small circle of wealthy customers whose special wishes were taken into account. The firms also serviced the products which they sold. The typical automobile factory of that time thus united place of production, sales agency, and workshop under one roof.[1] The few enterprises which were already producing for a regional and anonymous market sold their cars to independent dealers, who assumed the financial risk of further sale. The first automobile dealers often came from the realm of the bicycle or sewing-machine trade. They followed their former suppliers in expanding to include vehicles, for notable German automobile manufacturers like Adler, Brennabor, Dürkopp, Opel, Stoewer, and Wanderer had originally begun with the production of bicycles and sewing-machines.[2] These dealers now faced the difficult tasks of selling, servicing, and, if necessary, repairing automobiles, in addition to bicycles and sewing-machines.

After World War I, inflation, which was already in full swing, permitted the German manufacturers further to neglect the distribution sector. The galloping decline in the purchasing power of the mark created a protected domestic market which was commanded by the seller. The panicked refuge taken by the citizens in material values inflated the demand for automobiles. Because the buyers were striving to exchange their money at all costs for material goods, they did not make their decisions to buy at all dependent upon later customer service. The possibility of currency dumping also paved the way for German automobiles, despite their technical backwardness, to enter foreign markets. The economy, heated by hyperinflation, attracted numerous new suppliers to the market who tried their luck with the construction of primitive, spartanically equipped small automobiles. Many of them acquired old machines from the remains of former armaments plants, placed them in a backyard or in a shack, and called themselves from then on automobile manufacturers.[3]

Only the management of the firm Adam Opel AG made preparations for the time after the slackening off of the inflationary economy. The location of the enterprise actually lay in the French occupied zone. It was cut off for a while from the domestic German market and enjoyed no duty protection until 1924, so that Opel from the beginning was exposed to competition from French and American manufacturers. This market situation forced the firm's management to modernize its production procedures as early as 1923 and, following the American model, to introduce assembly line production.[4]

The economic problems of the postwar period left their imprint also on the automobile trade. Many dealers who had made good money on the sale of the vehicles left by the former imperial army wanted to remain in this line of business. Shops which had been transformed into workshops during the war now hoped for civilian business.[5] The urge to speculate, which was fired by inflation, served to multiply the circle of automobile dealers by numerous unqualified and often also numerous frivolous members.[6]

The stabilization of the German currency, which was concluded with the introduction of the Reichsmark in 1924, ended the automobile boom. Almost all of the over one hundred automobile firms which had been founded since 1919 had once again to close their doors. Only Hanomag, Maybach, DKW, NSU, Röhr, and Goliath outlived the year 1932, although even then only with the help of state subvention.[7] If Germany had counted eighty-six automobile manufacturers when inflation was brought under control, by 1930 there were only sixteen.[8]

Exports ran dry. The domestic market transformed itself into a buyers' market. The middle class, which formed an important layer of buyers in the U.S.A., and to some extent in England and France too, stopped for the most part demanding automobiles in Germany, since it had lost its savings through inflation. Moreover, German manufacturers were now confronted on the domestic market with the competition of foreign suppliers. The number of imported cars was triple the number exported as early as 1924. The number of foreign, mostly American, automobiles reached its high point in 1929 with almost 40 percent of the new registrations.[9]

II.

The head start of the American automobile manufacturers lay in their use of assembly line production, which, in conjunction with consistently executed standardization and typing, considerably reduced the costs of production. Despite the duty and the high costs of transportation, the automobiles imported from the U.S.A. could thus compete with those of the German manufacturers whose methods of production and construction techniques had not substantially improved since 1914.[10]

Moreover, the Americans considered the German automobile market capable of undergoing development, which, in the opinion of their experts, reached in 1929 only the level corresponding to the American market of 1911.[11] Although Germany clearly lagged behind Great Britain and France with respect to the production and supply of automobiles, on the other hand it disposed of the largest motorcycle industry and supply of motorcycles in the whole world.[12] The technically mature motorcycle proved itself superior to the small automobiles of the time in its driving properties, its acquisition price, and its maintenance costs. It embodied the German "people's vehicle" of the 1920s and '30s.[13] Therein lay the supposition that an increase in the income of broad layers of the population together with a decrease in the acquisition and

operation costs of automobiles would rechannel the large demand
for motorcycles to the automobile market.

The Americans based their export offensive not only on the
technical advantages and economy of their products. As an equal
condition for a successful turnover they considered the construction
of a network of sales offices, spread over the market, which would be
in a position to execute both the servicing and the repairing of the
automobiles sold. Above all, Ford and General Motors (GM)
succeeded within a short time in establishing a model marketing
organization on the German market. In 1926 Ford had thirty
dealers at its disposal; in 1930 the number was already 501.[14]

With their low-priced six-cylinder vehicles, the American firms
offered the German dealers a marketable model program, and they
guaranteed punctual delivery. While German manufacturers
granted the dealers sales commissions varying from 17 percent to
21 percent of the list price, the American producers went up to 25
percent and, in addition, offered financially weak dealers long-term
payment plans. In addition, the Americans, above all GM, cul-
tivated a new partnership relation between the manufacturer and
the dealer hitherto unknown in Germany. They worked together
exclusively with independent dealers, thus employing no dealer
agents, and, in opposition to the German producers, abstained from
any direct sales to the customers.[15] For these reasons, the German
automobile trade in the second half of the 1920s preferred to
represent American brands. In the political field, it supported a
reduction in import duties on automobiles.[16]

The German automobile manufacturers thereby lost not only
productive dealers to foreign competition. They observed with
astonishment the importance the Americans attached to "service
after sale," which they emphasized in their advertisements explicitly
as an argument to buy their cars.[17] Most of the German producers,
on the other hand, made the mistake of claiming in their advertisements that their cars did not need any repairs because of their
excellent workmanship.[18] For most of the German brands in 1925
there was neither a supraregional parts supply nor an efficient
network of repair workshops. Repairs to automobiles were often
made in the factory, at great cost in money and time.[19] If the German

automobile manufacturers did not want to be squeezed out of the home market, they not only had to modernize their production procedures and their construction technique, but their distribution organization as well.

The firm Opel which, thanks to its serial production in 1928 delivered 26 percent of all the automobiles sold on the German market, corresponding to 44 percent of the total supply from German production, followed the American model in the construction of its marketing organization. When it was bought up from GM in 1929, it already had at its disposal a network of 736 dealerships, which, with the exception of two factory branches, comprised only independent dealers and extended over all parts of the German Reich.[20] Its customer service suffered, of course, from the shortcoming that parts of the car types were not mutually substitutable. For this reason many of its dealers acquired costly machines and themselves produced the parts necessary for repairs. After the takeover of the Opel Works by GM, the parts were standardized. At the same time, fixed prices for individual repairs were introduced. In 1931 Opel/GM established its own "Opel Service School" which trained mechanics for the workshops of the dealers.[21]

In the other German automobile factories, the direction of the distribution policy was determined by the production program. The strong American competition in serial production moved most of the manufacturers to retreat to the construction of luxury, sport and representation vehicles. The purchasers of such vehicles attached importance to individual styling and special quality. Cars produced and sold in large series were rejected as run-of-the-mill. Their readiness to pay high prices for the fulfillment of individual wishes promised the manufacturer a profitable output also in the case of small series or even single production. Moreover, the wages in Germany lay far below those in the U.S.A.[22]

The sale and servicing of these expensive cars, offered in a large multiplicity of types, transcended the financial resources of most of the independent dealers. Since, moreover, poor regions hardly offered a market for these vehicles, sales shifted to the important cities, where the customers expected elegant showrooms in lively business streets. For this reason, firms started opening factory branches in different large cities in which their employees transacted sales and customer service. The "Community of German Automobile Factories," formed by the amalgamation of the manufacturers NAG, Lloyd, Hansa and Brennabor, disposed in 1927 of over twenty branches belonging to the factories. Daimler-Benz AG supported forty factory branches in 1930. Small manufacturers also introduced this distribution system. The firm Maybach, which produced decidedly luxury automobiles, possessed three branches, alongside nine representatives. The Wanderer factory established two branches in Munich and Berlin in 1929 whose costs undermined its financial base. In 1930 Horch supported branches in Berlin, Breslau, Cologne, Dresden, Essen, Freiburg, Hannover, Leipzig, and Stuttgart.[23]

In many cases, the factory branch formed the starting point for the establishment of a marketing and customer service organization. Future contract dealers were schooled in the salesrooms of the branches, and mechanics were trained in the adjoining model workshop. At the same time, the branch served as the central parts warehouse for a particular sales district.[24] Distribution through branches belonging to the factory, however, required a high expenditure of capital. Only a product policy tailored to large and expensive automobiles can explain why firms like Wanderer and Horch, which were constantly suffering from lack of capital and financed long-term investments with short-term credits, put money which was urgently needed for the modernization of production into the construction of a network of branches.[25]

The Zschopauer Motor Works, the largest German motorcycle manufacturer at the time, tried, on the other hand, to distribute its new small car "DKW" through its existing dealer network. It was soon found, however, that motorcycle dealers were not up to the requirements of the automobile business. For this reason, at least in the large cities, the firm tried to attract independent automobile dealers as representatives for the DKW.[26]

III.

The global economic crisis hit the German automobile industry hard. Where utilization of its production facilities constituted 55 percent in 1929, in 1932 it sank to around 25 percent. At the same time, sharp price competition set in. In 1932 the sales prices achieved consisted of only half the proceeds which the automobile market had yielded in 1925.[27] The German automobile manufacturers kindled the price struggle in their factory branches to the detriment of the independent dealers. In their branches they underbid the list prices which they prescribed for the independent dealers, and paid excessive prices for used cars which the customers gave in trade when purchasing a new car. This market strategy quickened the collapse of many independent trading firms.[28]

In the realm of customer service, the stiff competition forced the German firms on to the road which the American producers, including the Opel Works, had already taken.[29] Beginning in 1930, all of the larger manufacturers introduced the standardization of repair work which is still usual today. Added to this were the guarantee services performed by the respective dealers. The firm Stoewer, for example, in 1932 offered through its representatives two free inspections at 800 to 1000 as well as at 2500 to 3000 km mileage and offered a further one at 5000 km at the inclusive price of 7.50 RM.[30] The constructional improvement of automobiles, which reduced their susceptibility to repairs, soon resulted in many workshops being no longer fully employed. This situation deteriorated in the crisis years, because many of the locksmiths, mechanics, and chauffeurs who became unemployed began to take illicit jobs repairing automobiles.[31]

These difficulties became overshadowed by the hostile posture maintained against automobiles by the governments of the Reich and most of the "Reichsländer"—the states of the Reich—during the world economic crisis. The tax burden for vehicles and gasoline remained adamantly high. Road construction was further neglected and long-distance connections in the form of thoroughfares were lacking. Within the framework of public investments, the state on the other hand supported the "Deutsche Reichsbahn," at the time a modern and efficient enterprise providing a narrow-meshed railway network with low fares compared with other European state-owned railways.[32]

This attitude of the state, which hampered the growth of the automobile industry, fundamentally changed after the decline of the Weimar Republic in January 1933. The National Socialist dictator Adolf Hitler recognized the significance of the automobile for the successful execution of the war which he planned. But he also saw that Germany limped after the other industrial nations in motorization: in 1932 there was only one automobile for every 100 residents of the German Reich, whereas this relationship was 1 : 5 in the U.S.A., 1 : 25 in France, and 1 : 30 in Great Britain.[33] Immediately after its "seizure of power," his government, for this reason, granted tax benefits for the purchase of new automobiles. It further began laying a network of freeways—the "Autobahnen"—intended to allow the driver to travel longer distances quickly and safely.[34]

Strict state supervision and steering of foreign trade drove the foreign competition from the German automobile market. Even the firm Ford, which had been running an automobile factory in Cologne since 1931, was discriminated against in the first years of National Socialist rule as a foreign enterprise in the marketing of its products.[35] The German automobile industry, on the other hand, emerged strengthened from the economic crisis. In the meantime, many unprofitable enterprises had been forced from the market. Moreover, the manufacturers in Saxony—Audi, DKW, Horch, and Wanderer—had amalgamated into a group, the "Auto-Union," in 1932.[36] Supported by the market regulations of the National Socialist government, which prohibited price competition within the automobile trade,[37] there was formed on the supply side of the market the structure of an oligopoly. Alongside the product policy, the marketing organization developed into an important weapon in the marketing strategy of the individual enterprise.

Most German manufacturers continued to orient their distribution policy to the system of factory branches. There were two reasons for this decision. For one thing, the world economic crisis had considerably reduced the number of independent and efficient dealers. For another, in view of the demand for automobiles kindled by the state, the establishment of branches belonging to the factory proved to be a foothold in order to cover the provinces with a network of contract dealers from there. In 1938 even Opel/GM maintained four factory branches in Aachen, Düsseldorf, Magdeburg and Breslau, which mainly performed the tasks of the model workshop and the central spare parts warehouse. Alongside this, the firm had contractual ties with 1750 independent dealers. At the same time, Daimler-Benz AG conducted its marketing through 49 factory-owned branches to which about 300 representatives were subordinated. Adler, Auto-Union, BMW, Hanomag, and Maybach also chose the factory branch as the backbone of their marketing organization. In 1938, there existed altogether 166 factory-owned branches in the German Reich, of which 143 were in cities with a population of more than 100,000, which accounted for about one half of the total number of automobile sales.[38]

Since the crisis years, many independent dealers were indebted to their suppliers and continued to rely on their credit. As a return service the manufacturers now required the dealers to sell their products and their spare parts exclusively. This exclusivity clause put the dealer economically in the role of agent for the manufacturer, although his legal independence remained guaranteed. In 1935, 70 percent of the German automobile dealers sold the products of a single firm, only 1.5 percent offering more than three brands. In 1938, when the economic crisis had long been displaced by an armaments boom, 62 percent of the dealers were still tied by the brand bind.[39] Exclusive distribution not only deprived the dealer of the possibility of playing the individual manufacturers off against each other while working out the contract details, but also created an additional source of acquisition for the automobile firm, because in the contract workshops only its "original parts" were allowed to be used.[40] The striving of the manufacturers to secure a portion of the parts market for themselves by pretentiously advertising the uniqueness of their parts led to a conflict with the National Socialist regime. Since the military usefulness of civilian vehicles increased if the parts of the individual brands were mutually interchangeable, the National Socialists required that standardization should cover the entire economic branch. The entrepreneurs, however, did not want to give up their spare-parts business. Only beginning in 1938,

in the course of the immediate preparation for war, did the regime
succeed in having the manufacturers reduce the number of automobile types produced from 52 to 31.[41]

IV.

Between 1939 and 1948 the development of the distribution policy
in the German automobile industry came to a standstill. Until 1945
the factories and the workshops served the ends of the war economy.
After the end of the war, production, which started slowly in the
almost completely destroyed factories, was administered by authori-
ties subordinate to the instructions of the occupation powers. Only
in June 1948 did the currency reform in the three western occupied zones, which since 1949 have formed the Federal Republic
of Germany, create again a market for factory-new automobiles.
In the Soviet occupied zone, from which the German Democratic
Republic later emerged, the means of production on the other hand
were nationalized and a system of state planning and steering of
the economic process introduced. In this way the Auto-Union group
lost its production equipment; it had completely to rebuild its production in West Germany. Several factories of the firms Opel/GM
and BMW were also expropriated.

From 1948 until the beginning of the 1960s the West German
automobile market underwent a phase of "peaceful coexistence."[42]
In the territory of the later Federal Republic there had been 724,960
registered automobiles in 1938. Of these approximately 350,000
(more or less needing repair) survived the war.[43] A high pent-up
demand combined with the prosperity of the population, which had
been rapidly improving since the Korean War boom, accounted for
the fact that the production capacity of the automobile firms was
exhausted years in advance. For this reason, only limited competition
intensity existed on the partial markets, which were delineated by
the size classes of the automobiles.[44] In the lower middle class there
even existed the partial monopoly of a new supplier, the Volkswagen
Works (VW), which had already been founded in 1938 by the
National Socialist party organization "Kraft durch Freude"

("Strength through Joy"), although it manufactured only armaments until 1945.

The situation of the seller market explains why it did not lead to a fundamental reconstruction of the marketing organization in the German automobile industry after 1948. Since increasing in the quantity of production constituted the pressing problem, the distribution policy of the automobile firms were tied to the facilities existing from the prewar period. The tie between factory branch and contract dealer, characteristic of most manufacturers, was reestablished.[45] Moreover, the market situation strengthened the bargaining position of the manufacturer vis-à-vis the independent dealer. Even a middle-sized firm like Goliath could still afford to dictate its business terms to the dealer in 1951; it required the takeover of its entire production program, among which, alongside automobiles, were three-wheel delivery trucks and agricultural vehicles, and it insisted on the posting of a high amount of security.[46]

Beginning approximately in 1955 the opening of the export valve subdued the spread of competition on the domestic market. In the first place, the automobile manufacturers of Great Britain, whose factories had been comparatively little damaged during the war, covered the high pent-up demand on the world market determined by the war. In doing so, they made the mistake of delivering cars at any price, without very strictly attending to the quality of the workmanship and without establishing an efficient organization for customer service and the supply of spare parts. For this reason, repairing British cars proved to be a costly and time-consuming matter.[47] German exporters had apparently learned from their experience with the American competition during the 1920s. The firm VW, belonging to the state, which developed into a pioneer of German automobile exports, began selling its products abroad only after already establishing an efficient network of contract workshops. Beyond this, the foreign contract dealer was obliged to maintain the entire parts for a complete car in his warehouse. Moreover, the management of the firm tried to bring about a business size optimal for the customer among the foreign dealerships. According to its conception, a dealer in the U.S.A., for example, should sell at least 200 cars a year, but on the other hand not more than 400, because adequate customer service was not guaranteed when there was a larger turnover.[48] The distribution policy of the VW Works on export markets decisively contributed to the firm's being able to assert itself in the "difficult" U.S. market.[49]

Between 1948 and 1960 only the market for small cars experienced considerable structural changes. In the first postwar years the demand for motorcycles was still extraordinarily great.[50] Then, however, improvement in living conditions in the Federal Republic permitted more and more citizens to switch from a motorcycle to a little car.[51] For this reason, a whole series of entrepreneurs began to produce small and "smallest" cars. For the most part, motorcycle manufacturers were involved; they now tried to make up for the shrinking turnover of motorcycles with sales of smaller cars. Also numbered among the new automobile producers was the former agricultural machine producer Glas, who offered the tiny car "Goggomobil," and the former airplane factory Messerschmitt, which produced a three-wheeled cabin scooter—in a sense the transition from motorcycle to car.[52] Also such famous motorcycle manufacturers as BMW, DKW (Auto-Union) and NSU were faced with the problem of gearing their extensive and efficient network of motorcycle dealers and workshops, consisting mainly of smaller workshops, to the automobile business. After all, BMW had constructed a series of small and luxury cars in the meantime. The Auto-Union had even come out with a middle-class car. The firm NSU, however, had sold its automobile production to the Italian Fiat works in 1928 and since then exclusively specialized in the production of motorcycles. In view of the restructuring of demand, it only decided to produce cars again in the year 1957.[53]

V.

The peaceful oligopolistic behavior of the German automobile manufacturers on the domestic market ended in about 1960. The stimulus to change the market situation followed from the change in demand. Rising wages and salaries now also permitted the workers and the lower employees to buy a car of the lower middle class. The demanders and suppliers on the partial market for "sticking-plaster-

cars" quickly lost their way. The shrinking demand for small cars
was mainly met by French and Italian firms. On the other hand,
buyers who had still been happy with a VW 1200 in 1955 but who
now could afford a larger car thanks to their increased income, had
to change their suppliers who tended to represent only the lower
middle class.

Moreover, there appeared fewer and fewer buyers who were
acquiring a car for the first time. The need for a substitute determined more and more the size of the demand. At the same time,
the supply of used cars grew, which, although they no longer
corresponded to the latest fashion, were generally in technically
perfect condition—unlike the veterans of the years 1945 to 1948.
Often the dealers could only sell a factory-new car when they took
a used car in trade. Sharp price competition raged among the individual dealers in determining the price for a used car.[54]

On the side of the producers, their oligopoly prevented the
appearance of a price struggle. Instead of short-term price reductions,
the increasing saturation of the market led rather to a change in the
composition of the cars, an expansion of the production program,
an enlargement of the marketing organization, and an improvement in customer service. In their product policy, the manufacturers with the help of product designing and advertising strove
to offer as attractive a vehicle as possible, at a sales price which
remained constant with the trend. Cost reductions as a consequence
of technical progress were not passed on in the form of price reductions, but rather in the form of product improvements. Moreover,
product designing pursued the goal of awakening a premature need
for replacement by influencing fashion trends.[55]

One peculiarity of the German automobile industry, however,
might be the outstanding significance which was attached to the
distributional sector and retail policy in the marketing strategy of
the manufacturers beginning in 1960. The automobile producers
made an effort to cover completely all the regions of the market
with their dealers and workshops and, at the same time, to expand
their production program as much as possible to all partial markets.[56]
In doing so, new product development and distributional policies
had a mutual influence on one another.[57]

All the important German automobile manufacturers tried to

effect an exclusivity obligation in their marketing organization for their vehicles and their spare parts.[58] In the framework of an exclusive contract and in view of the growing market saturation, however, only a broad range of types guaranteed the dealer a profitable turnover and the full employment of his workshop. For this reason, the dealers preferred contracts with firms which offered a range of models extending from small cars to luxury vehicles. Such firms, for their part, could select the most efficient dealers from the circle of prospects. Smaller suppliers, who were only represented by one class of cars, on the other hand, had to be thankful for every prospective dealer who wanted to work with them.[59] The chairman of the board of the NSU Motor Works AG appropriately characterized this situation from the point of view of his firm: "The main factors in the car business are trade and service. One doesn't get good dealers as long as one delivers to only a limited circle of customers. In other words: We need a complete menu."[60]

Also many customers proceeded on the assumption that the big firms had better customer service at their disposal. The marketing difficulties of the Borgward group with its middle-class program supported this belief. The buyers praised the beauty and the technical innovations of the Borgward Isabella, but they then preferred to buy an Opel Rekord or a Ford Taunus.[61]

The change in the structure of the supply side of the German automobile market began as early as 1958, when Daimler-Benz AG, which only produced cars for people with high-class demands, took over the Auto-Union, which produced small and middle-sized cars. The BMW Works, which faced liquidation in 1960, saved themselves at the last minute, because their type "1500" opened the road to the middle class. The Borgward group, on the other hand, a typical technologically-oriented company, went bankrupt in 1961, and its models disappeared from the market. In 1961, VW dared to take the first step in the upper-middle class with the 1500 "Beetle." On the other side, however, the Opel Kadett succeeded in 1962 in breaking the partial monopoly of the VW 1200 in the lower middle class. In 1965 the VW Works bought the Auto-Union and won with its brand "Audi" shares of a segment of the market which had been dominated until then by Ford, and Opel. Glas expanded its program from "smallest" car to small car up to sporty middle-class cars and finally even to large luxury cars. NSU placed the RO 80 with Wankel motor alongside its small car "Prinz."[62]

This firm, however, no longer managed to solve its distribution problems. Many of its dealers, left over from the time of motorcycle production, were unable to cope with the care of the luxurious and technically demanding RO 80 together with the Prinz. Others, however, let themselves be recruited by those competitors who could offer them a richer selection of models. Especially in the large cities NSU with its narrow production program had a hard time finding qualified contract dealers. The firm was therefore forced to establish costly factory branches through which it transacted more than one third of its entire domestic turnover. It further tried to draw up a common distribution network with foreign importers. The distribution communities NSU/SIMCA and NSU/Alfa Romeo failed, though, after a short time. The respective products offered by both the partners differed considerably in their technical features, so that the required customer service placed high financial demands on a dealer in the hiring of qualified coworkers as well as in the acquisition of tools and parts. In 1969 NSU merged with the VW daughter Auto-Union to form the new firm "Audi-NSU."[63]

Glas, on the other hand, failed due to its multiplicity of types. As early as 1964 the firm manufactured 32 different models with between 250 and 1700 cc cylinder capacity. In 1966 Glas had to rely on the help of the BMW Works whose dealers also sold Glas automobiles. In 1967 BMW bought up the Glas Works in which only BMW models were soon manufactured.[64]

Of these, only Porsche, which built expensive and exclusive sports cars, was protected from the restructuring of demand because it could depend on a small but steady and liquid group of customers. It spread the marketing of its vehicles over a legally independent distribution company, the VW-Porsche GmbH.[65]

VI.

Although the marketing behavior of the German automobile producers is similar, differences in their distributional systems continue to exist to this very day.

Daimler-Benz AG still uses the method of immediate sales.

It covers the domestic market with a network of forty-two factory branches to which B and C dealers as well as contract workshops are subordinated. This organization proves to be advantageous, because besides automobiles, the firm offers a many-sided program of commercial vehicles, in particular trucks and buses in all dimension classes, whose sale and service for financial and technical reasons could hardly be mastered by independent dealers.[66]

In contrast to this, the VW Works strides along the indirect road to marketing according to which the wholesaler is always interposed between the manufacturer and the dealer. The wholesaler receives exclusive rights for a particular market region, while marketing in foreign territory is fundamentally open to the retailer. A "Works Foreign Service" supervises and cares for the marketing organization. Meanwhile, the dealers also offer vehicles of the subsidiary company Audi alongside VW products.[67]

In 1955 Ford-Cologne already introduced the American system of "franchising."[68] The firm turned down the establishment of wholesaling and began to distribute its products exclusively through independent dealers. Nowadays, the supporting network is completed by "Ford contract workshops." The caring for and the control of the marketing organization is conducted by a foreign service belonging to the factory.[69]

Adam Opel AG made the transition to "franchising" on January 1, 1967 against the opposition of its wholesalers. Since then their marketing proceeds only through direct dealers, with the right to distribute brands of the American mother company—Buick, Chevrolet, Cadillac, Oldsmobile, and Pontiac. The tasks of the wholesaler were taken over by the factory foreign service. By excluding wholesaling and abolishing exclusivity the firm hoped for a strengthening of its marketing organization, because the sales initiative of the middle-sized and small dealers would thereby be kindled. As a matter of fact, the former wholesalers had also simultaneously maintained retail businesses and therefore sometimes regarded the dealers affiliated with them as bothersome competitors.[70]

The decision of Ford and Opel to replace the threestage marketing chain with a two-stage one also naturally strengthened the power of the manufacturer vis-à-vis the trade. It was the wholesalers who, with their protected marketing region, could, when they amalgamated, build up an effective market strength against the producers.[71]

The BMW firm distributes its cars among wholesalers to whom retailers are subordinated, as well as to direct dealers. For the wholesalers there is an exclusivity agreement. Moreover, BMW opened factory branches in several large north and west German cities in order to better care for and steer the sales on regional markets. The sale of motorcycles was farmed out to a special organization of dealers.[72]

Seen as a whole, the distribution sector of the West German automobile industry reflects the degree of concentration which dominates the level of production. The higher the percentage of the market share of a firm, the thicker is its network of dealers and workshops. On the other hand, the density of the supporting points guarantees the maintenance of a high percentage of the market. Since the principle of the exclusive brand-bind forces the legally independent dealer into a "quasi-employee relationship" and since the efficient dealers are already tied to particular manufacturers, a high threshold in front of the entrance to the market is erected for a new supplier.[73] Apparently even this hurdle may be overcome with patience and toughness. It emerges from the official statistics that on the German automobile market in the first half of 1979, the Japanese manufacturers with 5.4 percent of the market of newly registered cars for the first time superseded the Italian competitors, who achieved just under 5 percent. The Japanese, who first appeared during the 1960s as suppliers of automobiles to the German market thereby occupy second place behind the French among the foreign automobile suppliers.[74] This success is noteworthy because the Italian Fiat works have been paying special attention to the German market since as early as the 1920s and maintain a strong service network in the Federal Republic.[75]

TABLE 1 Some statistical data concerning the development of the German car industry.

(1) Production of cars in Imperial Germany 1907–1912.

Year	Number of automobile factories	Production of cars (units)
1907	69	3,491
1908	71	4,142
1909	121	6,682
1910	114	8,578
1911	131	10,319
1912	124	14,296

Source: *Statistisches Jahrbuch für das Deutsche Reich*, Band 36, Berlin, 1915, p. 122.

(2) Sales of new passenger cars by German manufacturers 1927–1938.

Year	Domestic market (units)	Foreign markets (units)
1927	80,652	2,000
1928	97,016	3,862
1929	88,876	3,683
1930	72,683	3,539
1931	51,287	8,071
1932	37,186	7,214
1933	83,369	9,539
1934	133,330	11,212
1935	184,075	21,158
1936	210,687	29,843
1937	210,021	57,889
1938	211,486	64,238

Source: Tatsachen und Zahlen aus der Kraftverkehrswirtschaft. Auf Grund amtlicher und privater Unterlagen sowie eigener Erhebungen zusammengestellt vom Reichsverband der Automobilindustrie E. V., Berlin, 1931, p. 13; 1934, p. 14; 1937, p. 12; 1938, p. 12.

(3) Home registrations of cars and percentage share of foreign manufacturers 1928–1934.

Year	Number of registered cars	Foreign brands (%)
1928	69,564	19.8
1929	100,301	23.2
1930	125,250	25.0
1931	126,751	24.2
1932	113,725	23.9
1933	103,759	19.9
1934	117,504	17.4

Source: Tatsachen und Zahlen, 1931, p. 34; 1934, p. 42.

(4) Imports of new cars including buses from abroad 1931–1938.

Year	Cars and buses (units)
1931	3,343
1932	2,569
1933	2,371
1934	5,062
1935	7,429
1936	6,558
1937	7,585
1938	8,086

Source: Tatsachen und Zahlen, 1938, p. 66.

(5) Production, exports and imports of cars in the Federal Republic of Germany until 1977.

Year	Production (units)	Export ratio (%)	Imports including station wagons (units)
1949	104,054	9.4	—
1955	705,418	44.5	16,842
1960	1,674,298	47.8	89,349
1965	2,440,448	51.3	274,074
1970	3,129,112	54.8	660,226
1975	2,686,729	51.9	769,434
1976	3,301,352	52.8	853,676
1977	3,567,190	51.8	959,682

Source: Verband der Automobilindustrie E. V. (Ed.), Tatsachen und Zahlen aus der Kraftverkehrswirtschaft 21, 1956, p. 90; 41, 1977, p. 26 f.; 42, 1978, p. 26 f.

(6) Automobiles per capita in Imperial Germany (until 1914), the Weimar Republic (until 1932), the "Third Reich" (until 1938), the Federal Republic (since 1949) (in each case at the beginning of the year).

Year	Number of residents per automobile	Year	Number of residents per automobile
1907	2,300	1938	44
1914	720	1949	78
1921	510	1955	27
1925	244	1960	13
1931	94	1965	6.1
1932	100	1970	4.4
		1973	3.8

Source: H. C. Graf von Seherr-Thoss, *Die deutsche Automobilindustrie. Eine Dokumentation von 1886 bis heute*, Stuttgart, 1974, p. 559.

NOTES

1. A. Griep, *Entwicklung, Standorte und Absatzmärkte der westeuropäischen Automobilindustrie*, Diss. (Kiel, 1955), p. 161 (unpublished); By 1914, 124 manufacturers in Germany had begun to produce motor vehicles. K. Schneider, *Die Hauptprobleme des Kraftfahrzeugabsatzes in Deutschland* (Hamburg, 1933), p. 7.
2. O. Meibes, *Die deutsche Automobilindustrie* (Berlin, 1928), pp. 39–40, K. Schneider, p. 7.
3. W. Dungs, *Die Entwicklung der amerikanischen und der führenden europäischen Automobilindustrien und ihre volks- und weltwirtschaftliche Bedeutung*, Diss. (Köln, 1925), p. 106 ff.; E. Ruppel, *Die Entwicklung der deutschen Personen-Automobil-Industrie und ihre derzeitige Lage*, Diss. (Berlin, 1927), p. 12 ff.; V. Köhler, *Deutsche Personenwagen-Fabrikate zwischen 1886 und 1965*, in: Tradition 3, 1966, p. 135 ff.
4. F. Klemm, *Die Hauptprobleme der Entwicklung der deutschen Automobilindustrie in der Nachkriegszeit und der Wettbewerb dieser Industrie mit dem Ausland*, Diss. (Marburg, 1929), p. 42; H. Hauser, *Opel. Ein deutsches Tor zur Welt* (Frankfurt/M., 1937), p. 156 ff.
5. E. v. Pelser-Berensberg, *Der deutsche Motorfahrzeug-Handel*, Diss. (Würzburg, 1924) (unpublished), p. 62 ff.
6. F. Gercke, *et al.*, *Aufstieg oder Untergang von Automobil-Industrie und -Handel in Deutschland* (Berlin, 1931), p. 21.
7. Köhler, p. 138 ff., F. Blaich, "Garantierter Kapitalismus." Sub-

ventionspolitik und Wirtschaftsordnung in Deutschland zwischen 1925 und 1932, in: Tradition 22, 1977, p. 50 ff.

8. A. Becker, *Absatzprobleme der deutschen PKW-Industrie 1925–1932*, Diss. (Regensburg, 1979), p. 56.

9. Tatsachen und Zahlen aus der Kraftverkehrswirtschaft (Berlin, 1931), p. 62 ff.

10. Röhr-Auto AG, Ober-Ramstadt 1977 (reprint), p. 24 ff., Meibes, p. 102 ff., R. Adelt, *Die Krise in der deutschen Personenautomobilindustrie*, Diss. (München, 1931), p. 50.

11. A. P. Sloan Jr., *My Years with General Motors* (London, 1967), p. 349.

12. In the years 1928 and 1929 German manufacturers of motorcycles for the first time surpassed the British firms reaching first place in world production. During the Great Depression British manufacturers again took this place. Since 1934 Germany's production clearly exceeded that of Great Britain. From 1930 onward Germany disposed of the largest supply of motorcycles in the whole world. Tatsachen und Zahlen, 1932, pp. 113, 123; Tatsachen und Zahlen, 1938, pp. 118, 121.

13. Blaich, Die "Fehlrationalisierung" in der deutschen Automobilindustrie 1924 bis 1929, in: Tradition 18, 1973, p. 30 ff.

14. R. Hoenicke, *Die amerikanische Automobilindustrie in Europa*, Diss. (Berlin, 1933), pp. 47–48.

15. W. Schmidt, *Die General Motors Corporation unter besonderer Berücksichtigung ihrer Absatzmethoden*, Diss. (Leipzig, 1930), p. 48 ff., K. Schneider, p. 35 ff., A. Becker, pp. 32, 212 ff.

16. F. Zimmermann, *Die Lage der deutschen Automobilindustrie und der Kampf um den Automobilzoll*, Diss. (Heidelberg, 1926), p. 55 ff., H. Schneider, *Die Entwicklung der deutschen Automobilindustrie nach dem Kriege*, Diss. (Frankfurt/M., 1929), p. 70 ff., A. Becker, p. 30 ff.

17. T. Hoehne, *Eine kritische Untersuchung der absatzfördernden Faktoren in der deutschen Automobilindustrie unter besonderer Berücksichtigung der Absatzplanung*, Diss. (Frankfurt/M., 1936), p. 154.

18. Hauser, p. 178.

19. H. Bruns, *Die Deutsche Automobil-Industrie mit besonderer Berücksichtigung der Kleinauto-Industrie bei der Rationalisierung*, Diss. (Rostock, 1926), p. 51.

20. Adelt, p. 46, Sloan, p. 349.

21. Hauser, p. 178 ff., Sloan, p. 350, A. Becker, p. 220 ff.

22. Blaich, Fehlrationalisierung, p. 27.

23. K. Schneider, p. 20 ff., A. Becker, pp. 204 ff., 221.

24. H. Röttger, *Die Struktur des deutschen Automobil-Einzelhandels mit Personenkraftwagen*, Diss. (Köln, 1940), pp. 67, 96 ff.; H. Kreitmair, *Die Organisation einer deutschen Automobilfabrik* (München, Berlin, 1931), p. 117 ff.
25. A. Becker, p. 209.
26. *Id.*, p. 206.
27. Blaich, *Wirtschaftlicher Partikularismus deutscher Länder während der Weltwirtschaftskrise 1932:* Das Beispiel der Auto-Union AG, in: Vierteljahreshefte für Zeitgeschichte 24, 1976, p. 406 ff.
28. A. Becker, p. 206 ff., 214 ff.
29. P. Borgward, *Der Wettbewerb auf dem westdeutschen Automobilmarkt seit 1948*, Diss. (Kiel, 1967), p. 236.
30. A. Becker, p. 222 ff.
31. *Id.*
32. Blaich, Fehlrationalisierung, p. 28 ff.
33. Tatsachen und Zahlen aus der Kraftverkehrswirtschaft 1932 (Berlin, 1933), p. 119.
34. J. Stölzle, *Staat und Automobilindustrie in Deutschland*, Diss. (Freiburg/Br., 1959), p. 40 ff. Concerning the history of the "Autobahn" see: K. Kaftan, *Der Kampf um die Autobahnen* (Berlin, 1955).
35. M. Wilkins, *et al.*, *American Business Abroad. Ford on Six Continents* (Detroit, 1964), p. 270 ff. Opel, though owned by General Motors, was not regarded as foreign because of its long activity as a German firm.
36. P. Kirchberg, *Entwicklungstendenzen der deutschen Kraftfahrzeugindustrie 1929–1939.* Gezeigt am Beispiel der Auto-Union AG Chemnitz, Diss. (Dresden, 1964) (unpublished), p. 43 f.
37. See J. Hassinger, *Die Marktordnung der deutschen Automobilwirtschaft* (Berlin, 1939); J. H. v. Brunn, *Ein Konditionenkartell der Automobilwirtschaft 1931–1945*, in: L. Kastl (Ed.), Kartelle in der Wirklichkeit (Köln, Berlin, Bonn, 1963).
38. Röttger, pp. 67, 94 f., Hoehne, p. 6 ff.
39. A Klein, *Entwicklung und Aufbau des Deutschen Kraftfahrzeughandels*, Diss. (Berlin, 1940), p. 15 ff.
40. K. Laleike, *Struktur und Wettbewerbsprobleme der Kraftfahrzeug-Teile-Wirtschaft*, Diss. (TH Aachen, 1965), p. 147 ff. Only in March 1979 did the Federal Antitrust Division take offence at these contracts, judging them as restrains of trade. "Kampf ums Monopol. Der VW-Konzern will keine Konkurrenz der freien Ersatzteilhändler," in: Die Zeit, Nr. 2, Jan. 4, 1980, p. 18.

41. H.-D. Laag, *Typisierung als Mittel der Wirtschaftslenkung*, Diss. (Heidelberg, 1942) (unpublished), p. 29 ff., Wilkins, pp. 272, 279.

42. H. Jürgensen, *et al.*, *Konzentration und Wettbewerb im Gemeinsamen Markt. Das Beispiel der Automobilindustrie* (Göttingen, 1968), p. 133.

43. W. Becker, *Der Mann mit dem Vornamen Auto*, (Düsseldorf, Wien, 1979[2]), p. 25 ff.

44. Jürgensen, p. 149.

45. The factory retail outlets operated by Opel/GM and Auto-Union were remnants of the prewar years. P. H. Lang, *Das absatzpolitische Instrument Absatzorganisation. Darstellung seines Aufbaues in der Personenkraftwagenindustrie der Bundesrepublik Deutschland*, Diss. (Freiburg/Schweiz, 1973), pp. 137, 163.

46. W. Becker, p. 57.

47. K. S. Reader, *The Modern British Economy in Historical Perspective* (London, Harlow, 1969), p. 127; D. G. Rhys, *The Motor Industry: An Economic Survey* (London, 1972), pp. 136, 379.

48. Reader, p. 127, R. Bormann, *Möglichkeiten und Probleme des europäischen Kraftfahrzeugexportes nach den USA*, Diss. (Köln, 1963), p. 97; W. Bartram, *et al.*, Die Erschließung eines Exportmarktes—Eroberung des US-Marktes durch das Volkswagenwerk, in: H. Jacob (Ed.), *Exportpolitik der Unternehmung* (Wiesbaden, 1969), p. 80 ff.

49. Bormann, p. 96, K. W. Busch, *Strukturwandlungen der westdeutschen Automobilindustrie* (Berlin, 1966), p. 149.

50. H.-P. Rosellen, *BMW, Portrait einer großen Marke* (Gerlingen/Stuttgart, 1973), p. 51 ff.

51. K. Fiedler, *Lebenshaltung und Lebensstandard der deutschen Bevölkerung in materieller und soziologischer Sicht unter besonderer Berücksichtigung der Verhältnisse in der Bundesrepublik Deutschland von 1950 bis 1956/57*, Diss. (Tübingen, 1961), p. 95 ff.

52. Köhler, p. 141.

53. Lang, pp. 84, 160.

54. Borgward, p. 323, J. Jahn, *Automobilindustrie und Konjunkturwandel* (Kiel, 1967), p. 15 ff., W. Becker, p. 100.
    Wilhelm Becker, Düsseldorf, set a pioneering example for independent dealers of how to overcome the difficulties of the used car market. Based on the principle that second hand should not mean second class, he was the first dealer to propagate the "honest" used car which had been carefully checked and completely reconditioned before being exposed for sale. Customers were fully informed about

the actual condition of each car. Besides, these cars were presented in showrooms, and they were sold under a registered trademark showing the "Second Hand" as a quality designation. See W. Becker, passim.

55.   G. Maxcy, *et al.*, *The Motor Industry* (London, 1959), pp. 15, 139 ff., 196 ff., Borgward, p. 323 ff., O. Gempt, *Zukunftsperspektiven der europäischen Automobilindustrie—Zwang zu weiterer Konzentration?* (Göttingen, 1971), p. 323 ff.

56.   Gempt, p. 81, Jürgensen, p. 74.

57.   A useful survey of the product strategy of the German car manufacturers: F. Jagoda, *Die Produktpolitik der westdeutschen Automobilindustrie*, Diss. (Darmstadt, 1972).

58.   Busch, p. 151, Lang, passim, W. Becker, p. 108.

59.   Busch, p. 150, Gempt, p. 87.

60.   W. Berthold, *Die mobilen Manager, Glanz und Größe der deutschen Autoindustrie* (München, 1966), p. 241.

61.   Busch, p. 150.

62.   *Id.*, H. C. Graf von Seherr-Thoss. *Die deutsche Automobilindustrie. Eine Dokumentation von 1886 bis heute* (Stuttgart, 1974), pp. 424, 434 ff.

63.   Busch, p. 151, Jürgensen, p. 75, Gempt, p. 88, Lang, p. 161.

64.   Rosellen, p. 124, Seherr-Thoss, p. 446.

65.   Lang, p. 200.

66.   *Id.*, p. 174 ff. As regards the range of commercial vehicles produced by Daimler-Benz AG see G. Finger, *Das Wachstum von Unternehmen. Mit einem Beispiel aus der Automobilindustrie* (Tübingen, 1968), p. 53 ff.

67.   Lang, p. 120 f. Information of Volkswagenwerk AG, Sept. 11, 1979.

68.   B. P. Pashigian, *The Distribution of Automobiles, an Economic Analysis of the Franchise System* (Englewood Cliffs N. J., 1961), p. 11 ff.

69.   H. Hildebrand, *Die Absatzpolitik der deutschen Automobilindustrie unter dem Einfluß des Gemeinsamen Marktes*, Diss. (TU Berlin, 1966), p. 148, Lang, p. 149 ff.

70.   Hildebrand, p. 149, Lang, p. 136 ff.

71.   Gempt, p. 85.

72.   Lang, p. 189 ff.

73.   Busch, p. 152, see furthermore J. S. Bain, *Barriers to New Competition. Their Character and Consequences in Manufacturing Industries* (Cambridge, 1967[4]), p. 300 ff.

74.   "Japanische Erfolge," in: *Frankfurter Allgemeine Zeitung*, Nr. 178 (August 3, 1979), p. 11. "Automobile: Japaner drängen nach

Deutschland," in: Der Spiegel, Nov. 12, 1979, p. 74 ff.
75. M. Raisch, *Die Konzentration in der deutschen Automobilindustrie* (Berlin, 1973), p. 90.

118 — 21

p. 93

COMMENTS

6150
* 0441
5310
6314
Germany

1

Koichi Shimokawa
Hosei University

By reading this paper, I can understand the total historical situation of automobile distribution in Germany and its role in the development of the German automobile industry. The German automobile industry, originator of the internal combustion engine and gasoline-powered vehicle, has succeeded to an excellent level of industrial technology. Nevertheless, as a result of economic conditions prevailing in the Weimar Republic the first stage of development of the German automobile industry after World War I had some special characteristics. Among these was the delay in establishing mass production and mass distribution of popular cars because there was no significant market; this was due to the reduced purchasing power of the middle classes caused by heavy inflation during this period. Therefore, foreign auto manufacturers, especially American makers, made aggressive inroads into the German automobile market. German automobile manufacturers were greatly affected by the American makers' behavior, especially in introducing the moving assembly line and improving marketing methods. In confronting the Americans' entrance, the German auto makers responded in two ways. One was to increase motorcycle production, and the other was to specialize in luxury or sports cars. Dr. Blaich's paper analyzes how the auto makers' behavior, from the viewpoints of production or product strategy, affected automobile sales and distribution during the Weimar Republic, Hitler's dictatorship and after World War II.

From the paper I understand the special features of German automobile marketing to be as follows:

First, I can see how and why each auto maker specialized, thereby strictly separating the production system and product strategy of each automobile class, from high-class luxury car to popular car. This division was due to the abnormal economic situation in the Weimar "age" and the traditional high level of the German machine industry, and its effect remains today.

Secondly, the paper considers automobile marketing problems in Germany, especially after-sales service, maintenance, and parts supply.

Thirdly, I find that there was a degree to which some German auto makers could not develop adequate sales and dealer networks; they lacked adequate financial resources and German political and economic conditions had hampered the formation of a mass market for cars.

Fourthly, there was a tendency for the already existing auto repair shops, staffed by excellent craftsmen, to use their power to obstruct the auto makers' policy to organize and develop affiliated repair shops. This element might have been one of the factors delaying the development of German automobile marketing compared with that of America.

In this regard I would like to raise the following questions for Professor Blaich.

(1) According to the author, the first automobile dealers in Germany often came from the bicycle or sewing-machine trade. This was also true in the U.S. and to some extent in Japan. Both trades were pioneers in cultivating the mass market and establishing a modern dealership or special agent system. What about the distribution systems of these trades in Germany? And what kind of effect did they have on automobile distribution?

(2) In the 1920s quite different attitudes prevailed among U.S. and German auto makers concerning after-sales service and makers' responsibility. What was main reason for this difference? There were probably different perceptions between the two countries not only about mass production and mass sales but also regarding auto repair service. Where and how did these differences come about?

(3) In prewar Japan GM and Ford had complete systems of exclusive and single car line sales through their Japanese dealers.

Was this possible in Germany from the beginning? If not, what were the main reasons?

(4) Were there any obstacles or difficulties when the German auto makers trained mechanics independently and tried to organize auto repair shops and establish an auto parts distribution network?

(5) What about the difference between the general distribution pattern of the German automobile industry—something like an exclusive sales pattern (p. 104)—and the American franchise system which was introduced in Germany in the postwar period (p. 108)?

(6) In the United States, auto parts standardization had been advanced by SAE soon after 1910. Why was parts standardization by private auto industry delayed during the Weimar period in Germany?

(7) Was it specific VW policy to establish an optimal business size in the U.S. market during the postwar period? How about the dealer's optimal size in Germany related to dealer's sales turnover? In Japan if a dealer sold more cars and had a higher turnover, customer service would be guaranteed every time.

(8) Why was there a time lag in introducing the American franchise system in Opel and Ford in postwar Germany? In Japan it was introduced during the prewar period even though it was in an incomplete form.

(9) In Germany what was the main reason for the maker-dealer direct sales system not being developed by Benz and VW? In Japan it has been introduced and established as the main auto distribution pattern; its operation is very different from in the U.S. In my opinion, it is important to discuss whether the American system is superior to other systems or not, even though the American system is one of the model patterns in auto distribution.

(10) The author points out that distribution in the West German automobile industry reflects the degree of concentration (p. 109). Is this point of view valid for all countries and cases? In the Japanese case, even when there was a low degree of concentration I can find examples such as Honda Motors which operated a maker-dealer direct sales system by using aggressive marketing.

(11) In this paper, I see that German makers specialized according to the class and size of automobile. Why hasn't there appeared

a full-line producer in Germany so long after the full-scale development of the German popular car market in the postwar period?
In contrast, many Japanese auto makers followed a full-line policy
much earlier.

(12) I understand that auto repair and maintenance servicing
have had an important function in automobile sales and distribution.
But in the development of automobile marketing in Germany did
other marketing techniques—such as sales forecasting and mass
sales promotion—act as more active elements? I think this problem
would imply some evidence for transfer of American-type marketing
techniques.

(13) What was the role in Germany of sales financing which has
played an important part elsewhere in automobile sales?

Hisashi Watanabe
Kyoto University

Professor Blaich presented a very interesting and wide survey of
the development of the distribution sector in the German automobile
(passenger car) industry since the 1920s. I greatly appreciate his
contribution especially because I know that as yet very few economic
historians in Germany are engaged in studies of the automobile
industry, much less of the development of its marketing activities.

Concerning marketing, our discussion is based on two criteria:
the marketing activities of each firm and the market structure as
given conditions for them. The latter is inevitably influenced by
external factors, especially the cultural environment and industrial
policy of the government.

In my comments I would like to concern myself particularly with
the market structure of the German automobile industry in this
sense, and leave Professor Shimokawa to concentrate on marketing
activity as such. My comments consist of seven points.

1) In the first place, I am very interested in Professor Blaich's description of the German automobile industry in the 1920s. Therefore I would like to begin my comments also with market conditions in this decade as preconditions for the later brilliant development of the German passenger car industry. Frankly speaking, it is for me a little surprising that the German automobile industry showed such a remarkable backwardness as he mentioned compared with France and Britain, although Germany was the successful forerunner of the invention of the internal combustion engine and gasoline car and the German national economy had already reached a stage of maturity equal with Britain, France and the U.S.A. According to the paper this circumstance was caused by unfavorable conditions in the passenger car market. The motorcycle was regarded as the "people's vehicle" and railway fares were lower than in neighboring countries. Moreover the government's industrial policy did not encourage the new industry. Therefore I would like to ask Professor Blaich how we should now interpret such a painful market situation. From where did this relative backwardness of the German passenger car market come? Was it perhaps a result of backwardness in German economic growth? Does it simply mean that the living standard of the German people sank for a while more deeply than that of its neighbors after the catastrophe of World War I? Or is it to be considered rather as a certain typological difference in the concept of transport among European countries? I think this question is not irrelevant to an analysis of the conditions which enabled the German automobile industry to enlarge its domestic market so rapidly, especially after World War II.

2) My first question leads me to the second one, about government policy for the automobile industry in the periods under discussion, in particular policies covering highway construction and securing of a gasoline supply. On the one hand, the automobile industry is very sensitive to related government policies, which are on the other hand, of key importance to the whole system of economic policy, the later the more. Therefore I want to ask why the Weimar Government turned against the automobile industry, how the National Socialist Government *could* promote it so effectively, and

if one can certainly say that the Federal Government has *consistently* endeavored to enlarge the domestic market for passenger cars.

3) My third question is concerned partially with the second one. Now I would like to have Professor Blaich's supplementary explanation about the German government's oil policy in each period at issue, because the automobile industry in contemplating mass sales could not expect a rapid growth of its domestic market without a certain prospect of there being a stable supply of relatively cheap oil. But Germany has had neither oilfields in the North Sea nor in Texas. Germany has had to seek reliable foreign suppliers of oil. Of necessity German oil policy is thus an element of her diplomatic policy. Therefore I would like to know if and how these circumstances have characterized the orientation of the export and foreign investment strategies of German automobile manufacturers themselves.

4) My fourth question is concerned with market structure in the 1920s. Professor Blaich emphasizes that the middle class which should have created the widest domestic market for the mass production of passenger cars had not yet come into existence in Germany in the 1920s. According to him, German small car makers were engaged in the production of luxury cars or sports cars for a thin stratum of high society. On the other hand, however, he points out that an overwhelming offensive on the German market by American rivals, especially GM and Ford, was conspicuous in the latter half of the 1920s. This raises the question of which social class provided the American passenger car makers with their customers in the German market. Were American cars regarded in this period as superior to the German cars? Did American or German car makers best tap the middle class market in Germany?

5) My fifth question is concerned with market structure after World War II. Generally speaking, the German national economy is still characterized by its tenacious regional structure, which has proved unfavorable to more than a few young industries. This is especially the case with production of consumer goods whose location is usually oriented to the market. Therefore it seems to me to be a very interesting phenomenon that economic particularism has not

disturbed the development of a national market in the passenger car industry. For each oligopolistic car manufacturer a segmental rather than regional share for its own product is now the principal concern of marketing. In that case, what has enabled the German automobile industry to integrate the regional market so quickly? I should like to know if Daimler-Benz in Stuttgart ever had any peculiar difficulties in exploiting the northern German market for its output and if so, how the firm overcame that. I should also like to apply the same question to VW in Wolfsburg with respect to the southern German market, BMW in Munich with the western German market, Opel in Rüsselsheim with the eastern German market, and so on.

6)   Now I would like to concern myself with the marketing activity of VW which has brought about its spectacular achievements after World War II. Both Professor Blaich and Professor Wilkins have emphasized that the success of VW on domestic as well as foreign markets is due to the splendid marketing method which Nordhoff at one time learned from GM. According to Professor Blaich, however, there is a distinct difference between the marketing systems of VW and Opel. Yet it is not Opel, which is a subsidiary company of GM, but VW which has been so successful at exporting German cars to the American market. This fact leads me to my sixth question: whether or not Nordhoff modified what he had learned from GM, adapting not only to the domestic but also to foreign markets, just as Kamiya of Toyota modified the American method to suit the Japanese market, as Professor Udagawa illustrates in his paper. I would like to have Professor Blaich's opinion about Nordhoff's probable modifications of the American method. On the whole I feel that historical German characteristics in the distribution system and marketing concept have not been mentioned enough in his report.

7)   My seventh and last question is related to VW again. Although VW is not a typical state-owned enterprise, it is not a typical private enterprise like Toyota and Nissan either, which probably makes one of the biggest differences between the representative automobile manufacturers of Germany and Japan. The Federal Government and the government of Lower Saxony are the

largest shareholders in VW. Therefore the government (especially the former) can maybe exercise some influence upon the decision making of this firm internally through the supervisory board. Therefore I would like to ask Professor Blaich whether, in which way and to what extent government intention can be materialized in the firm's strategy, especially when it concerns investment abroad.

French Automobile Marketing, 1890–1979

6150
5310
0441
6314
France

Patrick Fridenson
Université de Paris X—Nanterre

Introduction

It is well worth remembering that for most French car makers production has remained the major challenge from the beginning of the industry up to the present years, with only one significant exception: the depression of the 1930s (when car makers were forced to search for ways to sell to consumers). At first, their chief interest was directed toward refinements in the product itself. Then it often shifted toward the expansion of their production capacity and the improvement of their shop organization. Almost always, the French motor car industry was obsessed with the problems of trying to keep up with the demand, both national and international. This is one of the main reasons why management and marketing never received as much attention in France as they did in the U.S. from the mid-1920s onward, when most Americans who could afford a car had bought one. It also explains why American innovations in motor car marketing, whenever they were introduced in France, were not reproduced in every feature, but were adapted to French needs.

The market characteristics, distribution structures and commercial practices that prevailed in France in the period 1890–1914, when the French motor car industry experienced its first boom, are still not well known. Yet a few points may be stressed. In wholesale trade, the growth of the railways had permitted a simplification of the commercialization networks and a concentration of the dealings in certain cities. In retail trade, large department stores had been growing since the 1850s. More recent were chain stores, created after 1860 and especially after 1887, and most active in the grocery trade. Their success relied (as in the case of Félix Potin) on two methods which were at the basis of modern French distribution: they developed vertical integration and became their own manufacturers for the products they sold on a large scale (some American wholesale merchants selling French-made products on the U.S. market did the same by investing in French factories); and they insisted on the specificity of their trademark, enhancing its fame by conducting wide publicity campaigns. Their managers were no doubt among the founders of mass consumption in France. However, in the same period, small retailers did not decline, but, in fact, increased in number. In general, the French market remained fragmented, each social group and each region keeping most of its own consumption habits. This differentiation of consumption stood in the way of mass distribution.[1]

Historians do not know much about the marketing strategies devised in France by American and French producers of consumer durable goods such as sewing machines, reapers, cash registers and typewriters. But, again, we may dwell upon some features. The French-born bicycle industry, which reached large-scale production rapidly after 1885, adapted its marketing strategy to the existing decentralized commercial structure. For instance, the Peugeot firm, when it entered this industry, used its own widespread network of hardware dealers. In contrast, the main French cotton firms did not sell their goods directly to dealers or small merchants. After the Napoleonic wars they had created their own sales organization, consisting of regional warehouses which they ran. These agencies enabled them to "internalize the market," to use Alfred Chandler's famous phrase. However the atony of the French market in the 1880s hindered the spreading of this organization to other sectors by French businessmen. But American firms selling in France such consumer durables as typewriters, cash registers or cameras created their own sales agencies and even (in the case of Eastman Kodak) their own network of retail shops. So did the French and foreign firms for sewing machines and, in some instances, for bicycles, heating devices, gramophones, agricultural machinery. Yet for all these products, a part of the market remained in the hands of independent tradesmen who got their supplies from several makers.[2]

Lastly, it should be observed that France in the years 1871–1914 did not see a major development of exclusive dealing commitments, as was the case in Germany for the wholesale trade of coal, iron and steel, and printing paper.[3] In France also there were cartels, many more than is commonly known, but generally they did not completely control distribution. This was partly due to French legislation, but more importantly to the remaining divergences between industrial firms. Yet it should be observed that the largest grocery company, Félix Potin, introduced exclusive dealing in retail trade by placing contracts with provincial independent tradesmen giving the latter the exclusive right to sell the Potin products within a well-defined area.

The history of the marketing of French cars may be divided into three periods: from 1890 to 1914 the age of free and open franchises for a luxury market; between 1919 and 1939 the regulation (and Americanization) of salesmanship; from 1944 onward the application of modern management rules and techniques to the marketing of mass-produced products, a marketing now led by the manufacturers themselves.

I. To 1914

The pattern which most directly influenced the early marketing of the French motor car industry was that of the bicycle industry. Many of the early French car makers had first worked in that industry and they could use their network of bicycle dealers for cars, as Peugeot did from the beginning. It was also there that a new production device had been adopted: the assembly of mass-produced pieces on specialized machine tools. Many of the pioneer French car dealers had been previously or were simultaneously bicycle dealers. A striking exception was Panhard, which initially sold cars through its woodworking machine dealers.

In the early years manufacturers sold their cars at their factories, where they also provided service and production facilities. However, provincial companies had to establish their own sales and repair shops in Paris, since their largest market was in the capital. One third of the price of the car was paid in cash with the order, and the rest on delivery. But when the number of customers grew, companies had to dispose of their cars through dealers, and direct sales by the manufacturer declined. Usually cars were marketed through regional distributors who were the exclusive representatives of the maker for a certain number of departments and were forbidden to trade in other regions. In their territories the distributors themselves dealt with local agents or sub-agents who operated at the city level. Distributors and agents often handled several makes. The manufacturer sold the cars to the distributor or dealer at the price of the retail catalogue minus a discount of 10 to 20 percent. When they ordered cars, the dealers had to pay in cash about 20 percent of their value and the rest on delivery. There was no discount on replacement parts, but "the agent is always free to raise their prices to increase his profit." The early contracts lasted a year and a half. The Renault company reduced their validity to one year in 1906. Under these conditions, the manufacturers were able to organize quite elaborate networks of agents. By 1903 Renault had 120 of them. In 1913 Panhard had 58 regional distributors, and Renault 94.[4]

The distribution process of cars in the U.S. at the same time was almost identical, although there were numerous experiments by manufacturers to determine which method would best meet their requirements.[5]

In France the growth of the market led to several changes. Following the example given in 1903 in London by Charles Rolls, who took the initiative of selling Panhard cars on credit, a minority of French dealers decided to ask 20 percent in cash and the rest in four quarterly installments at an annual interest rate of 5 percent. Soon several small financial institutions specialized in installment loans to automobile buyers. The first to be established was the Automobile Bank, founded around 1906 by a diamond merchant (Hugues Citroën, the brother of young André Citroën) and by a car dealer. Through this bank a medium-sized company, Unic, arranged for credit sales.[6]

The larger manufacturers began to found their own branches for distribution and after-sale services. Peugeot started first, in Paris in 1897 and 1901 and shortly afterwards in the other major French cities. A smaller company, Lorraine-Dietrich, soon followed this example.[7] Renault, which for a long time refused to do so, finally created four regional branches between 1910 and 1913. Panhard by 1913 also had four provincial branches. In the U.S., the Ford company created branches from 1905 onward, but most of the other car makers did so only in the 1920s. Their French counterparts were obviously keener on commercial integration, the benefits of which they also experienced in foreign markets.

Marketing divisions came into being within the structures of the French motor car companies. They were soon subdivided to cope with the quick growth and variety of the demand. At Panhard the marketing division after 1906 was divided into three parts: Paris, the provinces, and foreign countries. At Renault there were two sections after 1908, one for cars sold in France and one for foreign sales and taxicabs.

A second-hand market developed slowly.[8]

From the beginning of the industry, demand was stimulated by a series of devices. The companies issued handbills, illustrated catalogues and picture posters. They advertised widely in the newspapers. They paid for sign-posts and direction-plates. The major car makers owned the daily newspaper *l'Auto*, founded in 1900, which sold 125,000 copies in 1913.[9] France was where automobile journalism began. Companies took part in yearly national and regional motor car exhibitions and shows. Commercial success sprang also from the development of automobile races, which made the public familiar with the motor car and provided the firms with an excellent commercial showcase.[10]

The publicity brought by the races and motor shows was all the more necessary as competition between firms was strong and, in most cases, not restricted by agreements and ententes. Moreover, French tariffs did not impede the penetration of foreign cars into the French market; French customs rates were 8–12 percent of the value of the car—a level much below the American one (45 percent).[11] Therefore the small sales of Ford's Model T before 1914 can be attributed not to the tariff, but to the insufficient marketing activity of Ford's European manager, H. B. White, and of his French dealers, and to the fact that in France Fords did not range in the lowest price. Therefore, despite encouraging signs such as *l'Auto*'s favourable comments, Ford could not overcome the resistance of French taste. All these factors prevented Ford from repeating its English success in France. Despite the great activity of Henri Depasse, Ford's first main agent, Ford's entry on the French market from 1907 onward did not alter the marketing pattern of French motor cars. The same can be said about Ford of England. Only in its marketing "was there any significant divergence from American methods. . . . A dealer was permitted to sell other cars as well as Fords." Ford established a small assembly plant in Bordeaux in 1913, but the war broke out before its operations had reached a significant level.[12]

In 1914 the French car market was drained by an already wide and dense network of agents, most of which had belonged since 1904–1906 to a National Union of Agents which defended their cause vis-à-vis the manufacturers.[13] But French marketing had two weaknesses. One was the free and open franchise policy. The other was the price and product policy of the car makers. The large majority of models sold in the middle and high ranges. Cars in the low-price range made up only 15 percent of the total production.

Why did French manufacturers not adopt a bolder marketing strategy? A partial explanation lies in the rapid growth of their exports. It enabled France to keep the leading position in the international commerce of motor cars up to the First World War. In 1907 French exports of motor cars and parts amounted to 50 percent of the country's total car production. By 1912 and 1913 it still remained at 44 percent, in spite of American competition in the English market. Exports were very profitable indeed. It should be noted here that much of their success did not come from manufacturers' policies but from the autonomous activity of foreign-born importing agents and also of wealthy tourists who purchased cars in France and brought them into their native country. Only a few French firms (especially Renault, Panhard, Darracq) had developed good marketing organizations abroad. Others let their product speak for itself. Another reason is that French manufacturers knew by experience that the large car is more profitable than the small car. Lastly, most of them kept focusing on the urban clientele. Let us give at this point a breakdown of the French domestic market. In 1901 the urban areas accounted for 63 percent of motor car registrations, for 51.5 percent in 1905, the same in 1907, and for 48 percent in 1910 and 44.5 percent in 1913. It looks as if the urban markets were soon satisfied, and as if the effort to penetrate the rural areas declined after 1905. Precisely, the expansion of the French motor car industry from 1919 onward (if we let exports aside) would rest on the clientele of small towns and rural areas.[14] Experts since 1905 had advocated the mass production of ordinary cars at a cheap price, and there was also the example of the bicycle industry, the expansion of which came in part due to lower prices (by 1913 there were 3.5 million bicycles in France). But managements in the motor car industry, despite the interesting success of the taxicabs, preferred to compete "on the basis of designs that emphasized reliability and elegance." Most of them had but a small interest in marketing and did not believe French customers were ready for especially large sales.

II. 1919–1939

The conditions of competition in the French market changed considerably in this period.[15]

First, protective tariffs were raised in 1916 to 70 percent of the value of imported cars. This was done at the request of French car makers who were becoming anxious about the growth of American production. After the end of the First World War the tariffs became lower, but they were still at a higher level than in the pre-1914 period: 45 percent minimum. In April 1930 they were raised to 70 percent minimum and 220 percent maximum, once again after a campaign led by the automobile lobbies. The same reaction against American hegemony occurred in all European countries. Taxes on horsepower were used to attain the same result.

Secondly, the structure of the French motor car industry itself changed. The most important car makers converted their factories to large-scale production and introduced the American-born assembly line. This move had been announced as early as 1916: at that time "half a dozen" firms were "making plans to manufacture popular-priced cars when the war is over" thanks to "quantity output." In 1917 a public report, the draft of which had been discussed with the manufacturers, advocated the same goals, and so in 1918 did an influential book written by Georges Cote, former general manager of Automobiles Pilain, in Lyons.[16] Thus the share of the Big Three (Renault, Peugeot and the newcomer Citroën) rose rapidly to 63 percent of sales in the French market (1929). The Big Three were highly integrated firms. The other car makers were mostly assemblers of parts produced elsewhere, and their output consisted generally of medium and high-priced machines for the upper middle class.

Thirdly, in 1927 the State reduced by half the road tax for cars of more than 9 years of age. This decree was a strong incentive to the development of the used car market, which outranked the new car market by 1930.[17]

The marketing problems which the motor car industry would have to face and solve in this new era had been well described in the 1917 and 1918 publications to which I have already referred. The previous system did not often make cars conveniently available for consumer inspection and testing in advance of purchase; the delay between order and delivery was uncertain; installment plans were established only by large distributors; replacement parts were provided conveniently only for the larger makes; the customers' practice of selling to the dealer their used car as partial payment for a new one on a trade-in basis had led the dealers to obtain from the manufacturers higher discounts on prices, at first to cover the risks in such trade, but also often to sell the new car at a greatly reduced price. These shortcomings were mostly related to demonstration, credit and repairs, services that traditional French merchants were not in a position to offer. Georges Cote suggested some remedies. An agreement between the car makers should intervene. It would set a uniform system of discounts, at a lower rate but with a bonus for high sales. But the firms should also increase the number of their own direct selling agencies. The dealers' retail outlets should be developed, together with a better availability of repair services and replacement parts, and storage facilities for the cars to be sold. Advertising should make great strides. Aňd financial institutions should be developed in common by banks and car makers (despite the recent failure of the Automobile Bank) to allow the widespread use of installment sales.[18]

How was this program implemented in the 1920s? The major companies subdivided the structures of their sales departments. At Citroën the "Service Commercial France" included the service of regions, consisting of (1) the four commercial regions of France and Algeria, the divisions of branches, installment sales and travelers, and (2) the commercial office, which took in documentation, prospection, advertising, road signs and toys. It included two other services, one for attendant parts and one for repairs. The sales department at Renault in 1932 also divided France (outside Paris) into four regions. But it was much more fragmented; it was composed of 37 sections and employed 795 persons.[19]

So much for management. Let us examine the changing relationship between the car maker and the dealer.

The number of the dealers grew rapidly. They were now as numerous—and important—in small towns as pharmacists, who were often their neighbors. By 1932 the total number of motor car, motor bike and bicycle dealers was estimated to be 15,000. Renault had 94 dealers in 1914, 277 in 1921, and 1,165 dealers and subdealers in 1929. Citroën in 1926 had 400 dealers (374 in 1934) plus 3,000 subdealers and stockists.[20]

The motor car companies improved their control of the financial liability of the dealers they chose, a point which had been underlined in 1918 by Georges Cote. The dealers had to deposit caution-money, the amount of which soon became proportional to the number of cars allotted to each dealer for the year. At Renault, with the yearly contract the dealer had to send a first payment on account for his future sales. It was followed by three other quarterly payments on account, so that the factory always would have the dealers' deposits for one term of orders.[21]

The companies also tried to settle the matter of dealers' commissions. In 1919, in the days after Citroën's entry on the market, two larger manufacturers, Peugeot and Renault, and two smaller pro-

ducers, Berliet and Ariès, signed an agreement on the distribution
of their vehicles. From now on dealers should sell at listed catalogue
price. There should be only one intermediary between producer
and consumer. The discount should be limited to 10 percent, and
one third of it would be settled at the end of each season, to induce
the dealer to carry out his engagements. However, the companies
signatory to this convention did not succeed in convincing many
other car makers, as they faced Citroën's competition, the "used
car-evil," and the slump of 1920–21. The agreement was probably
short-lived. Following the American trend, the percentage of
discount rose during the 1920s, from 12 percent to 18–25 percent
on average. In 1929 the Big Three agreed on the terms of a standard
dealers' franchise contract: it would last one year; the replacement
parts should be bought from the same manufacturer; the commission would be raised from 19 percent to 22 percent. Soon after,
however, the companies violated their own rules.[22]

The companies were more fortunate when they insisted upon
exclusive representation on the part of their dealers in each region.
Citroën, with its large expansion program, was a newcomer; it
chose to import American methods in every field, and was the first
French car maker to systematically regulate the distribution of its
product through exclusive franchise agreements with a sales quota
system. It started to do so in 1919. By 1923 every Citroën dealer
had accepted the restricted franchise, and the other larger manufacturers were developing the same practice. It should be noted that
Ford of England adopted the exclusive agencies pattern in 1919 too,
a few months later than Citroën. In exchange, dealers had to provide
the level of service the factory prescribed: large and well-lighted
premises, an inventory of replacement parts as determined by the
factory, the necessary tool outfits, and so on.[23]

The companies not only increased their supervision of the dealers
appointed by the factory; they also developed their technical, commercial and financial assistance to them. Once again Citroën was
in the vanguard. It divided its network into large regions, each of
them supervised in the factory by a region manager. If sales were
not sufficient, he could now send an inspector, rather than terminat-
ing the franchise. But the real commercial help came with the crea-

tion of a group of travelers who could be sent to the provinces to look for potential buyers, and with the launching, in 1922, of commercial caravans which displayed the latest designs through small cities. The firm also issued various pamphlets to advise the dealers in their prospecting and marketing activities. In 1927 it published its first sales handbook for dealers. Technical assistance relied on the sending of lecturers and demonstrators who gave advice to the dealers. Committees of dealers also met at the factory in Paris, where they codified every repair. In 1926, Citroën published the first dictionary of repairs and was soon able to issue a standard repair tariff, and later a tariff for replacement parts. The dealers' accounting systems were also unified and modernized. Citroën created in Paris three schools for its dealers and their workers: one for repairs, one for sales promotion, one for accountancy. But Peugeot and Renault took the lead in financial assistance to dealers. In 1929–1930 Peugeot established a company, and Renault two companies, whose aim it was to extend to the dealers loans on mortgage either for their sales or for building new garages. Just as had been the case in the U.S. from 1921 onward, the dealers had become so valuable to the manufacturer that the latter became interested in their survival "to the point of furnishing capital."[24]

At the same time, companies developed their network of retailing branches. From 1921 to 1929 Renault added 27 branches to its 4 prewar ones. Citroën had 3 branches in 1919, its incipient year, 9 in 1929, 11 in 1932, 20 in 1934. The branches were meant to display the best business practices, to provide a thorough knowledge of marketing costs and, of course, to yield direct profits. In the case of Renault, their creation was decided especially when the local market lacked dealers of high quality.

On the whole, the integration of the distribution system was more fully developed by Renault than by Citroën, as we can see from the percentages of sales attributed to each method of distribution in 1938:

	Direct factory sales	Retailing branches	Dealers
Renault	6.0	29.6	64.4
Citroën	1.4	22.4	76.2

In the U.S. too a tendency existed toward closer supervision of the distribution sector.[25]

Another response to the new conditions of trade lay in the provision of services to consumers. In order to sell more cars, the major companies (with Citroën again in the lead) developed installment plans. From 1922 to 1928 they set up satellite finance companies with the help of banks and insurance companies, following once more the American pattern. As in the U.S., a number of local credit companies also financed the time purchase of motor cars. The new companies made installment purchases of motor cars easier. However, the adoption of installment buying accounted only for a minority of new car sales in France:

1926	1927	1928	1929	1930	1931	1937
3%	7%	14%	20%	23%	23%	35%

These relatively low percentages cannot be explained only by the difference in incomes between the U.S. and France. Several factors are responsible. One is the high proportion of rural car buyers; they are said to have been reluctant to borrow and to make time payments. The second is the nature of the French banking and financial system, which is less diversified than that in the U.S. or the U.K. Finally, one may also set forth the attitude of car makers other than Citroën, which adopted installment plans later and to a smaller extent (among them, Ford SAF). Louis Renault, for instance, remembered the dangers caused by credit to his father's textile commercial affairs and also considered capital engaged in credit as insufficiently productive. When he resolved to create a finance company distinct from his corporation, he met resistance within his own administration, which was afraid of the new company's possible independence from Renault's main management. Yet sales on the deferred payment system had been developed in France by tradesmen since the 1870s, especially under the impulse of Georges Dufayel. Even then, though, peasants and unmarried men had always been reluctant to enter into credit arrangements. The French State intervened only in 1934, by enacting a law which gave the car makers a right to mortgage each car sold on time payments.[26]

The other services were also inaugurated by Citroën. He created a network of stockists, which made replacement parts easily available almost everywhere. He solved the difficult matter of repairs. He initiated the standard exchange of a used component. He adopted the one-year guarantee for all cars and the free overhaul of all cars after 500 km. He founded his own insurance company, which led to a reduction of the premiums by 30 percent. The other makers could but follow suit.

Advertising was widely developed. There again Citroën was the most active and often the first. It is worth noting that he used in the beginning the services of an American advertising agent who had settled in Paris. By the 1930s, the proportion of the turnover devoted to advertising had risen to 2 percent by Citroën and Renault (1.5 percent for American car makers, 1921–1927). There were a few major innovations. One was the use of films (as early as 1922), gramophone records and broadcasting. Another was the making of toy cars for children. A third was the sponsorship of spectacular journeys across Africa and Asia. A fourth was the use of prospection letters addressed by mail to potential customers; 15 percent of the recipients responded by buying cars. Manufacturers soon had their own advertising departments (24 persons at Renault in 1932). Occasionally they launched flashy operations (such as André Citroën having his name permanently illuminated on the Eiffel Tower between 1924 and 1934, or his reception of Charles Lindbergh in his factory). In the 1930s two things changed. The accent of the advertising campaigns often became xenophobic, with the public being asked to buy only French cars. The new management at Citroën from 1934 onward considerably reduced the company's advertising effort, doubting—like Louis Renault—its impact and preferring to invest in technical research.[27]

On the whole, the Americanization of French marketing policies remained uncompleted. Though General Motors' success in marketing was known in France, at least in the academic world, the forecasting of demand and statistical and financial controls on sales were not as sophisticated as Donaldson Brown and Richard Grant's elaborate analytical techniques. As late as 1934 Louis Renault still regretted that forecasts over "4 or 5 months" were "absolutely aleatory." And whereas General Motors had taken the lead in bettering dealer relations, French car makers did not move quickly to overcome their difficulties in this respect.[28]

In addition to domestic sales, the expansion of French car production (18,000 in 1919, 254,000 in 1929) also relied on the rapid growth of exports. This was mostly due to the weakening of the French franc, which gave French manufacturers a favourable position on foreign markets. When the franc was stabilized in 1926, French car exports began to decline, a decline that was increased by American and Italian competition. The car makers' counter-strategy was to develop their exports to the colonies. But from 1930 onward the colonial market also declined, though it became larger than the foreign markets. The network of dealers and branches in the colonies was considerably increased during these years.[29]

In the 1930s the problems experienced by the dealers worsened with the economic depression, and these played a central role in marketing policies.

France now had a selling market. Used cars accounted in 1930 for 52 percent and in 1935 for 68 percent of the registrations. In 1937 70 percent of new cars were partly paid for by trade-ins and 50 percent of them were sold in 2 years' time. Forty-five thousand used cars were sold each month. A difficult question for both customers and dealers was to determine the real value of the various used makes and models. From 1927 onward a weekly newspaper, *l'Argus*, published standard prices for used cars. But an attempt in 1930 to establish a statistical bureau furnishing schedules of prices and information cards on each vehicle on a voluntary basis soon failed. Therefore the trade-ins were often burdensome for the dealers, all the more so as they were slow to sell at lower prices. The special discounts with which some car makers provided dealers to aid in liquidating their stock (a method also used at General Motors) were not always sufficient or identical. The National Dealers Association persuaded the Parliament and the governments to put pressure on the manufacturers, in order to obtain an agreement on fair and standard selling prices and discounts. But it finally failed to reach its goal, and the market was in a state of chaos in 1939— contrary to what happened in some foreign countries. The dealers were also angry because manufacturers had reduced their discounts during the depression. Peugeot dealers had a 20 percent markup in 1914. By 1936 it had declined to 16 to 18 percent. On Renault's cheapest car, it was 15 percent by 1935.[30]

The weak financial condition of most dealers was the main reason why the Big Three cancelled in 1935 their intended introduction of smaller and cheaper models they had prepared. The dealers were not equipped for a larger output and for the lower discount necessary on small cars. Yet one lesson was drawn from General Motors' experience. In 1935 the Citroën company launched its first market survey on both the potential buyers' wishes and the social structure of customers. It conducted the same enquiry each year up to 1940. The survey paved the way for management's decision to prepare a popular car, the 2 HP, which was ready in September 1939 when war broke out.[31]

III. Since 1945

Several changes occurred after 1945, some of which had been anticipated by French manufacturers during World War II.[32]

Customers became more preoccupied with buying new cars. Selling was no longer their major concern, at least up to the mid-1950s. Their buying appetite was stimulated by the automobile press, which proliferated and found more and more readers up to 1974. It was now financially independent from the car makers and oriented toward the defense of the car drivers. The growth of replacement demand was a later phenomenon. It accounted for 20 percent of French registrations in 1963, 50 percent in 1969 and an estimated 80 percent in 1980.[33] The protective tariff barriers, still very high after the war, were progressively reduced to relatively low levels after the creation of the Common Market; a 17.6 percent common external tariff went into effect in 1968, and this was reduced to 11 percent in 1972. By 1968 free trade had been achieved within the European Economic Community. Initially reluctant, the French car manufacturers (under the lead of Renault) had accepted at the end of 1956 the lifting of barriers and quotas for the sake of expansion, as they contemplated enlarging their foreign outlets. The French motor industry consequently came under greater competitive pressure from the outside, accompanied by an expansion of foreign investment in assembling cars or components in France.[34]

Government regulation in other areas was greatly increased. In the long run, the two most significant measures were the control of retail prices, which ended in 1978, and the strict supervision of credit conditions. In comparison, the instituting of French national economic planning in 1946 did not really alter the behavior of the motor industry. Either the firms did not abide by the production levels and goals set by planning, or, because of the power of the companies, these production figures simply reflected the car makers' targets. This was even true of Renault, a firm that the State took over in October 1944 but whose policy ever since has always been largely autonomous. State ownership only encouraged the Renault Company to show more active entrepreneurship and to concentrate at first on inexpensive mass-produced models.[35]

The strategy of the Big Four (Renault, Citroën, Peugeot, Simca) adjusted itself to the new national and international environment. Up to the late 1950s it focused on models aimed at lower income groups, a trend which had begun to emerge in the late 1930s. The French car market became more democratized; by 1955 workers and employees accounted for 15.9 percent of new car registrations.[36] Then a Fordist pattern prevailed in France. It was supplanted at the end of the 1950s by a Sloanist strategy, i.e., the production of a diversified range of models, with frequent model changes.

Conversely, most manufacturers laid a greater emphasis on marketing issues. This time Renault took the lead. It created in 1945 a market studies department, which in 1946 launched its first survey on the potential market for the 4 CV, including interviews with 3,525 people all over France. This first survey was followed by a confirmation inquiry and by various quality inquiries. The result of these studies led a few years later to the establishment of a Quality Department, which considerably improved the reliability of the Renault models. A further pathbreaking move was, in 1967, the opening of a Department of Economic Surveys, which became in 1970 a Division for Planning and Information. To be sure, it capitalized on all the planning efforts Renault had engaged in since 1945 and even more since 1955. But it was also very innovative—thanks to its multidisciplinary teams—in its treatment of the global economic and sociological environment and of long-range (5- to 8-year) forecasts, and in its setting of mathematical and statistical patterns. Renault was one of the first French firms to advance in this area. The American-led Simca (Chrysler) soon followed. Renault had already been one of the pioneers of integrated management by introducing the computer in 1960 to regulate both stocking and production.

Renault during the whole period expanded advertising to stimulate the growth of demand in cooperation with the leading French advertising agency, Publicis. The content of automobile advertising changed from a preoccupation with fantasies to more practical content. In 1968 advertisers gained access to French TV, but Renault and the other car makers devoted a smaller part of their advertising budget to TV ads than many other French corporations did. By 1979 TV accounted for only 10 percent, while radio absorbed 16 percent and the press still accounted for 73 percent. In 1979 Renault spent 0.7 percent of its car sales income on advertisement. From the 1960s onward Renault became more preoccupied with styling and rationalized the choice of colors for its various models. The company also entirely rebuilt its network of dealers and agents after the war and enlarged it to 5,000 agents in the early 1970s and 7,500 in 1979. These were now supervised by company officials whose offices were in the main town of each region and who managed each of the 12 Area Marketing Departments (Directions Commerciales de Zone). They supervised simultaneously the retail branches and subsidiaries existing in the area. Renault indeed developed both the number and the size of its network of branches and subsidiaries. These numbered 60 in 1977 and had a share of 30 percent of the make's total sales in France. Departing from its prewar policy, Renault since 1945 has avoided multiplying branches, in order to reserve its available capital for industrial investment. Like Citroën, it creates branches only in towns where a large dealer gives up the game for lack of commercial and financial means. Renault's marketing strategy has so far resulted in only two failures, both in the 1950s: a large model called the Frégate, and a short-lived attempt to penetrate the U.S. market.

TABLE 1 The Proportion of French Auto Exports Accounted for by Each Maker (%).

	Passenger & light commercial cars				Trucks				Total			
	Renault	Citroën	Peugeot	Chr. France	Renault	Citroën	Peugeot	C.F.	Renault	Citroën	Peugeot	C.F.
1960	44.9	11.8	16.9	15.4	29.8	37.1	18.5	—	50.5	14.3	17.1	—
1961	43.6	15.6	20.1	13.6	29.6	45.8	17.9	—	46.6	18.8	20.0	—
1962	48.5	14.0	19.0	17.6	31.5	43.4	14.9	—	46.8	16.8	18.6	—
1963	47.1	16.8	20.5	25.9	29.3	46.8	16.2	—	48.6	20.3	20.0	—
1964	38.9	15.4	17.7	22.8	29.8	46.9	14.8	—	43.3	19.0	19.1	—
1965	42.3	16.7	18.8	21.9	35.4	43.1	13.5	—	43.6	19.9	18.3	—
1966	42.7	14.7	17.1	25.5	38.8	36.4	16.9	—	43.6	16.9	17.1	—
1967	46.9	12.8	19.0	21.3	32.5	39.6	16.0	—	45.9	15.5	18.7	—
1968	46.4	14.3	16.3	23.0	31.8	32.2	19.9	—	45.2	16.0	16.6	—
1969	45.9	15.0	16.5	22.7	33.5	34.2	19.3	—	44.8	16.7	16.7	—
1970	46.4	17.0	16.9	20.1	34.6	47.2	22.6	—	45.5	19.1	17.3	—
1971	42.5	17.8	17.9	22.1	29.1	58.1	24.2	—	41.5	20.2	18.4	—
1972	41.0	18.9	18.3	21.7	29.6	32.0	26.5	—	40.3	19.7	18.7	—
1973	43.0	17.4	18.5	20.8	26.5	26.6	26.6	—	41.9	18.2	18.9	—

Source: S. Soares-Ferreira, *op. cit.*, p. 149.

Simca was also rather keen on marketing, probably because of its financial links with foreign makers and its new management teams. On the other hand, in the 1940s and 1950s Peugeot and especially Citroën maintained conservatively-oriented commercial policies, inspired by an excess of caution and sustained by the exceptional (Ford-like) faithfulness of their customers. For instance, Citroën's first Marketing (in the modern sense) Department opened only in 1968; it was responsible for the development of computers in the firm. The main effort was directed toward expanding the distribution network. By 1966 Citroën had 27 branches, 300 dealerships, 4,400 agents. However, in the late 1960s and 1970s a younger management group pulled the two firms toward more expansionary decisions, particularly in the fields of modern marketing, and they partly made up for lost time.[37] By 1979 the total number of Citroën's branches, dealerships and agents had risen to 5,500. The same year the advertising expenses of the Peugeot-Citroën group occupied the fourth rank of all French corporations; Renault, which only had to advertise for one brand, was fifth, spending 30 percent less. The proportion of cars exported by Peugeot and Citroën also grew.[38]

Manufacturers offered better services to their customers. Renault again was the most enterprising, and to this day offers the best services. In 1954 it created the credit saving program, a system by which a customer paying for his car in 25 monthly installments takes possession of the vehicle as early as the ninth month. Citroën followed suit in 1959–1961, with delivery of the car taking place in the twelfth month. In 1964 it decided to include as part of the installment payments the trade-in of a used Citroën car. But Renault had gone further in 1963, with the free saving scheme. The customer deposits what he wants before ordering his car; when the savings reach a designated amount, his car is immediately delivered to him. Then in the early 1970s leasing was introduced. By 1973 leasing represented 9.8 percent of new car sales in France, installment sales 30.7 percent and personal loans 10 percent; 50 percent of new cars were bought on time (the proportion being higher for economy cars). Technical services for the customer also expanded. They were under control of the new and fast growing After Sale Department of the companies. The length and conditions of product guarantees were

increased. Microprocessors were introduced by Renault's maintenance stations in 1978. Lastly, Renault developed car rental facilities
by buying the Europcar company and assimilating it with its network.[39]

The used car problem was partly solved. In 1944 the State recognized the current used car price-list published by *l'Argus* and established by the National Chamber of Motor Traders as the official
standard basis for dealings. Other reliable lists of prices are still
published by *l'Argus'* rival newspapers and by a Parisian brokerage
organization, which—in contrast to *l'Argus*—publishes a list drawn
up from real transactions. The existence of these lists was one of the
causes of the increase in the percentage of direct transactions, i.e.,
those without any intermediary: it had risen to 50 percent by 1974.
Renault's network now sells second-hand cars of other makes which
arrive as trade-ins, after having reconditioned those it intends to sell
rather than destroy. They are given a special guarantee for 3 or 6
months after electronic control check. After 1958 Citroën also revised
and renovated its second-hand Citroën cars as a means of facilitating
the sale of new cars. Car makers in France were all the more anxious
to regulate the used car market as it represents 80 percent of all
transactions on cars. However, used-car transactions are sometimes
still marred by frauds.[40]

The dealer-manufacturer relationship was not settled by a law,
as it was in the U.S. A 1955 bill was rejected because of a strong
lobbying effort by garage proprietors, who fought efficiently against
the extension of the contract to 9 years and closer supervision of the
dealer's commercial business by the manufacturer. But though the
bill was rejected, the dealer's freedom generally declined. So did
the amount of his discount. For Renault's popular car in the 1950s
it fell to 8 or 9 percent of the selling price. This was but one sign
of the Renault company's tighter grip on its agents. They are carefully selected people and a rather stable group. The Area Marketing
Management department follows closely their commercial activity
and since 1965 it has offered them assistance in business administration and in accountancy. The company also helps in financing stocks
thanks to a special subsidiary firm. The Marketing Division, thanks
to the information and suggestions provided by the network,

produces a pluri-annual development plan of distribution. And, as in Sloan's General Motors, the chairman of Renault often spends time on field trips, to explain his policy personally to the dealers and to ask for their comments. After all, is not the French motor industry adopting General Motors' and Sloan's major lesson?[41]

Conclusion

Obviously, the history of French automobile marketing followed the general trend epitomized by the American industry. But this was not due to the presence of American-owned motor car firms or of American specialists in France. The exceptions were Citroën's start in advertising (in the early 1920s) and Simca's vigorous marketing policy (in the late 1960s). Rather, it was mostly the result of a deliberate strategy which French car makers adopted as a response to their own changing competitive situation. Whereas initially there was a market ready for them and they only had to meet its demand, they progressively discovered that it was necessary for them to do part of the distribution themselves through branches and, even more, to reach a better understanding of the market, of its own rules and changes.

Yet four special features of the French case are worth underlining. One is the slow growth of installment sales. It is all the more striking since, as we have noted, there was an important national tradition of time payments, even for expensive goods such as furniture. In addition to the explanations we have already mentioned, two more reasons may be relevant: the early development and strength of the second-hand car market provided an alternative to buying on time, and the conditions of credit for cars in France may have been less favourable than for other goods or in other countries. The other interesting point is the strength of State regulation of marketing conditions (more than of actual policies) from the 1930s onward. A third point we should emphasize is that French dealers—like their European colleagues—long had a stronger position (both in society and vis-à-vis the manufacturer) than their American counterparts. This was partly due to the number of brands available on the market. It left them the ultimate possibility to change from one make to another which offered better terms—a common practice in the 1960s.[42] Therefore the manufacturers could not exert on dealers the same type of pressures as Ford could in the years of the Model T. Finally, France's consumerist movements were much weaker and developed later than those in the U.S., leaving much more freedom for car makers to develop their customary policies. Thus the selling contracts remained ambiguous on several points; the date of delivery was not always certain; the data on speed or gas consumption were sometimes subject to discussion; and spare parts were too expensive. It would have been an easy solution to explain these original features by the peculiarities of French culture. I would rather speak of a response to new problems by a rational combination of available resources and factors within the existing economic and social frame-work.

In the French case, we should also stress the variety of the channels of distribution which have been used by car makers. As we have seen, such a variety characterized French distribution prior to the advent of the motor car. The French car makers adapted their policy to these indigenous traditions. Even today, we still find independent dealers (in small proportion, however).

In modernizing its marketing strategy and structures, the French motor industry not only achieved vertical integration by contracts, it also often set pioneering examples for other firms in the twentieth-century consumer durables revolution. A fine example of this is Renault's Planning Division. Citroën's collapse in 1934 was not caused by its pioneering marketing policy, which had enabled the company to dominate the French market. Its main source lay in an ill-timed renovation of the factories; it had been delayed too long, and its financial weight was too heavy in the heart of the depression.

However, it is clear that there are problems that French car makers have not been able to solve entirely. They have built a nationwide sales organization to generate a high volume of replacement sales, and yet official statisticians have observed since the early 1970s a trend toward demotorization in a minority of French city dwellers. The manufacturers have coped with the development of a basically replacement demand, but they have not reached total harmony in their relations with their dealers; neither have they offered a final

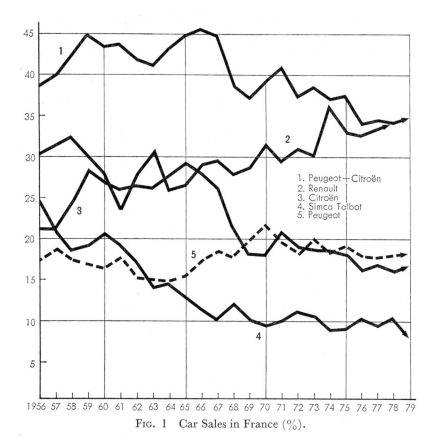

FIG. 1   Car Sales in France (%).

solution to the used car problem. Therefore marketing is still on the agenda of French car makers today.

NOTES

1. P. Passama, *L'intégration du travail. Formes nouvelles de concentration industrielle*, Paris, Sirey, 1910, pp. 21–142 and 220–222.
T. Zeldin, *France, 1848–1945*, Oxford, University Press, I, 1973, and II, 1977; A. Faure, "L'épicerie parisienne ou la corporation éclatée," *Le Mouvement Social*, July-September 1979, pp. 117–119; F. Caron, "Le développement des échanges," in F. Braudel and E. Lab-

rousse (eds.), *Histoire économique et sociale de la France*, Part IV, vol. 1, Paris, P.U.F., 1979, pp. 155–169.

2. C. P. Kindleberger, "Origins of United States direct investment in France," *Business History Review*, Fall 1974, pp. 382–413; M. Lévy-Leboyer, *Les banques européennes et l'industrialisation internationale dans la première moitié du XIXe siècle*, Paris, P.U.F., 1964; P. Passama, *op. cit.*, pp. 37–38.

3. F. Blaich, "Ausschließlichkeitsbindungen als Wege zur industriellen Konzentration in der deutschen Wirtschaft bis 1914" in N. Horn and J. Kocka (eds.), *Recht und Entwicklung der Großunternehmen im 19 und frühen 20 Jahrhundert*, Göttingen, Vandenhoeck und Ruprecht, 1979, pp. 317–342; M. Gillet, *Les charbonnages du Nord de la France au XIXe siècle*, Paris, Mouton, 1973, esp. pp. 261–262; M. Rust, *Business and Politics in the Third Republic: the Comité des Forges and the French Steel Industry, 1896–1914*, unpublished Ph. D., Princeton University, 1973; H. Morsel, "Contribution à l'histoire des ententes industrielles," *Revue d'Histoire Economique et Sociale*, January-March 1976, pp. 118–129; P. Passama, *op. cit.*, p. 131.

4. See the documents kept in the archives of Panhard (Paris), Peugeot (Sochaux), Renault (Billancourt), Berliet (Vénissieux), the year-books of the Chambre Syndicale des Constructeurs d'Automobiles, plus two contemporary pamphlets: *Société Anonyme des Anciens Etablissements Panhard et Levassor, 1905* (National Archives, Paris, 65 AQ N 69); T. Bernard, *Une visite chez Berliet à Lyon*, Paris, 1908, and P. Fridenson, *Histoire des Usines Renault*, vol. I, Paris, Le Seuil, 1972, pp. 19–82; M. Flageolet-Lardenois, "Une firme pionnière: Panhard et Levassor jusqu'en 1918," *Le Mouvement Social*, October–December 1972, pp. 27–47; J. M. Laux, *In First Gear. The French Automobile Industry to 1914*, Liverpool University Press, 1976, pp. 7–8, 13, 18, 40–43, 70–71, 133–135.

5. J. B. Rae, *The American Automobile. A brief history*, Chicago University Press, 1965, pp. 18–19; R. P. Thomas, *An analysis of the pattern of growth of the automobile industry: 1895–1929*, unpub. Ph. D., Northwestern University, 1965, pp. 44–47, 73–79, 138–139, 170–173.

6. J. M. Laux, *In First Gear*, *op. cit.*, p. 148.

7. P. Passama, *op. cit.*, p. 37.

8. H. Mortimer-Mégret, *La voiture automobile d'occasion*, Paris, 1908.

9. N. Spinga, *L'introduction de l'automobile dans la société française entre 1900 et 1914*, unpublished M. A. thesis, University Paris X-Nanterre, 1973, pp. 19–20, 22, 24–25, and 31.

10. See, for instance, G. Hatry, *Renault et la compétition. L'époque héroïque*, Paris, Lafourcade, 1979.

11. L. Massénat-Déroche, *L'Automobile aux Etats-Unis et en Angleterre*, Paris, 1910.

12. *L'Auto*, 10 December, 1910. M. Wilkins and F. E. Hill, *American business abroad: Ford on six continents*, Detroit, Wayne State University Press, 1964, pp. 31, 33, 50–51, 54, 66, 466, 468.

13. J. Bouvier, "L'automobile et les transports," *Journal de la Société Statistique de Paris*, January 1933, pp. 4 and 9.

14. For exports, cf. J. M. Laux, *In First Gear, op. cit.*, pp. 71–72, 75, 98–102, 116, 142, 203, 209. For profits: *ibid.*, pp. 210–217. For the breakdown of the demand, cf. N. Spinga, *op. cit.*, pp. 51–88.

15. Useful contemporary studies: P. Weinberger, *L'industrie automobile en France et à l'étranger*, Paris, 1931; J. L. Platet, *L'industrie automobile française depuis la guerre*, Paris, 1934; M. Schwartz, "L'industrie automobile," *Journal Officiel, Documents Administratifs*, 26–27 August 1936, p. 32; M. Ehrmann, *L'automobile de tourisme en France*, Bordeaux, 1938. Historians' studies: Fridenson, *op. cit.*, pp. 131–295, 319–321, 325; G. Declas, *Recherches sur les usines Berliet (1914–1949)*, unpubl. M. A. thesis, University Paris I, 1977, pp. 12–43 and appendix 4; J. L. Loubet, *La Société Anonyme André Citroën (1924–1968)*, unpubl. Ph. D., University Paris X-Nanterre, 1979, pp. 31–317, 600–604, 606.

16. I. F. Marcosson, *The war after the war*, New York, John Lane, 1917, pp. 99–100; National Archives (Paris), F[12] 7713, report by Lucien Périssé, 1917; G. Cote, *L'automobile après la guerre*, Paris, Dunod, 1918, pp. 70–73.

17. J. Morice, *La demande d'automobiles en France*, Paris, Colin, 1957.

18. G. Cote, *op. cit.*, pp. 114–122.

19. F. Sabatès and S. Schweitzer, *André Citroën: les chevrons de la gloire*, Paris, E. P. A., 1980, p. 285; P. Fridenson, *op. cit.*, p. 325.

20. H. M. Astruc, *L'automobile à la portée de tous*, Paris, 1920, and 60th edition, 1938; J. Bouvier, *op. cit.*, p. 9; J. A. Grégoire, *L'aventure automobile*, Paris, Flammarion, 1953, pp. 19–20; P. Fridenson, *op. cit.*, p. 143. J. L. Loubet, *op. cit.*, pp. 140, 142–143.

21. J. L. Platet, *op. cit.*, pp. 94–95; C. Rocherand, *L'histoire d'André Citroën. Souvenirs d'une collaboration*, 2nd edition, Paris, Christian, 1979; P. Fridenson, *op. cit.*, pp. 182–183; J. A. Grégoire, *Cinquante ans d'automobile*, Paris, Flammarion, 1974, pp. 244–247.

22. J. L. Platet, *op. cit.*, pp. 95–97; P. Fridenson, *op. cit.*, pp. 149–150.

23. J. L. Platet, *op. cit.*, pp. 94–95; C. Rocherand, *op. cit.*, p. 28; M. Wilkins, F. Hill, *op. cit.*, p. 97; J. L. Loubet, *op. cit.*, pp. 143–148.

24. C. Rocherand, *op. cit.*, pp. 54–56; M. Norroy, *op. cit.*, p. 128; P. Fridenson, *op. cit.*, pp. 145–147; R. P. Thomas, *op. cit.*, p. 210; F. Sabatès and S. Schweitzer, *op. cit.*, pp. 225–279.

25. P. Fridenson, *op. cit.*, pp. 142 and 183; J. L. Loubet, *op. cit.*, pp. 139–141; V. Schweizer, *Die Französische Automobilindustrie*, Zurich, 1952, p. 60; R. P. Thomas, *op. cit.*, pp. 237–238. On Renault: Paul Guillon's account in G. Hatry (ed.), *Témoignages*, Billancourt, S. H. U. R., 1980, p. 15.

26. C. Couture, *Des différentes combinaisons de vente à crédit dans leurs rapports avec la petite épargne*, Paris, 1904; A. Peytel, *La vente à crédit et les automobiles*, Paris, Dalloz, 1932; A. C. Dédé, *Traité pratique de la vente à crédit des automobiles*, Paris, 1937, pp. 59, 63; J. L. Platet, *op. cit.*, pp. 106–121; M. Ehrmann, *op. cit.*, pp. 207–213 and 357–364; National Archives, Paris, 91 AQ 8, note by Citroën's marketing department, 1927; M. Wilkins, F. Hill, *op. cit.*, p. 140; E. Fuchs, *Louis Renault*, Billancourt, Renault, 1935, p. 49.

27. J. L. Platet, *op. cit.*, pp. 76–91 and 103–105; M. Norroy, *op. cit.*, pp. 93–122; C. Rocherand, *op. cit.*, pp. 57–66, 129–137, 219–228; J. L. Loubet, *op. cit.*, pp. 110–127, 137–138 and 283, 285; P. Fridenson, "L'idéologie des grands constructeurs dans l'entre-deux-guerres," *Le Mouvement Social*, October–December 1972, p. 62; R. P. Thomas, *op. cit.*, pp. 235–236; P. Fridenson, *Histoire . . .*, *op. cit.*, p. 173; F. Sabatès and S. Schweitzer, *op. cit.*, pp. 177–216 and 277–285.

28. A. D. Chandler Jr., *Giant Enterprise*, New York, Harcourt, Brace & World, 1964, pp. 146–148 and 157–170; P. Weinberger, *op. cit.*, pp. 75 and 170 ff; National Archives, 91 AQ 4, note from L. Renault to F. Lehideux, 25 September, 1934.

29. Interview of André Citroën, *L'Europe Nouvelle*, 13 January, 1923; P. Pellé, *L'industrie automobile française et l'empire colonial durant la crise des années trente*, unpubl. M. A. thesis, University Paris VIII-Vincennes, 1978, pp. 16–18; 28–40, 55–59, 76–83.

30. J. L. Platet, *op. cit.*, pp. 96–103; L. Daries, *Autos d'occasion. Piraterie moderne!*, Toulouse, 1937; E. Mattern, *Etude de la crise*, Montbéliard, 1936; P. Fridenson, *Histoire . . .*, *op. cit.*, pp. 210, 244–246, 319; S. Macaulay, *Law and the balance of power: the automobile manufacturers and their dealers*, New York, 1966; D. Gaucher, *La presse automobile de 1945 à 1973*, unpubl. M. A. thesis, University Paris X-Nanterre,

1976, p. 59.

31.   P. Fridenson, *op. cit.*, pp. 199–200; J. L. Loubet, *op. cit.*, pp. 292–293.

32.   J. P. Bardou et al., *la révolution automobile*, Paris, Albin Michel, 1977, pp. 200–204, 210–213, 225–228, 232–251.

33.   B. Chevalier, "L'automobile, la presse et la presse automobile," *Presse-Actualité*, February 1969, pp. 20–23; D. Gaucher, "La presse automobile," *Presse-Actualité*, November 1979, pp. 49–51; J. Peronnin, "Renouvellement du parc automobile en France," *Arts et Métiers*, March 1979, p. 17.

34.   M. Wilkins, "Multinational automobile enterprises and regulation: an historical overview," in D. H. Ginsburg and W. J. Abernathy (eds.), *Government, technology and the future of the automobile*, New York, McGraw Hill, 1979, pp. 235–236; J. M. Laux, "Les capitaux étrangers et l'industrie automobile," in M. Lévy-Leboyer (ed.), *La position internationale de la France, XIXe-XXe siècles*, Paris, Mouton, 1977; J. Szokolóczy-Syllaba, *Les organisations professionnelles françaises et le Marché Commun*, Paris, A. Colin, 1965, pp. 224–269.

35.   J. Sheahan, *Promotion and control of industry in postwar France*, Cambridge (Mass.), Harvard University Press, 1963, pp. 102–126; M. Peyrard, "L'industrie automobile européenne face à la concurrence internationale," *L'Actualité économique* [Montreal], October–December 1966, pp. 496–627; J. P. Anastossopoulos, *The strategic autonomy of government-controlled enterprises operating in a competitive economy*, Columbia University, unpubl. Ph. D., 1973, pp. 238–295; P. Fridenson, "La bataille de la 4 CV Renault," *L'histoire*, February 1979, pp. 33–40.

36.   Chambre syndicale des constructeurs d'automobiles, *L'automobile en France*, Paris, Riss, 1956, pp. 22–23.

37.   G. Toublan, "Etude du marché de la 4 CV," *De Renault Frères à Renault Régie Nationale*, December 1978, pp. 238–247; P. Dreyfus, *La liberté de réussir*, Paris, Simoën, 1977, pp. 89, 94–108, 133–134; "Histoire d'une campagne publicitaire: le lancement de la Renault 14," *Renault Magazine*, October 1976, pp. 15–18; J. Chouty, "Quatre roues sous du jaune tilleul," *Le Monde Dimanche*, 18 November, 1979; "La D. C. Z. Paris à la rencontre de sa clientèle particulière," *Renault Magazine*, April 1974, pp. 10–21; R. Moreau, "Physionomie du groupe Simca," *Economie et Politique*, June 1961, pp. 38–56; J. L. Loubet, *op. cit.*, pp. 525–528, 547–552, 558, 563–564, 588–589; E. Seidler, *Les grandes voix de l'automobile*, Paris, L'Equipe, 1970, pp. 46–49, 83–88, 102–104; Régie Nationale des Usines Renault,

Compte rendu d'activité 1978, Villancourt, 1979, p. 20; L. Bardin, "Le panier à salade," *Le Monde Dimanche*, 6 April, 1980, p. XIX; H. Lauret, "Comment la R5 est devenue un fait de société," *Le Matin de Paris*, 28 July, 1980, p. 15. Advertisement data kindly provided by Sécodip.

38. *Citroën Année-Modéle 1980*, Paris, S. A. Automobiles Citroën, 1979, p. 30. Advertisement data provided by Sécodip. S. Soars-Ferreira, *Caractères des exportations de l'industrie automobile française*, Montrouge, Prospective et Aménagement, 1974, pp. 144–172.

39. E. Seidler, *Le roman de Renault*, Lausanne, Edita, 1973, pp. 79, 101, 172; J. L. Loubet, *op. cit.*, pp. 538–539; J. J. Chanaron and S. Soares-Ferreira, *1973–1975: l'automobile en crise*, Grenoble, IREP, 1975, vol. II, p. 49 and vol. III, pp. 52–59; Régie Renault, *op. cit.*, p. 35; Institut National de la Consommation, *Guide pratique de l'automobile . . .*, Paris, Le Seuil, 1974, pp. 26–27, 36–38, 61–66.

40. D. Gaucher, *op. cit.*, p. 59; J. Wagner, *la méthode de distribution par concessionnaires et son application dans l'industrie automobile*, Geneva, Georg, 1968, pp. 131–146; J. L. Loubet, *op. cit.*, pp. 542–544; J. J. Chanaron, S. Soares-Ferreira, *op. cit.*, vol. II, pp. 62–71; "La voiture d'occasion chez Renault," *Renault Magazine*, October 1973, pp. 31–34; "La D. C. Z. Paris . . .," *op. cit.*, p. 18.

41. D. Gaucher, *op. cit.*, pp. 137–138; J. Wagner, *op. cit.*, p. 90; P. Dreyfus, *op. cit.*, pp. 132–136; A. D. Chandler Jr., *op. cit.*, p. 164; Renault Archives (Villancourt), "tarif clientèle métropolitaine," 26 February, 1951 and 27 November, 1961.

42. J. J. Chanaron in: J. P. Bardou et al., *op. cit.*, p. 233; P. Bercot, *Mes années aux usines Citroen*, Paris, 1979.

p.127;

COMMENTS

6150
* 0441
5310
6314
France

1

Roy Church
University of East Anglia

In the history of marketing motor cars the similarities between French, British and even American experiences appear to be more striking than the differences, though the similarities between British and French experiences are greater, for obvious reasons. It would not be productive to enumerate them in detail; merely to observe that while in degree the evolution of the French (and British) markets occurred more slowly than in the United States, and while marketing strategies developed later and to a more limited extent than in the United States, the similarities are sufficiently revealing of the uniformities to be found in the dynamics of market formation and marketing methods in Western societies as to justify our concentration upon the contrasts. I shall focus in particular on the dissimilarities revealed by the comparative histories of the two cases which in most respects resemble each other—France and Britain—and take as my starting point the general remark made by Professor Fridenson that "Almost always, the French motor car industry was obsessed with the problems of trying to keep up with demand"—though he excludes the Great Depression of the early 1930s. It is, he says, because French car makers were in a sellers' market for most of the period before the Great Depression that "management and marketing never received as much attention in France as they did in the United States . . . ."

I am in agreement with Professor Fridenson's remark that the market characteristics, distribution structures and commercial practices that prevailed in France before 1914 are not well known, a statement which applies equally to the British industry, but it is

useful to compare the evolution of the two markets to highlight the
significant factors explaining the differences in development in two
similar societies.

In 1913 France produced 45,000 cars; Britain 34,000. The number
of cars registered on French roads in 1913 has been estimated at
125,000; in Britain the figure was 250,000—and figures for registration, rather than production, show the extent of the two markets.
Clearly, Britain's relatively low output cannot be explained by
differential market sizes. Neither can the size of the market explain
why the experimentation with small, low-priced cars should have
been more highly developed in France before 1907 than in Britain.
Thereafter, the rate of growth in British car output exceeded that in
France, though French cars continued to dominate British imports
until shortly before 1914. Why then did French production exceed
British output by about 33 percent? It has been suggested, by
The Times article in 1914, that the French market was more democratized, less exclusive, than the British, a view repeated by Professor
Saul. Recent estimates by Professor Laux now suggest that less than
15 percent of total French production in 1913 consisted of small,
low-powered, low-cost motor cars, a figure which included single
and two-cylinder as well as four-cylinder vehicles. A comparable
estimate for Britain is difficult to make, but seems unlikely to have
fallen much below 15 percent. This suggests that the unfavorable
comparison between the structure of the car market in the two
countries has been overdone, at least for the period immediately
preceding World War I. In both countries the evolution of the
market for the lighter weight, low-powered, low-cost cars was slow
in comparison with the United States. Renault had been successful
with the 8–9 h.p. two-cylinder taxi before 1909 though less so with a
two-cylinder 10 h.p. car; Austin's 10 h.p. car, introduced in 1911,
also proved less successful than the larger more expensive cars. After
1909, an Anglo-French Company—Darracq—operating in both
countries began to founder on a policy emphasizing cars in the
lower half of the price range. Not surprisingly, both Renault and
Austin concentrated on larger models in supplying the private
passenger car market after 1911. It was left to other manufacturers
in both countries to develop the compact lower-priced models,

first by experimenting with cycle-cars and then from 1912 with small cars proper—those produced by Zebré, Unic, and the Peugeot Bébé, the cars of Singer, Standard, Hillman and in 1913 Morris leading the way. Both in Britain and France *manufacturers* can be criticized for a relative disinterest in aggressive marketing methods before 1912, but in Britain the aggressive agents who imported cars into Britain, praised for their effectiveness by Professor Laux, were instrumental in developing a market for cars considerably more extensive than in France, although French production was larger. Why did not French manufacturers or agents develop the French domestic market in a similar way?

Renault seems to have earned relatively high rates of return on turnover and might have been expected to be less interested in marketing initiatives, though Renault was losing momentum from 1910. It may be significant that Peugeot's rapid rise to prominence occurred during the critical period between 1910 and 1914, when profits as a percentage of sales were very much lower than those received by Renault, paying dividends of between 5 and 7 percent, and that publicity-seeking activity combined with a new model strategy (which surely adds up to an important marketing initiative) may be regarded as important factors at this time. One question which will need attention, therefore, is whether the industry as a whole was sufficiently profitable to justify French manufacturers' apparent disregard for marketing before 1914? And in view of the dispersion of profitability levels among French firms, is there any connection between profit performance and attention to marketing strategies? It is true that French exports were the largest in the world, but between 1907 and 1913 exports from the United States and from the U. K., though still below those of French manufacturers, had increased both relatively and in absolute terms. We might deduce that export markets were becoming more competitive, and that this provides a partial explanation for French manufacturers establishing plants in other countries, a marketing strategy well in advance of other European and British manufacturers. It is possible, of course, that exports may have been more profitable than selling in the home market. There is certainly evidence to suggest that entrepreneurial effort was being directed towards this goal in the years immediately preceding World War I, similar to contemporary development in the British industry, and that 1919 might be too late to identify the turning point in the changing perceptions of the market potential for non-luxury cars.

Perhaps the principal difference was that there was no one in the French industry comparable with Percival Perry, the British importing agent who perceived the market potential of a car which (as in France) was universally condemned in Britain before 1911, as cheap and nasty. By 1913 no fewer than 7,000 Model T cars were sold in England, whereas in France fewer than 700 found buyers. Perry, it seems, broke through the prejudice against the poor image established by American automobiles, whereas in France it is suggested that pride in the home-manufactured product prevailed. By 1914 the British market had probably become at least as "democratized" as the French.

> This sequence of events, however, does not accord with the views expressed by Professor Wilkins that the small sales of Ford's Model T before 1914 are attributable to French taste. This is an interpretation which Professor Fridenson appears to accept so far as it refers to consumer resistance, but which he qualifies so far as it relates to the reception accorded both to the idea of the popular car and then to the Model T. In Britain, too, the breakthrough came only when Perry successfully penetrated the British consumer's resistance. Tastes can be changed; this is surely a basic tenet of marketing lore.

Leaving the pre-1920 period, I am puzzled by the alleged relationship between the growth of demand for cars in France in the interwar period, and installment selling. Significantly, perhaps, it was an Englishman, the Honourable C. S. Rolls, who introduced the practice by selling French Panhard cars on credit to British customers as early as 1903, and yet during the interwar years installment selling accounted for a tiny proportion of total car sales in France as compared with the United States, and perhaps more surprisingly in Britain too. Professor Fridenson describes this as a weakness in French marketing, yet I will remind you again of his remarks in the introduction that the French car manufacturers' basic problem was to keep up with, rather than to stimulate, demand. I infer from this that the lack of extensive installment selling did not hamper demand seriously enough to cause concern to manufacturers; or is the earlier statement relating to the buoyancy of the French market throughout the period to 1938, excepting the depression, misleading? I would value his comments on what seems to be something of a paradox. Perhaps the figures for French car production, and in particular French car registration, might provide a clue.

Another point which relates to the overall condition of the market for cars is the remarkable inclination of the French manufacturers, from a very early stage, to set up assembly plants in other countries. How is this explained, and does this not reflect a concern with marketing and penetration even before World War I? Or does it reflect growing competition from the United States and other producers in export markets? It would be interesting to discuss these factors.

A lack of finance is seen to pose a problem for dealers in the 1930s, and I would like to know why dealers experienced this difficulty which, again, might be related to overall demand. Was their reluctance to accept lower margins on small cars more than a lack of perception of the potential capacity of the French market to expand further? Austin's dealers actually requested him to build a smaller, cheaper model which eventually turned out to be the huge-selling Austin Twelve, and subsequently the basic design for the Austin Seven, the biggest-selling car in Britain between the wars. Professor Fridenson notes the increased attention to market surveys following the important dealers' revolt in the 1930s, though he does not indicate whether this may be regarded as cause or effect.

Turning to a later period, in what ways did the weakness of consumer movements hitherto "leave French car makers greater freedom to develop their customary policies"?

Finally, we have identified less than perfect stereotypes of the technologically-oriented firm and the commercially-oriented firm in Britain, the United States, Japan, and possibly Germany. In the case of Britain and the United States, the explanation seems to be fairly simple, with the earlier Ford and Austin influenced most strongly in the pioneering stage of the motor industry by the technical problems of producing a machine which was functionally successful. Morris and General Motors evolved later in this stage of the industry's history when volume selling was critical for low cost production and the fuller exploitation of the potential market for motor cars. Would Professor Fridenson explain why this dichotomy should also have existed in the early French industry, with Renault and Citroën? Is there a similar paradigm which casts Renault in the role of inventive engineer-entrepreneur, and Peugeot or Citroën as firms where the primary imperative was commercial rather than technical?

2

Terushi Hara
Waseda University

I.

Professor Fridenson shows us very clearly the three periods of French automobile marketing and includes many interesting historical facts. The first period is from 1890 to 1914, the period of free and open franchises for a luxury market. The second period is from 1919 to 1939, the age of salesmanship regulation, in other words, the age of Americanization. The last period is from 1944 to the present day, and in this period modern management rules and techniques began to be applied to the marketing of mass-produced vehicles. I am entirely in agreement with the logic of this classification.

After analyzing these three periods, he shows us three characteristics of French automobile marketing: the slow growth of installment sales; the strength of state regulation of marketing conditions from the 1930s onward; and finally, the weaker consumer movement which developed later than in the United States and thus left car makers much more freedom to develop their policies.

II.

Professor Fridenson shows us that the economic behavior of the

French people is very different from that of other nations. For example:

He writes that car demand was always greater than the production ability. This means the French car makers were not so eager to pursue maximum profits.

He says that the small sales of the Ford Model T before 1914 cannot be attributed to the tariff but to French taste, which prevented it from repeating its English success.

He writes that since 1905, technical experts advocated the mass production of ordinary cars at a cheap price, but that management in the motor car industry preferred to compete "on the basis of designs that emphasized reliability and elegance" (quotation from J. Laux).

He shows that the adoption of installment buying was relatively slow in comparison with that of other countries.

III.

What are the main reasons making the economic behavior of French people so particular? Can we explain it in terms of the particular cultural traditions of the French people? I would like to know if Professor Fridenson agrees with this kind of explanation, which has been made well known to us through the works of David Landes. Or, as a member of the younger generation, does Professor Fridenson want to offer another kind of explanation?

IV.

Taking the history of automobile marketing as an example, I hope to discuss these problems.

(A)   Professor Fridenson gives us three reasons for the relatively slow adoption of installment buying (p. 138).   1) A high proportion of rural car buyers are said to have been reluctant to borrow. 2) The French banking and financial system was less diversified than those of the United States and the United Kingdom.   3) French car makers were opposed to the introduction of the installment system. These answers are correct but raise further questions. Why were rural car buyers reluctant to borrow? Why was French banking less diversified? Why did most of the French car makers not adopt the installment system? How can we answer these questions? Can we explain them in relation to French culture or are there other explanations?

(B)   I have the impression that Professor Fridenson considers that the American method of automobile marketing was introduced into France after some hesitation. He gives the example of Citroën in the 1920s. Why did this company adopt American-style marketing so actively? Professor Fridenson does not mention the collapse of this company. But it is said that one of the causes of the crash of Citroën was the application of American-style marketing policies, so American methods did not always have favorable influences on French marketing activities.

(C)   Professor Fridenson stresses the importance of the second-hand car market in the 1930s. Second-hand cars account for 52 percent (1930) and 68 percent (1935) of registrations (p. 140). I would like to ask not only Professor Fridenson but also other participants about the importance of the second-hand car markets in other countries. If this is peculiar to France, why did it happen?

Japan's Automobile Marketing:
Its Introduction, Consolidation, Development and Characteristics

Masaru Udagawa
Hosei University

I.

Since the Meiji Restoration in 1868, Japan has succeeded in gradually transplanting modern industries from advanced countries, and in establishing and developing these industries. At the same time, Japan has also learned from and imported systems and methods of management and administration from those industries. However, the introduction of marketing techniques came at an extremely late date. It is said that the full-fledged introduction and establishment of marketing techniques were not achieved until the period of rapid economic growth after World War II. The most important reason for this delay is the fact that while elaborate wholesalers' commercial organizations had been already established in the Edo era, the size of the Japanese market itself was small. Manufacturers, therefore, depended on the existing wholesalers' network for marketing and concentrated all their activities on production.

The situation was different, however, with respect to the new consumer industries which began to be introduced in and after the Taisho period (1912–1925). The commercial organizations then existing were completely inexperienced in dealing in these commodities, and sometimes even refused to deal in them, thus obstructing the distribution process itself. The manufacturers of these new products, therefore, had to develop markets and organize outlets by themselves, and there emerged some who partially imported and put into practice modern marketing techniques. These industries, then, had experience in marketing; they put this experience to practical use and played a leading role in marketing in the postwar era, when marketing techniques were imported and developed on a large scale.

This report will consider the case of the automobile industry, one of the newly arisen industries, for whose establishment the activities of modern marketing were indispensable. In analyzing how this industry introduced, established and developed marketing systems and methods, I wish to refer mainly to the business activities of the Toyota Motor Company, and the Nissan Motor Company.

II.

The economic boom during World War I and the process of reconstruction after the 1923 Great Kanto Earthquake led to the spread of automobile use in Japan (Table 1). There began to appear a large number of automobile importers, while pioneer entrepreneurs began to produce automobiles domestically to meet the demand.

Many of the automobile importers had, up to then, imported bicycles and machinery. At the end of the Taisho period, some large-scale importers and distributors of foreign motor vehicles such as the Yanase Motor Company and the Nihon Motor Company were established. They signed import and sales contracts with foreign automobile makers, but were independent with respect to their sales activities and did not necessarily form sales networks for their particular makers.[1] Domestic makers in this period could not compete with imported automobiles because they lacked the technical and financial bases for mass production, which itself was fundamental to the motor industry, and because their sales activities depended on personal connections through friends and relatives.[2]

In the Showa period (1926 and after), the demand for automobiles greatly increased. The market, however, was dominated neither by importers of foreign automobiles nor by domestic makers, but rather by big motor companies of the United States, Ford and General Motors (GM) in particular. Ford established Japan Ford in Yokohama in 1925, and General Motors set up Japan GM in Osaka in

TABLE 1   Volume of Motor Vehicles in Japan, 1908–1930.

(Unit: Vehicles)

	Passenger cars (incl. buses)	Trucks	All motor vehicles
1908	—	—	9
1909	—	—	19
1910	—	—	121
1911	—	—	235
1912	—	—	512
1913	—	—	892
1914	—	—	1,066
1915	—	—	1,244
1916	1,624	24	1,648
1917	2,647	25	2,672
1918	4,491	42	4,533
1919	6,847	204	7,051
1920	9,355	644	9,999
1921	11,228	888	12,116
1922	13,483	1,383	14,866
1923	10,666	2,099	12,765
1924	17,939	6,394	24,333
1925	21,002	8,162	29,164
1926	27,973	12,097	40,070
1927	35,775	15,987	51,762
1928	44,660	21,719	66,379
1929	52,829	27,541	80,370
1930	57,827	30,881	88,708

Sources: Annual Statistics, Police and Security Department; Ministry of the Interior.

1927; they started to produce motors by KD (knock-down) assembly. The mass production of automobiles by these two companies not only worsened the lot of domestic makers, but also seriously weakened the position of importers of foreign automobiles, and the Japanese automobile market quickly fell into their hands (Table 2).

Furthermore, both Japan Ford and Japan GM not only introduced the mass production system to Japan, but also transplanted the corresponding mass sales system. Ford and GM were competing furiously in the U.S. market at that time, and this competition extended directly to the Japanese market, where both Japan Ford

TABLE 2   Motor Vehicles Supplied in Japan, 1916–1935.

(Unit: Vehicles)

	Domestic-made	CBU imports	KD imports	Japan Ford	Japan GM	Kyoritsu Motors
1916		218				
1917		860				
1918		1,653				
1919		1,579				
1920		1,745				
1921		1,074				
1922		752				
1923		1,938				
1924		4,063				
1925	376	1,765	3,437	3,437		
1926	245	2,381	8,667	8,677		
1927	302	3,895	12,668	7,033	5,635	
1928	347	7,883	24,341	8,850	15,491	
1929	437	5,018	29,338	10,674	15,745	1,251
1930	458	2,591	19,678	10,620	8,049	1,015
1931	436 (2)	1,887	20,199	11,505	7,478	1,201
1932	880 (184)	997	14,087	7,448	5,893	760
1933	1,681 (626)	491	15,082	8,106	5,942	998
1934	2,247 (1,170)	896	33,458	17,244	12,322	2,574
1935	5,094 (3,913)	934	30,787	14,865	12,492	2,612

Sources: Industrial Affairs Bureau, Ministry of Commerce and Industry; others.

Notes: 1. Figures in parentheses are numbers of small cars.
   2. Total number of KD imports and total of breakdown for KD imports differ but follow the statistics on record.

and Japan GM competitively introduced updated sales systems and marketing techniques developed in the United States, and fought with each other for domination of the Japanese automobile market. As a result, by about 1930 the great majority of Japanese automobile dealers—who had been persons of property in local areas and importers of foreign automobiles—entered into franchised contracts with either Japan Ford or Japan GM, and were organized under the control of these companies. Japan Ford and Japan GM each had between seventy and eighty dealers.

Japan GM established dealers for each type of automobile in each prefecture, whereas Japan Ford established them only in places where it was thought necessary, irrespective of location. The qualifications and regulations for Japan GM's dealers were as follows:[3]

1) The dealers should set up showrooms and efficient service stations, while keeping a supply of necessary parts. The dealers should also employ a sales manager and salesmen as defined.

2) The dealers should always, on the basis of the contract, stock a certain number of new automobiles that could be sold immediately. Furthermore, orders should be made at the end of each month and should contain details of amounts for four months; fixed amounts for the first two months and estimated amounts for the last two months.

3) Payment to Japan GM should be made in cash or by a check for the full amount.

4) The dealers should send to Japan GM a report every ten days of the total sales, type of automobiles sold, names of buyers, methods of payment (cash or a monthly installment).

Japan Ford also made similar requirements of its dealers.

Both Japan Ford and Japan GM adopted a policy of demanding that their dealers strictly follow these conditions and of canceling franchise contracts where dealers did not observe the conditions or did not achieve a good sales record. There was, therefore, a large turnover of dealers, and for the ten years from the time both Japan Ford and Japan GM started production, approximately 300 dealers were newly established.[4] One Japan GM dealer of that time stated as follows:[5]

"Many of the dealers in those days repeatedly 'started up in Spring, continued until the business slump at the end of the year, and then hung out a signboard by a different name the next year.' This was because both Japan Ford and Japan GM did not extend any parental assistance in the form of financial support to dealers, but instead tried to find replacements or other dealers as soon as the business of the original dealers declined."

Before Ford and GM began operations in Japan, there were no sales agents dealing in such durable consumer goods as automobiles. For this reason, they were able to transplant franchise methods which they had developed in the United States—methods where the makers took the initiative without meeting resistance from the existing distribution routes. In that sense, the automobile industry in Japan had from its outset an extremely modern and rational sales organization, including marketing techniques.

On the other hand, it is also a fact that these methods were imported directly to Japan, and Japan Ford and Japan GM applied them so mechanically that no attempt was made to adapt them to the Japanese situation and commercial practices.

III.

To counter the monopolistic domination of Japan's automobile market by Japan Ford and Japan GM, the Ministry of Commerce and Industry and the Ministry of the Army became eager to produce automobiles domestically; the former aimed to improve the balance of payment and the latter asserted their case for military reasons. Both of them repeatedly requested the three big *zaibatsu*, Mitsui, Mitsubishi and Sumitomo, to expand their businesses to include automobile production. These *zaibatsu*, however, consistently refused to accept the request, because even they judged that it was extremely difficult to enter a business completely dominated by foreign makers, and to compete successfully with them.

What was fortunate, however, for Japan's automobile industry was that there were two entrepreneurs full of enterprising spirit: Yoshisuke Aikawa and Kiichiro Toyoda. Aikawa was the president of the Nissan Konzern, a new *zaibatsu*, and Toyoda was the first son of Sakichi Toyoda, who was known as Japan's "Weaving King," and himself central manager of the Toyoda Konzern, a local *zaibatsu*. Both of them were graduates of the technical engineering department of Tokyo Imperial University and possessed professional know-how. Their motive was nationalistic, aspiring as they did to foster by themselves an industry that had not yet been established in Japan—and also to catch up with the big *zaibatsu* through success in this field.[6]

Furthermore, these two entrepreneurs chose the automobile industry as one which might best meet their business ideals and

TABLE 3 Motor Vehicle Production by Nissan and Toyota, 1934–1945.

(Unit: Vehicles)

	Nissan			Toyota		
	Passenger Cars	Commer-cial Cars	Total Produc-tion	Passenger Cars	Commer-cial Cars	Total Produc-tion
1934	650	290	940	—	—	—
1935	2,631	1,169	3,800	—	20	20
1936	2,562	3,601	6,163	100	1,042	1,142
1937	4,068	6,159	10,227	577	3,436	4,013
1938	4,151	12,440	16,591	539	4,077	4,616
1939	1,370	16,411	17,781	107	11,874	11,981
1940	1,162	14,763	15,925	268	14,519	14,787
1941	1,587	18,101	19,688	208	14,403	14,611
1942	871	16,563	17,434	41	16,261	16,302
1943	566	10,187	10,753	53	9,774	9,827
1944	9	7,074	7,083	19	12,701	12,720
1945	—	2,001	2,001	—	3,275	3,275

Sources: *30-Year History of Nissan Motors.*
20-Year History of Toyota Motors.

aspirations quickly, and they chose as their target the domestic production of a popular passenger car that could rival foreign cars. For this purpose the establishment of the mass production system was indispensable. Unlike the pioneer entrepreneurs described above, however, they did have existing business bases that brought in high profits, and thus succeeded in mobilizing the necessary capital, technology and human resources to establish the industry. After long and deliberate preparations for the founding of a new business, Aikawa established the Automobile Manufacturing in 1933 (renamed Nissan Motors the following year), and Toyoda established an automobile division within the Toyoda Automatic Weaving Machine Works in 1935 (made independent as the Toyota Motor Company in 1937). They succeeded, within two to three years, in developing a mass production system which matched Japan Ford and Japan GM in terms of the number of units produced (Table 3).

The establishment of the mass production system by Nissan and Toyota delighted the Ministry of Commerce and Industry and particularly the Ministry of the Army, which had eagerly hoped for the domestic production of automobiles. In 1936 the Ministry of the Army took the initiative to obtain the passage of the Auto-mobile Manufacturing Business Law, which provided for (1) the control and exclusion of foreign automobile companies and (2) a licensing system for the setting up of automobile businesses. Nissan and Toyota immediately obtained licenses under the Law. The Diesel Motor Company (renamed Isuzu Motors after World War II), which originated in the activities of the aforementioned pioneer domestic makers but had managed to survive, also obtained a license later.

Both Aikawa and Toyoda had solid technical backgrounds, but they were equally aware of the importance of the sales problem in the automobile industry, and believed that business success could only be achieved when a mass production system and a mass sales system functioned as two parts of one operation. Nevertheless, both they themselves and the enterprises they managed had up to then no experience in sales activities.

How then did Nissan and Toyota form their respective sales networks and secure capable sales personnel?

Once Nissan Motors finished establishing a mass production system for its small-sized automobile, the "Datsun," it entered a sales agents' contract with seven large auto importing companies and dealers, and commissioned the sales of the Datsun in December 1934. Further, in the next year when truck production went into full operation Nissan, to promote mass sales and a strong monthly installment financing system, established the Datsun Truck Sales Company. This was financed by the seven companies noted above and by Nihon Sangyo, the holding company of the Nissan concern, which provided 50 percent of the capital.[7] In this way, Nissan Motors depended on existing sales institutions when it started its sales activities. With respect to sales, therefore, the salesmen could raise a stronger voice than the maker.

However, Nissan Motors did not continue this marketing system, dominated by salesmen, for long. As Nissan Motors began to produce the "Nissan," a line of standard-size automobiles, by importing in February 1937 a complete set of production facilities from a U.S. Company, Graham Paige, it abolished the existing sales agent system in order to establish its own marketing system. The Nissan Motor Sales Company was established, Datsun Truck Sales was annexed to it, and all Datsun and Nissan models and parts began to be sold through this company.[8]

Nissan Motor Sales was both a distributor and a sales financing institution. In order to carry out these two functions, Nissan Motor Sales extensively sought personnel from large foreign automobile sales companies, particularly Nihon Motor Company, and at the same time it imitated Japan Ford and Japan GM in an effort to establish a nationwide sales network.[9] As a result, it was able to set up one dealer in each prefecture by 1939. Furthermore, dealerships in major areas such as Tokyo and Osaka were directly managed by Nissan Motor Sales, while those in other areas were established with local capital and managed by local manpower.

In discussing the marketing activities of Toyota Motors, it is impossible not to mention Shotaro Kamiya. The marketing activities of the company have been developed, from the founding of the company to the present, according to the sales ideas of Kamiya.

Kamiya had worked for Japan GM as regional manager and manager of the sales and advertising departments, and was one of the few experts in the motor marketing field in Japan. Kiichiro Toyoda asked Kamiya to join his company, promising that he would be entrusted with all sales activities. Kamiya, who sympathized with the desire to promote domestic production of automobiles, joined Toyota Motors, in spite of the fact that his salary was reduced to one-fifth of that which he had received from Japan GM.[10]

Kamiya had recognized the superiority of GM's dealer management techniques from the time when he worked for Japan GM. But, at the same time he had his doubts about the mechanistic application of the franchise method which, above all, attached importance to the contract. For this reason, although Kamiya mapped out a franchise system led by the maker along the lines of Japan GM when he set out to formulate the Toyota sales network, he attempted to revise the system to suit Japanese managerial customs as much as was practically possible. To this end, he stressed that the relationship between maker and dealers should be shifted from the "contract-first" idea of the American system to a community of common destiny, where human factors such as mutual understanding and the spirit of cooperation should be taken into consideration when administering dealers.[11]

In concrete terms, Kamiya advocated a sales slogan which said: "The profits reaped through sales of automobiles should first benefit the buyers, secondly the dealers and lastly the maker." He also persuaded Chevrolet dealers, with whom he had had connections since his time with Japan GM, and who had similar misgivings about the management policies of the American company, to become contracted agents for Toyota by explaining to them the significance of the sale of domestically-produced automobiles. He adopted the policy of forming a dealer network by combining local capital and local human resources.[12]

Kamiya's ideas and policy met with much sympathy among the dealers of Japan GM; this, plus the bad prospects looming over the makers affiliated with foreign capital because of the Automobile Manufacturing Business Law, led many of them to shift to Toyota. As a result, Toyota Motors organized an almost nationwide sales network composed mostly of dealers who had turned away from Japan GM by 1939. At the same time, corresponding to this organization of the sales network, Toyota founded a Toyota Financing Company and set up a monthly installment payment system.

In this way, Nissan Motors and Toyota Motors adopted "maker-led" mass sales systems to correspond to their mass production systems. In order to provide tough competition for Japan Ford and Japan GM which had together dominated Japan's automobile market, and to expand the share of domestically-produced automobiles in the market, there was no other way than to adopt the same sales system as the American producers had. Nissan was able to secure the organization and management know-how of these systems by recourse to importers of foreign automobiles and dealers for foreign motor companies, or by hiring employees from Japan Ford, while Toyota was able to secure them by hiring Kamiya and his men from Japan GM. These two companies were therefore able to form a nationwide sales network in a short period of time.

Of course, they modified the sales systems they took from the foreign automobile companies; that is, the system was revised so as to adapt to the Japanese situation and to their respective company situations and structures. In comparison with Toyota, Nissan's modifications were relatively minor since it was stronger and had more technical expertise and since its founder had lived in the United States when he was young and was familiar with American ideas and methods.

IV.

The Japanese economy had deteriorated in World War II, but the acquisition of special procurement contracts during the Korean War marked the beginning of a return to stability. It achieved miraculous development during the economic boom beginning in

TABLE 4   Number of Motor Vehicles per 1,000 Persons in Japan, 1959–1977.
(Unit: Vehicles, %)

	Total Vehicles	Passenger Cars	Vehicles per 1,000 Persons	
			Total Vehicles	Passenger Cars
1959	1,009,122	318,758	10.9	3.4
1960	1,353,526	417,333	14.5	4.9
1961	1,763,555	663,951	20.9	7.1
1962	2,729,304	889,032	28.7	9.4
1963	3,762,352	1,233,651	39.2	12.9
1964	4,988,450	1,672,359	51.5	17.3
1965	6,300,020	2,181,275	64.3	22.3
1966	7,921,372	2,833,246	80.1	28.7
1967	10,029,024	3,836,409	100.4	38.4
1968	12,482,266	5,209,319	123.6	51.6
1969	15,126,666	6,933,732	148.0	67.8
1970	17,581,843	8,778,972	170.1	84.9
1971	19,857,877	10,572,122	189.8	101.0
1972	22,408,513	12,531,149	209.5	117.2
1973	24,999,281	14,473,630	230.7	133.6
1974	26,781,306	15,853,548	244.2	144.6
1975	28,090,558	17,236,321	251.0	154.0
1976	30,069,260	18,475,565	265.9	163.4
1977	32,007,950	19,825,712	278.0	172.0

Source: Japan Automobile Manufacturers Association.

TABLE 5   Production Record of Motor Vehicles and the Shares Taken by

	Industry Total		Main Manufacturers' Share		
	Total Vehicles (Passenger Cars)		Toyota	Nissan	Isuzu
1950	32,459 (	2,396)	36.0 (19.8)	38.4 (36.1)	12.8 (—)
1952	38,994 (	4,839)	36.2 (38.4)	35.8 (49.1)	13.3 (—)
1954	70,103 (	14,472)	32.4 (29.3)	28.3 (32.1)	14.0 (13.2)
1956	111,066 (	32,056)	41.8 (37.4)	30.2 (40.4)	10.3 (6.4)
1958	188,303 (	50,643)	41.9 (41.9)	29.1 (33.3)	9.1 (5.9)
1960	481,551 (	165,094)	32.1 (25.5)	24.0 (33.3)	7.9 (4.8)
1962	990,706 (	268,784)	23.3 (27.1)	21.4 (33.1)	6.7 (5.7)
1964	1,702,475 (	579,660)	25.0 (31.4)	20.5 (29.1)	6.3 (5.9)
1966	2,286,399 (	877,656)	25.7 (36.0)	22.6 (24.9)	4.7 (3.7)
1968	4,085,826 (2,055,821)		26.9 (32.1)	24.0 (27.8)	3.6 (1.9)
1970	5,289,157 (3,178,708)		30.4 (33.6)	26.0 (28.3)	2.8 (0.6)
1972	6,294,438 (4,022,289)		33.2 (37.0)	29.6 (33.6)	2.9 (0.3)
1974	6,551,840 (3,931,842)		32.3 (37.8)	27.6 (31.9)	3.8 (0.7)
1976	7,841,447 (5,027,792)		31.6 (34.4)	29.4 (32.0)	4.3 (1.8)
1978	9,269,153 (5,975,968)		31.6 (34.1)	25.8 (29.0)	4.4 (1.7)

Source: Japan Automobile Manufacturers Association.

the 1960s. This economic recovery and expansion increased the demand for trucks and commercial passenger vehicles, and with the increased national income through rapid economic growth, the era of the popular passenger car came into being in the latter half of the 1960s and in the 1970s, when demand increased very rapidly (Table 4).

The increased demand for automobiles not only drove the advanced automobile makers such as Nissan Motors, Toyota Motors and Isuzu Motors to adopt a strategy of expansion, but also made possible the emergence of many new makers such as Mitsubishi Motors, Toyo Engineering, Prince Motors and Honda Motors, all of which expanded into automobile production from bases in shipbuilding, machinery and aircraft or two-or-three-wheeled vehicle production. The postwar automobile industry developed rapidly, centered on mass production and mass sales by new and old makers and on furious competition among them (Table 5). Automobiles truly came to have a leading position in the Japanese industrial economy.

Main Manufacturers.

(Unit: Vehicles, %)

Main Manufacturer's Share				
Mitsubishi	Toyo	Prince	Honda	Others
1.9 (—)	0.1 (—)	— (—)	— (—)	10.8 (44.1)
2.3 (—)	— (—)	1.1 (1.9)	— (—)	11.3 (10.6)
7.1 (—)	— (—)	5.2 (5.1)	— (—)	13.0 (20.3)
3.1 (—)	— (—)	6.8 (4.0)	— (—)	7.8 (11.8)
4.3 (—)	2.0 (—)	7.3 (9.8)	— (—)	6.3 (9.1)
5.1 (3.2)	9.0 (14.2)	6.4 (6.6)	— (—)	15.5 (12.4)
7.3 (3.1)	16.4 (15.6)	4.2 (4.8)	— (—)	20.7 (10.6)
8.0 (5.1)	14.4 (10.4)	5.0 (7.7)	1.3 (0.9)	19.5 (9.5)
10.4 (8.6)	13.1 (10.5)	— (4.0)	2.5 (0.4)	21.0 (11.9)
8.8 (6.3)	11.3 (8.7)	— (—)	7.8 (9.1)	17.6 (14.1)
8.6 (7.7)	8.1 (7.1)	— (—)	7.4 (8.7)	16.7 (14.0)
7.1 (5.5)	10.2 (9.4)	— (—)	5.3 (5.8)	11.7 (8.4)
7.6 (5.9)	11.3 (9.6)	— (—)	6.6 (8.1)	10.8 (6.0)
8.3 (8.0)	9.1 (8.9)	— (—)	7.1 (9.4)	10.2 (5.5)
10.5 (10.5)	9.2 (8.3)	— (—)	8.0 (10.5)	10.5 (5.9)

In establishing this mass production and mass sales system, in inter-company competition, and in the reorganization of the business world, Nissan and Toyota took the lead. However, particularly with respect to marketing activities, Toyota led Nissan, and in fact took the initiative in automobile marketing in postwar Japan. Toyota's preeminence in the marketing field was the most important factor in enabling it to catch up successfully with its rival, Nissan, and to bring about the rapid growth of the company.

Before World War II, as mentioned above, Nissan and Toyota introduced and revised the American-style sales system. When Japan suddenly entered a wartime economic system, each maker's sales activities were centrally controlled by the Automobile Control Association. But with the close of the war, the automobile sales organizations once again came to be affiliated with each maker, which in turn concentrated its efforts on the maintenance and strengthening of its sales system. Here Toyota took the lead. First of all, in reorganizing the automobile sales system, Toyota was able to take more positive action than Nissan, which had been more

severely affected by the war and the postwar reform. Moreover
Toyota absorbed dealers affiliated with Nissan who felt dissatisfied
with Nissan's high-pressure management. In this way, Toyota
completed a network whereby one dealer was promptly set up in
each prefecture.[13] The opportunity for Toyota to take a decisively
preeminent position in automobile sales activities arrived in 1950.
At that time Toyota was faced with a serious management crisis
because of the economic recession which resulted from the Dodge
Plan deflationary policies, and a bank syndicate forced it to adopt
organizational reform with the main aim of separating the sales
department from Toyota Motors. As a result, the sales department
became independent, as the Toyota Motor Sales Company
(T.M.S.).

What the bank syndicate intended was to make Toyota Motor
Sales function both as a distributor and as a sales financing company. However, Toyota was not satisfied with imposing only these
two functions on T.M.S. and insisted on adding another one,
that of promoting the overall marketing activities of Toyota as a
whole, including those involving the maker and the dealers. The
bank syndicate accepted this proposal. Shotaro Kamiya, who had
been engaged in Toyota's sales activities, had long thought that
an independent organization should be established to integrate the
three functions noted above and to put them into practice, while
an equal partnership between the sales and production departments
should be set up.

In other words, the following seven advantages were expected
from the separation of T.M.S. from Toyota Motors.[14]

1) The establishment of a production system capable of meeting
   demand.
2) The establishment of a dual fund-raising system for production and sales, and the rational use thereof.
3) The development of a balanced commodity policy through
   cooperation between the marketing-oriented T.M.S. and the
   technology-oriented Toyota Motors.
4) The avoidance of friction between Toyota Motor Company
   and its dealers, since T.M.S. would function as a buffer between the two.

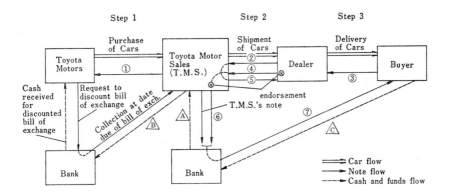

1 Acceptance of bill of exchange
2 Drawing of promissory note
3 Installment-sales note
4 Installment-sales note
5 Payback of promissory note
6 Carrying of installment-sales
   note as collateral
7 Collection at date due of
   installment-sales note

A Collateral financing for
   installment-sales note
B Payment of bill of exchange
C Receipt at the date due of the
   proceeds of installment-sales note

FIG. 1   Sales Financing Procedure Followed by Toyota Motor Sales Company.

Source: Koichi Shimokawa, "Marketing and Sales Financing in the Automobile Industry: U.S. and Japan," in Keiichiro Nakagawa, ed.,
Marketing and Finance in the Course of Industrialization. The International Conference on Business History (3), Tokyo, University of
Tokyo Press, 1978.

5)   The firmer establishment of Kamiya's leadership in sales
activities.

6)   The acquisition of updated information through T.M.S.

7)   Employee acquisition of marketing-oriented attitudes and
skills through the activities of the Toyota Motor Sales Company.

In this way, Toyota Motor Sales was established under
Kamiya's leadership. T.M.S. set out various policies and put them
into practice: modernization of dealer management, improvement
of the sales system and reinforcement of sales financing in order to
utilize the merits found in the system of division of labor between
production and sales.

Toyota Motor Sales first drew up a comprehensive manual on accounting for dealers to start off with after examining GM's standard dealer management methods, and adopted an integrated system whereby each dealer was required to adopt a uniform method of managing finance, credit and debt, and inventory, and to present every ten days a sales report on vehicles sold.

The adoption of the above system made it possible to change from the old system which called for the sale of only as many units as could be produced, to a new system stressing the production of only as many units as could be sold. At the same time it made it easy to draw up and adjust a plan of production, sales and profit through Toyota Motors, T.M.S., and dealers. This system helped to enhance the cooperative consciousness of these three parties and to create among them an integrated body.[15]

This "trinity" was further reinforced and promoted with the support of the Bank of Japan and the bank syndicate and through the establishment of a sales and financing system centered on Toyota Motor Sales, as shown in Figure 1. In other words, by adopting this system, Toyota Motors could collect the payment for a product without fail if it forwarded cars. Dealers, in turn, who were always beset by financial problems due to the poorly developed consumer financing system and the low evaluation of the distribution business by financing institutions, could secure both wholesalers' and retailers' financing at the same time by the establishment of installment sales financing routes, that is, bank→T.M.S.→dealer→ buyer, so that they could concentrate all their energies on sales while being relieved of any anxieties.[16]

The outbreak of the Korean War and subsequent special procurements formed the direct impetus for the rehabilitation and further development of Japan's automobile industry. Each automobile maker, having amassed large profits through special procurements, was busy importing technology through technical association with foreign automobile makers in order to adapt to the forthcoming era of the passenger car, an era that required advanced technology. Toyota also tried once to establish a technical association with Ford, but later gave it up and instead followed the same principle of self reliance in technical development that it had maintained from the beginning.

It was, however, a considerable gamble for Toyota to make this decision and it tried to succeed by reinforcing and promoting its marketing strategy and resolving to put two further policies into action in 1952–53.[17] One of these was to increase demand by lowering the price of cars; thus Toyota lowered the price of its only passenger car, the "Toyopet," from ¥1,200,000 to ¥950,000. This measure involved serious problems in terms of cost, but Kamiya's aim to create demand and achieve mass production on a remunerative basis was persuasive to Toyota Motors. This resolute decision was accepted and received full support from taxi drivers, who accounted for 75% of the total demand for passenger cars at the time, and Toyota secured a foothold for the full-scale expansion of its passenger car business.

Another policy was to open a showroom, Tokyo Toyopet, under direct management. There were two objectives here: to establish a foothold for sales strategy in the Tokyo area, which represented 30% of the entire national passenger car market at the time; and to make the store a model for dealers to use in their modernization plans. For this reason, Toyota Motor Sales changed the distribution system from the one-dealer-one-prefecture system, and further expanded direct sales stores. This decision made possible the full-scale employment of university graduates as salesmen by Tokyo Toyopet, and allowed a complete sales system of home sales areas and management sales to function effectively so as to secure a maximum number of customers, to tap new demand in dense urban areas, and to bring Toyota to the top position in the Tokyo market. These policies were immediately diffused to dealers affiliated with Toyota.

Toyota succeeded, by means of these positive marketing strategies, in winning out in furious competition with makers who imported foreign technology. It then set out to organize driving schools to increase the number of drivers and to eliminate middlemen in the sales of automobiles by adopting a set-price sales system, in an effort to provide a suitable environment for the era of the passenger car.

In the latter half of the 1950s, Toyota was able to anticipate developments in automobile use and adopted the policy of diversifying production in correspondence with the varied demand structure ranging from top of the line models to popular cars; it decided to stress the popular car in its publicity. Toyota established mass production plants for new types on the basis of this policy of compartmentalization of the market, and also, by 1968, had set up a sales network for these new types of cars along with a sales channel composed of four dealers in each prefecture.[18]

Thus Toyota's sales channel changed to a multiple dealer system and a sales system in which one passenger type and other commercial types of cars could be handled in each channel. At the same time, Toyota Motor Sales expanded and reinforced the three functions noted above and strove for more rapid communication and closer cooperation with Toyota Motors. It kept new dealers informed of its sales ideas and policies, and by stressing a spirit of cooperation between Toyota Motors, T.M.S., and dealers, it succeeded in unifying them.

This vertical integration system connecting the maker, T.M.S. and dealers brought into full play the benefits of group management, firmly raising it to the top position in industry. The preeminence of this system was reinforced by the automobile industry itself as demand for cars increased rapidly and the passenger car market became firmly established.

Toyota's achievements in sales naturally drew the attention of other automobile companies, and other makers went on to imitate or follow much of the marketing system or methods that Toyota had adopted and put into action. Nissan Motors, a rival of Toyota, was no exception.

Since Nissan Motors was a leading affiliate of the Nissan Konzern, one of the most powerful new *zaibatsu*, it was severely affected by the war and the postwar reforms. Nissan, therefore, was inevitably beaten by Toyota in the reconstruction of its dealer network, and was forced to lose many of its executives because of the General Headquarters' (GHQ) policy of removing business leaders from their positions. It may have been due to this situation that Nissan's course of action in formulating a rationalization policy in face of the management crisis caused by the Dodge Plan differed from that of Toyota. Whereas Toyota separated its sales department and set up Toyota Motor Sales, Nissan absorbed Nissan Motor Sales which was reconstructed soon after the war and incorporated into the main company as the sales department.[19] Nissan's organizational reform strengthened the voice of the production department more than ever and reportedly created the groundwork for high-pressure management of dealers.

From this time on, Nissan adopted a management plan attaching more importance to production, which stressed the preeminence of its technical prowess, than to marketing activities, and those who evaluated the business characteristics of Toyota and Nissan used to call Toyota "the company of sales" and Nissan "the company of technology."

Nissan's technology-first principle bore fruit with the introduction of the famous "Bluebird," and for a time Nissan led Toyota in the passenger car market. This success further reinforced Nissan's production-oriented characteristics, forced the production department's Bluebird-centered production and sales plans onto the sales department, and at the same time reinforced a tendency to regard dealers simply as sales agents.

In the end, however, Nissan was forced to reexamine its structure once the passenger car market was firmly established and to change its production line. In the process of trying to differentiate according to market demand and because of intensified competition as passenger car sales in general went up, Nissan's top position in the passenger car market was usurped once again by Toyota, which adopted a full-line policy and a corresponding marketing system. Nissan also had to face a situation where its market share was further reduced as new makers entered the market.

Especially as a result of this situation, Nissan adopted a full-line policy in the latter half of the 1960s, and as a part of this new policy took over Prince Motors in 1966, one of the more powerful companies in the automobile industry, thereby broadening the type of cars it produced. At the same time, Nissan began to try to improve marketing in order successfully to promote its new full line.[20] The first point was to organize and strengthen the multiple sales channel system in order to eliminate differences between maker and dealers and to create a cooperative system based on mutual trust. The second point was the strengthening of the sales department. The aim here was to correct the lack of cooperation between the production department and the sales department, to systematize demand and sales forecasting through an equal and cooperative relationship between the two departments, and to coordinate forecasts with production plans, thus establishing a unified marketing system in the company as a whole.

In promoting this marketing policy Nissan deliberately adopted Toyota's policies. This change in Nissan's management strategy and improvement of its business structure produced fairly good results and profits as the passenger car market grew, and made it possible for it to remain, with Toyota, one of the two giants of Japan's automobile industry.

V.

Automobile marketing in Japan had its origins in the American-style sales channel policy and techniques which were imported by Ford and General Motors at the end of the Taisho period and in the early Showa period. These policies and techniques took root in Japan through Nissan Motors and Toyota Motors, which began with the domestic production of automobiles.

Distribution organizations were unified under a control association during wartime but were reorganized by each maker after the war. From then on, Toyota Motors took the lead in automobile marketing. It studied GM's sales methods more at this time than in the prewar period, modified them and put them into practice. These were well suited to the postwar process of rehabilitation and expansion of the automobile industry, and a motive force for Toyota's great leap. Most other automobile companies learned a lot from Toyota's marketing strategy and system and followed in its path.

It is in the developments noted above that the processes of introduction, consolidation and development of automobile marketing in Japan can be understood. At the same time, these processes were also the processes of emergence and growth of Japanese-style automobile marketing. In fact, automobile marketing in Japan came to have remarkably different characteristics from in America, which was its origin, although of course the degree of difference naturally varied among makers.

With regard to the major characteristics of automobile marketing in Japan, it is, first of all, possible to point out the intimate cooperation or unification of makers (including the motor sales companies in this case) and dealers. This cooperation between makers and dealers first started prior to World War II, when makers tried to develop sales routes for domestically-produced automobiles. The automobile market at the time was so completely dominated by Japan Ford and Japan GM that in order to sell domestically-produced cars in competition with foreign ones it was indispensable for Japanese makers (who strongly aspired to produce automobiles themselves) and dealers to cooperate on the basis of mutual interest. The relationship between them in the postwar period took the form of affiliations between makers and dealers. The close nature of their relationship was reinforced by the establishment of the "maker-led" sales financing system, set up to compensate for the under-development of consumer financing institutions, and with the adoption and use of modern sales techniques that the maker introduced and developed. The process of affiliation of dealers with makers, however, should not be conceived of as a one-sided domination of the former by the latter; rather, it should be regarded as a process of systematic combination in a marketing structure based on close interdependence of both parties.[21] For this reason, except for the period of reorganization of distribution immediately after the war and the period of reconstruction of the dealers' network followed by the reorganization of the automobile industry, it has been extremely rare for dealers to change their affiliation with makers. Unilateral cancellation of contracts by makers has been even rarer.

The second characteristic lies in the large scale of dealerships. This is because each maker, on principle, set territories on a prefectural basis and adopted a policy of constructing a dealer network on the basis of the strategic positioning of a small number of dealers. For this reason, a high number of units were sold per dealer. For example, new cars sold per dealer by Toyota, Nissan, Mitsubishi and Toyo in 1968 numbered 3,117, 2,944, 2,445, and 3,379, respectively.[22]

The fact that large territories were set may be due in part to the fact that Japan's automobile sales network took over that of Japan Ford and Japan GM or that it was set up in imitation of these foreign companies, but the basic reason is that demand itself was small in the early stages of popular automobile use. However, this large territory and the large-scale dealership system was maintained unchanged even after each maker increased its line as the passenger car market grew. It became necessary to reorganize sales channels in line with this development, although makers established multiple dealer networks in the same territory so that each dealer specialized in one type of vehicle. This large territory system was good for protecting the rights and profits of existing dealers, and the most effective way to set up large dealerships at strategic points, in order to attract customers and to explore potential sources of demand through cooperation between dealers and maker.

There was another more positive reason for adopting and maintaining such a large dealer system: Japanese society does not accord the distribution business much in the way of prestige. The automobile sales business, a relatively new distribution business, is no exception. For this reason, dealers try to improve their social position in two ways: to strengthen their relationship with makers and to expand the scale of their own business. This effort to expand advantageously works to reinforce the mobilization of finance, winning customers and securing personnel.[23]

The third characteristic is a firmly established home sales method. It is customary for Japanese buyers to prefer to purchase commodities through salesmen who come to their homes. This tendency is strong particularly when buying expensive durable consumer goods. For this reason, this kind of automobile retailing has been a central sales technique in the automobile industry from the beginning even up to now. However, its relevance has changed over the years; between the prewar period and the period soon after the war, the number of customers was so limited that sales depended largely on the personal intuition and ability of salesmen, and their commission sales constituted the main part of automobile sales. However, with the advent of the era of mass production and mass sales, such methods have reached their limit. Each dealer now employs a massive number of salesmen, mainly university graduates, in principle one salesman for each sub-area composed of 2,000–3,000 households in one large territory, and uses a very detailed management-sales method.[24]

The fourth characteristic is the existence of general sales companies, usually called motor sales companies, which stand between makers and dealers. The general sales company usually acts as a brother company or affiliate of the makers and is mainly responsible for distribution, sales financing and marketing. A typical example is Toyota Motor Sales. Approximately half the makers have this kind of organization.

These general sales organizations have been set up out of necessity. Because distribution routes for durable consumer goods, consumer financing institutions and other facilities that normally accompany the growth of the automobile market have not yet been fully established or developed, makers themselves have had to develop and reinforce these functions. At the same time, they have functioned as organizations for importing, developing and practicing modern marketing techniques, instructed and directed dealers, and played a role in promoting market development itself.

In this way, Japan's automobile marketing, although it took that of America as a model, has been conditioned by its peculiar social and cultural background, by the process of economic development, by commercial customs and financing conditions, and has undergone a great transformation through positive adjustment to these conditions; as a result it has come to have characteristics that can be referred to as Japanese-style automobile marketing. Japanese-style marketing has been strikingly effective in helping to develop the passenger car market in a rapidly growing economy, and, with establishment and reinforcement of the mass production system, has been a forceful feature in the rapid development of Japan's automobile industry.

NOTES

1. Hiromichi Osuga, "Jidōsha hanbai kikō no shiteki kōsatsu" (A Historical Analysis of the Automobile Distribution Organization). *Jidōsha to sono Sekai*, no. 108, 1975, p. 4.
2. Jidōsha Kōgyō Shinkōkai, "Nihon Jidōsha Kōgyōshi Kōjutsukiroku-shu" (Oral Record on History of Japan's Automobile Industry). *Jidōsha Kōgyō Shiryō Shiriizu* (2) (Tokyo, 1975), p. 5.
3. Masaru Udagawa, "Nissan Zaibatsu no Jidōsha Sangyō Shinshutsu ni tsuite" (On the Development of the Automobile Industry of the Nissan Zaibatsu) (1). *Keiei Shirin*, vol. 13, no. 4, 1977, pp. 107–109.
4. Toyota Jidōsha Hanbai (KK), *Mōtorizeishon to tomo ni* (With the Process of Motorization) (Nagoya, 1970), p. 33.
5. Aichi Toyota (KK), *Aichi Toyota Nijūgonenshi* (25-Year History of Aichi Toyota) (Nagoya, 1969), p. 83.
6. Masaru Udagawa and Seishi Nakamura, "Japanese Business and Government in the Inter-war Period" in Keiichiro Nakagawa, ed., *Government and Business*, The International Conference on Business History 5, (Tokyo: University of Tokyo Press, 1980), pp. 83–100.
7. Nissan Jidōsha (KK), *Nissan Jidōsha Sanjunenshi* (30-Year History of Nissan Motors) (Tokyo, 1964), pp. 46–47; Nissan Jidōsha Hanbai-ten Kyōkai, *Nijūgonenshi* (25-Year History) (Tokyo, 1974), pp. 5–7.
8. *Nissan Jidosha Sanjunenshi*, *op. cit.*, pp. 64–66.
9. Keizō Uchida, *Onjō—Kuruma to tomo ni* (Paternalism—in the Automobile Industry) (Tokyo, 1966), Nissan Jidōsha Hanbaiten Kyōkai, p. 101.
10. *Mōtarizeishon to tomo ni*, *op. cit.*, pp. 35–37.
11. Kōichi Shimokawa, "Toyota Jihan no Māketingu" (Marketing of the Toyota Motor Sales Company), in Shimokawa and others eds., *Nihon Keieishi o Manabu* (Learning Japanese Business History) [3] (Tokyo: Yūhikaku, 1976), pp. 220–223.
   Osuga, *op. cit.*, "The Automobile Distribution Organization—," pp. 11–12.
12. *Mōtarizeishon to tomo ni*, *op. cit.*, pp. 38–41.
13. *Ibid.*, pp. 105–110.
   Toyota Jidōsha Hanbaiten Kyōkai, *Sanjūnen no Ayumi* (30-Year History) (Tokyo, 1977), pp. 25–28.
14. *Mōtarizeishon to tomo ni*, *op. cit.*, pp. 94–95.
15. *Ibid.*, pp. 114–117.

16. *Ibid.*, pp. 120–123.
    Kōichi Shimokawa, "Marketing and Sales Financing in the Automobile Industry: US and Japan," in Keiichiro Nakagawa, ed., *Marketing and Finance in the Course of Industrialization*, The International Conference on Business History 3 (Tokyo: University of Tokyo Press, 1978), pp. 136–137.
17. *Mōtarizeishon to tomo ni, op. cit.*, pp. 151–156.
    Tokyo Toyopet (KK), *Tokyo Toyopet Nijunenshi* (20-Year History of Tokyo Toyopet) (Tokyo, 1973), pp. 14–15.
18. Hidemasa Morikawa (under the editorial supervision), *Sengo Sangyōshi eno Shogen* (A Witness to Postwar Industrial History) [2] (Tokyo: Mainichi Shimbunsha, 1977), p. 43.
    Mōtarizeishon to tomo ni, op. cit., pp. 487–504.
19. *Nissan Jidōsha Sanjūnenshi, op cit.*, p. 200.
20. Nissan Jidōsha Kabushiki Kaisha, *Nissan Jidōsha Shashi* (The Company History of Nissan Motors) (Tokyo, 1975), pp. 88–97.
21. Shimokawa, "Toyota Jihan no Māketingu," *op. cit.*, p. 228.
22. Nihon Jidōsha Kaigishō, Nikkan Jidōsha Shimbunsha, *Jidōsha Nenkan* (Yearbook of Automobile) (Tokyo, 1970), p. 82.
    Mōtarizeishon to tomo ni (Shiryohen [Data Collection]), *op. cit.*, p. 870.
23. Osuga, "The Automobile Distribution Organization—," *op. cit.*, pp. 11–12.
24. Minoru Fukuda, *Jidōsha no Māketingu* (The Marketing of Automobiles) (Tokyo: Tōyō Keizai Shinpousha, 1974), pp. 18–19.

188

COMMENTS

Fritz Blaich
Universität Regensburg

In his very interesting paper Professor Udagawa has approached his subject from two aspects. First he explains the development and the characteristics of Japan's modern automobile marketing. He then examines the management policy of the two big motor companies, Toyota and Nissan, in order to determine how much significance had been attached to the distributional sector and to retail policy in the managerial decisions of each firm.

I would like to emphasize two dominant characteristics of the Japanese automobile market:

(1) Obviously the Japanese banking establishment took practically no interest in financing the stock keeping of the individual automobile dealers or the purchasing by individual buyers. Due to a poorly developed consumer financing system, the manufacturers, partly forced by bank syndicates, began to establish legally independent sales companies, thus separating distribution from production. These sales companies carried out two functions. Besides selling automobiles, they became active in wholesale and retail financing by introducing installment payments.

(2) When intending to buy a car Japanese customers do not attach great importance to elegant showrooms. Rather, they expect trained salespeople to come to their homes. Because of this custom the Japanese automobile dealer cannot be satisfied with just a salesroom in a desirable location and an effective repair shop. He must also take great care to maintain a staff of qualified sales agents. For this reason I think that only a relatively large sales territory would guarantee the Japanese automobile dealer a profitable turnover and the full employment of his workshop.

Now I want to raise some questions:

(1)   At the beginning of the 1930s American manufacturers completely dominated Japan's automobile market. With regard to the distribution sector, they introduced the American system of franchising. Yet the two principal companies showed an important difference in their application of the system: General Motors of Japan established dealers for each type of automobile in each prefecture, whereas Ford of Japan established them only in places where it was thought necessary. As far as I can see, Ford's procedure offered the dealers better sales opportunities, for I suppose that the volume of demand differed considerably from prefecture to prefecture.

(2)   On the whole both the American firms, however, failed to adapt their distribution systems to the conditions of the Japanese market. The author repeatedly stresses in his paper that Ford and GM applied the franchise method mechanically without paying attention to Japan's commercial practices. Above all the Japanese dealer always stood in fear of the immediate cancellation of his contract if he could not reach a certain sales revenue. Therefore it was no wonder that Toyota and Nissan, which entered the automobile market just before the outbreak of World War II, succeeded in establishing their own outlet systems within a short time. They took over the franchise method but attempted to revise it by strengthening the corporate ties between manufacturer and dealer.

I would like to ask why Ford and GM did not make greater efforts to assert themselves on the Japanese market, after having already set up assembly plants in Yokohama and Osaka. Was it too difficult for them to work out a sales system that would be appropriate to Japan's business manners? In Europe, for instance, American investors usually knew well how to adapt modern American business methods to the national peculiarities of the European markets. Sometimes even formalities were taken into account as the following example will display: John H. Patterson, the founder and general manager of the National Cash Register Company, would give orders that the name of a foreign subsidiary company be translated into the language of the country where it was set up. Thus the German corporation became "Nationale Registrier-Kassen GmbH," the French company emerged as "La Nationale

Caisse Enregistreuse SA," the Spanish as "Cajas Registradoras 'National'," and the Italian as "Societa Anonima Registratori di Cassa 'National'."

To be sure, GM of Japan lost its able sales manager Shotaro Kamiya to Toyota Motor Company, and it was he who modified the "imported" franchise system by cultivating a new partnership relation between the manufacturer and the dealer. On the other hand, it was also a former GM employee, Heinrich Nordhoff, who managed to transform Volkswagen from a heavily bombed armaments plant into a prosperous automobile factory by applying American management methods. Yet neither Opel nor Ford lost its position on the German automobile market.

(3) Let me now move on to the managerial strategies applied by Toyota and Nissan in the postwar years. During this period Toyota was often called "the company of sales" and Nissan "the company of technology." I suppose that Nissan had no choice but to concentrate all its forces on the reconstruction of the production sector because of its comparatively heavy damages due to the war. To some extent the management policy of Nissan seems to me to be comparable to the development of the German Borgward Group, which after the war included the firms of Borgward, Goliath and Lloyd. The founder and manager of this group, Carl Borgward, an excellent engineer, had a good start in the postwar period by inventing or introducing new technologies. In 1948, for instance, he was the first German automobile manufacturer to come out with the "pontonform," which was gradually imitated by all his competitors, at last even by Daimler Benz AG. While putting much money into expensive technological research he had to neglect the expansion and modernization of his sales organization. When the saturation point of the market was reached, his group went bankrupt in 1961. The management of Nissan, however, succeeded in keeping its strong position on the Japanese market by imitating the sales system of Toyota. I think it would be interesting to know whether this result might be attributed to a clear decision taken by Nissan's management, or was it simply caused by the favorable situation of the market, which was still dominated by the seller?

PART III

AUTOMOBILES AND INTERNATIONAL MARKETS

Automobiles and International Markets

Mira Wilkins
Florida International University

I.

There are two kinds of "international" automobile marketing. They are not entirely distinct and, in fact, blend when seen in a historical context. The first involves exports and (for the recipient country) imports; the second, *national* production and marketing of a "foreign" car. Historically, the process of "international" marketing began with exports. A few cars could be sold without a marketing network—by individual orders, through an "agent," or from a single showroom.

Advertising and brand name identification came early in this industry. Integral to "mass marketing" was advertising. The exporter soon discovered that if the car was to be sold in quantity, a marketing organization was required. Selling internationally involved defining a differentiated product and ultimately establishing a wholesale and retail network where volume sales occurred or could be anticipated.

Exports are only one form of international marketing. A second is associated with sizeable foreign investment. Automobile producers discovered that they could not reach certain foreign markets solely through exports, because of costs (of transportation and production), competition from the host country or other firms, or political considerations (tariffs, or nontariff barriers to trade; import substitution policies of government). None of these reasons was mutually exclusive. Thus, an automobile company invested in more than a sales office (or marketing organization); it assembled and did some manufacturing, and then perhaps made a complete car within the host country. It marketed this car in that nation and perhaps even exported it. To the extent that the car was made and sold locally, it was a *domestic* product—the Ford made in England, the Opel in Germany, the Volkswagen in the United States.

In this paper, I am going to interpret the words "international automobile marketing" to include (1) exports and imports and also (2) the marketing operations *abroad* of *international* automobile companies—even when their activities abroad are almost entirely "domestic," that is, within a particular foreign country.

II.

In the 1890s, shows and races were the way to advertise new automobiles produced in the United States and Europe. At these events, customers and manufacturers compared products. From their origin, exhibitions and races had international participation.[1]

At the turn of the century, Europeans produced more cars than Americans.[2] Their units were custom-made and tailored to the needs of an elite market. They were priced accordingly. Wealthy Americans preferred the European car to less well-constructed domestically-made units. Measured by dollar value, imports of cars and parts into the United States exceeded exports until 1906.[3]

European cars were identified as quality products. Thus, it is not surprising to find early ties between Daimler and Steinway. In 1888, William Steinway—already a well-known maker and marketer of pianos—entered into an agreement with Gottlieb Daimler, wherein the latter authorized Steinway to act on his behalf and to form the Daimler Motor Co. in New York. Steinway held most of the shares in the Daimler Motor Co.[4] Why did the German manufacturer choose Steinway to market his products in the United States? Probably Steinway's experience with expensive high-priced merchandise was crucial. Steinway owners might well buy a Mercedes. Moreover, as Cyril Ehrlich points out, pianos were an early, expensive consumer durable sold on credit.[5]

In time, after William Steinway's death, the German Daimler company obtained a direct equity interest in its New York agent. In 1905, the Daimler Manufacturing Company (a successor to the

Daimler Motor Co.) began to manufacture Mercedes in the United States. Imports faced a 45 percent U.S. tariff. U.S. manufacturing meant that Mercedes benefited from the tariff protection. The American Mercedes was advertised as "a faithful reproduction . . . of the foreign car."6

The sequence of events is instructive. First came the independent agent (Steinway), then the affiliate (Daimler Manufacturing Company—in which the Steinway *family* still participated), and finally the manufacturing in the United States of the Mercedes automobile.

Meanwhile, in Europe Daimler through marketing and licensing agreements entered France (Panhard and Levassor had a license from Daimler) and England. In each country, distinct *domestic* marketing structures emerged. Other European manufacturers had representatives abroad to market their cars.7

American manufacturers engaged in export at the same time as the United States was a net importer of cars. Ford, for example, sold abroad the sixth car that it produced. Very quickly, in the nearby Canadian market, Ford established a manufacturing facility. A 35 percent tariff encouraged import substitution. A marketing organization to sell Ford cars in Canada was established, founded with the initial distributor of Ford cars in the Dominion. In time, Ford-Canada developed a marketing organization for Ford cars in the British empire—Great Britain exempted.8

Ford's export business outside Canada was first handled by an independent New York-based agent (R.M. Lockwood), who arranged with independent export houses to handle the trade. These often appointed foreign agents. Ford soon learned that if its international business was to expand, more than independent agents were required; salaried officials were needed to handle the international marketing and to appoint dealers.9 As Ford developed its domestic marketing, so it pursued exports and international marketing. The basic difference was that in time it discovered that in its *major* foreign markets it had to manufacture near its customers. Thus, in Canada and England—and later in Germany and France—and much later in Australia, Brazil, and Argentina, Ford manufactured within the sovereign nation. In every case that it did so, it had the rudiments (and sometimes far more) of a marketing organization in place.

In England, when the marketing was developed by Ford, the product was at first a replica of the U.S. car—although as early as 1913, Fords made in England had right-hand drive. In England (unlike in the United States) the early dealers were permitted to handle competitors' products—a concession to local practice, but more important an initial means of enabling a dealer to survive. By 1914, Ford had 1,000 dealers in England. The car made there was in first place in the British market.[10]

III.

Mass production and mass marketing in the automobile industry go together. Ford Motor Company has traditionally been credited with the assembly line and mass production. Of equal, or greater, importance was the idea of a *cheap* car that would be widely owned (mass consumption). To market this car domestically, advertising was required and a network of dealers. To market it internationally, the requirements were identical. Export from independent agent to independent agent could not suffice.

In my *American Business Abroad: Ford on Six Continents*, I showed how Ford initiated in country after country direct representation. In each locale, it developed a marketing organization and distinct advertising. Ford was not alone; General Motors followed. The larger the market, the more the need for investment in a marketing organization to sell the cars. Sometimes assembly followed, and sometimes full production. In that case, international marketing became *national* marketing as investment substituted for trade. Chrysler was a late participant in this patterned development, but it too followed the exact same sequence.[11]

In each country as sales rose, a marketing organization of salaried men supervising company-associated dealers came to be required for the automobile maker to get nearer its consumer: to demonstrate the car, to provide service, to offer credit.

In the 1920s, managers at Ford and General Motors (GM) recognized that the product sold in the United States was not fully satisfactory in European markets. In Britain, taxes, road conditions, gasoline costs, and competition indicated to the U.S. companies the need for design changes. General Motors responded first. In 1925, GM bought Vauxhall—a small British manufacturer. As Ford, once the leader in British industry, fell behind Morris and Austin in sales in Britain, Ford's British manager in 1925 asked the home office for a small, low-powered car designed for the British market (not until 1932 did Ford actually offer such a unit).[12]

On the European continent, taxes, road conditions and gasoline costs meant that most customers preferred the smaller, lighter units. In 1929 General Motors acquired the first-ranking German car maker, Opel. Ford's "European-Type" car—designed initially for the British market—far outsold its "U.S.-Type" car in the European market in the 1930s.[13]

IV.

Ford and General Motors had to respond to the requirements of European markets or lose sales. As American producers developed mass production, European manufacturers had imitated: Morris, Austin, Citroën, Renault, Peugeot, Opel, Fiat introduced assembly-line production—following American practice. By 1929, each had abandoned the custom-made models of early years. By the 1930s, the idea of the Volkswagen took shape in Germany. The concept was totally in keeping with American mass production ideas; it was in every sense to be a German Model T.[14]

Yet, whereas in the United States in the 1920s mass marketing by automobile manufacturers had become well established, despite their introduction of interchangeable parts and the moving assembly line, European car makers still sold in relatively limited markets. Whereas one person in five owned a car in the United States in 1939, the figures for Great Britain were one in 23, for France one in 20, and Germany one in 56.[15] Nonetheless, the European-designed small, light, low-powered, gas-efficient car had pushed American companies to provide similar specialized products for Europe (and Europe alone).

European automobile producers in the inter-war years were

involved in international marketing. Renault by 1929 was represented in 49 countries and had assembly plants in Belgium (1926) and England (1927).[16] Austin, at the initiative of Rosengart, licensed the latter to produce in France. To penetrate the U.S. market, Austin licensed the output of the "baby" Austin in western Pennsylvania. This car was, however, a total failure in the U.S. market—despite its low operating costs. Austin did not manage to develop a product appropriate to the U.S. market, nor did Austin create an effective U.S. marketing organization.[17]

Indeed, in the interwar period the American automobile industry had worldwide supremacy. It was American products that were sold in the U.S. market. Imports had virtually disappeared (Mercedes were no longer made in the United States, production having ceased in 1913). Throughout the interwar years, the dollar value of U.S. automotive exports exceeded imports by a ratio of never less than 138 to one (1938) and in 1935 when imports were less than $500,000, the ratio soared above 464 to one![18] In Canada, affiliates of U.S. producers made cars and sold them through their own marketing organizations. In Europe, American companies had manufacturing and assembly plants and well-developed domestic marketing networks in each country. Worldwide, U.S. companies had assembly plants in numerous nations and a global network of sales office, distributors, and dealers.

In the 1920s, in the heyday of the Model T, Ford dealers, whose commissions were extraordinarily generous, came to be among the wealthiest individuals in many countries (often Ford chose for its foreign dealers individuals already well situated; for example, a wealthy sugar planter in Jamaica would also sell Model Ts).[19]

In short, in the interwar years, the American automobile industry was supreme. Nonetheless, European manufacturers were developing products that forced U.S. businesses *abroad* to modify *their* European designs. In a world of high tariff barriers and autarchy, U.S. automobile makers—if they could not export built-up cars— assembled or produced abroad and sold through their developed marketing organizations.

V.

World War II disrupted the world economy. Civilian automobile production ceased. Dealers went to war. Internationally, marketing networks fell apart.

When the war was over, a rebuilding process began. Dollar shortages were ubiquitous. Throughout Europe, governments urged producers to export. Automobile manufacturers responded. Indeed both U.S.-owned and domestically-owned car builders in Europe sought simultaneously to resume civilian production and domestic and foreign sales.

In 1950, the United States produced 76 percent of the world's motor vehicles.[20] It was a net exporter of cars and in fact all automotive products. But the year before, in 1949, British makers of cars (including U.S. multinational corporations in England) surpassed the "U.S." domestic makers, reaching first place in *world exports*.[21]

In England, the government pressured automobile builders to export. British-owned *and* U.S.-owned automobile companies did so. American multinational corporations imported the products made in England and sold them in the United States (and elsewhere around the world) through existing dealers. But the demand for the imports in the United States was small, and the U.S. companies soon stopped importing the so-called "captive" imports once British dollar shortages abated.

The British-owned companies that tried to penetrate the United States market in the immediate postwar years found it impenetrable. The problem was their absence of attention to developing a marketing network. The U.S. market was the largest in the world. Yet, in the postwar years until 1957, imports represented less than 1 percent of total car sales.[22]

During the 1950s, European automobile output grew as economies in Europe were rebuilt. By 1957—the very year when the Treaty of Rome was signed and the European Common Market was established—European car companies began to see the potentials of a mass market. The British car industry was challenged by a healthy

German and French industry. In 1956, German car exports for the first time exceeded those of the British and took first place in the world.[23] The reason lay in the extraordinary success of the Volkswagen.[24]

The Volkswagen triumph was a marketing achievement. It is fascinating to trace the learning experience. Not until after World War II did the Volkswagen, which was planned and designed in the 1930s, actually go into commercial production. Occupying forces in Germany put Heinz Nordhoff in charge of the German Volkswagen business in 1947. Nordhoff had been employed by General Motors' German subsidiary, Opel. As noted, when GM acquired Opel in 1929, Opel was the leader in the German automobile industry; it retained that position throughout the pre-World War II years. From his experience with that subsidiary of General Motors, Nordhoff had realized the importance of organizing a marketing and service network. Indeed, when in the 1950s Volkswagen started to export to the United States, it coached its representatives on the failure of British (and French) cars to maintain good sales in the United States, because of a deficiency in their marketing organization.[25] No British or French car maker had been able to develop a satisfactory sales and service network in the United States. Perhaps the inabilities of the British and French companies in this respect were grounded in their not yet having fully concentrated on mass marketing *at home*. Perhaps it was more fundamental—for in the early post-World War II years the British and French cars failed to match the requirements of the American market.

While the European consumer wanted a small, light, gas-frugal, low-priced car, Americans wanted power and speed (to cover long distances on good roads); they wanted large cars (remember the baby boom). While most European cars remained small, American-built cars became bigger, more powerful, heavier, and more expensive.[26] Consequently, *they* became less competitive in world markets. In one sense it did not matter, since U.S. companies had subsidiaries worldwide that offered appropriate-sized cars for European and other markets.

Nordhoff had an excellent product in the Volkswagen Beetle.

The design was distinctive. He made important engineering and cosmetic improvements. Volkswagen in the United States established a distribution organization, sending in salaried representatives, appointing distributors and dealers. As early as 1950, Volkswagen had appointed a New York foreign car dealer as its exclusive agent for the United States east of the Mississippi. This man selected a network of dealers. In 1953 Volkswagen decided it needed direct representation, did not renew the New York agent's contract, and dispatched salaried men to New York and San Francisco. By 1956 Volkswagen's New York office had fifty-four employees and was prepared to move its U.S. headquarters across the Hudson River to Englewood Cliffs, N.J. Volkswagen appointed a formidable network of dealers in the United States.[27] The effort to develop a marketing organization and to engage in advertising proved well justified. Because American makers were selling the "big" cars, there was a segment of the U.S. market that was ignored by the U.S. producers. Volkswagen cars filled that unmet demand. In the 1950s U.S. imports of other European makers also rose. By 1957 U.S. car imports exceeded U.S. car exports for the first time in at least a half century.[28] Volkswagen imports contributed importantly to the rising total.

1957 is important as the post-World War II year when (1) (measured by number of units) the U.S. balance of trade in passenger cars went into deficit, and (2) imports of cars obtained over 3 percent of the U.S. market. From 1957 on, U.S. car imports have exceeded exports; since 1957, imports (excluding those from Canada) have soared to over 18 percent of the U.S. market.[29] The rise of imports from Europe reflected the coming of age of the European automobile industry.

As imports rose, American producers responded to the obvious demand for a small car. American Motors introduced the Rambler. General Motors and Ford once again started importing cars from their British and German affiliates—the "captive" imports. As soon as they could, they introduced new domestically-produced "compact cars" (and cut back on their own imports).

In 1959 imports—primarily from Europe—captured 10.2 percent of the U.S. market. Then they dropped to 4.9 percent in 1962 as

U.S.-made products—Falcons, Valiants, and Corvairs—substituted.
Neither Renault nor Fiat—both large exporters—had developed
sales and service organizations in the United States. Faced with
the U.S. "compacts" as competition, their sales fell sharply. By
contrast, Volkswagen—with its marketing network—was able to
increase its U.S. volume—albeit at a slower rate than in earlier
years.

Volkswagen provides a case of a European small car maker
which behaved just like a U.S. multinational corporation. It
recognized that mass production required mass marketing and
created in the United States and in world markets a comprehensive
new network to sell and service the car.

Whereas Volkswagen built its own distribution system—as
had Ford in the United States and worldwide—Daimler-Benz
took a different route. Its Mercedes—with its limited high-income
market—was reintroduced into the post-World War II U.S. market
through the Studebaker distribution system. When Studebaker and
Packard merged in 1954, Studebaker added a quality top-of-the-
line car. The Mercedes and the Packard appealed to similar markets.
In 1965 Daimler-Benz's subsidiary Mercedes Benz of North America
Inc. bought Studebaker's distribution organization. (Studebaker
ceased production.) The German firm terminated all except 300
of Studebaker's 1,200 dealers. Subsequently from that base, it
added new dealers.[30]

In the 1950s the United States was the world's largest market,
as it had been in the past and would be in the future. With the
rise of the European automobile industry and the low U.S. tariffs
(in 1956 the duty was 9.5 percent, it dropped thereafter), the
American market had become open to imports.

Worldwide, however, the pattern was different. American
exports were not competitive. If American companies wanted to
reach world markets, they had to produce abroad. In Australia,
and then in less developed countries—Argentina, Brazil, Mexico—
new automobile industries arose. It was not only U.S. companies
that invested within these nations; Volkswagen, for example, built
a major automobile plant in Brazil.

Wherever there were sales, the multinational corporations

formed (or re-formed earlier) marketing organizations—to sell imports or, more often now, locally-assembled or-produced products. The marketing organizations varied in extent—and the scale correlated positively with the degree of market penetration.

Before World War II, the Japanese automobile market had been served by imports (generally assembled in Japan). Ford and General Motors both had assembly plants, built in 1925 and 1926 respectively. Japanese manufacturing developed in the 1930s—Nissan and Toyota—but on a very modest scale. Indeed, in 1938 in Japan there was about one car for every 1,200 persons.[31] After World War II, however, Japanese industry developed. The market was virtually closed to imports and totally closed to investment. Multinational corporations could not establish foreign-owned domestic production. The Japanese industry began to export; by the late 1950s Japanese car imports began to trickle into the U.S. market. (Toyota sold 288 cars in the United States from October 1957 to December 1958.)[32]

Just as the U.S. companies and Volkswagen recognized the need to integrate forward and to develop international marketing organizations staffed by salaried individuals, so the Japanese companies followed the same pattern. In October 1957, Toyota Motor Sales Company Ltd. of Japan formed Toyota Motor Sales, U.S.A., headquartered in California. In its first fourteen months of existence, it had appointed 45 dealers and opened a parts warehouse (with an inventory of 2,800 different parts). Sales rose very slowly, only to fall in 1960 when the U.S. compact models were introduced. The company still did not have a satisfactory product for the U.S. market. Its earliest offering was "under-powered, overpriced and built like a tank." There was nothing automatic, or easy, or routine about the Japanese entry into the U.S. or world markets. Japanese executives learned from the experiences of other multinational corporations. In large markets products might have to be specially designed. A marketing network was essential.[33]

VI.

In the 1960s, U.S. cars once again grew in size and horsepower.

The cars were built for the affluent American consumer, who wanted comfort, roominess, style, and power. Gasoline was cheap. American engine designers did not worry that these were "gas guzzlers." In 1968 no U.S.-made car had a manufacturers' list price of under *$1,800*, while seventeen different models of imports sold in the American market for less than that price.[34]

Once the United States had produced low-priced cars; now the tables were turned. Europeans and Japanese began to compete on the basis of price. Moreover, European car makers had become accustomed to "mass markets." The European Economic Community had created a giant market and given continental European producers a new experience with a large tariff-free market.[35] In 1967, for the first time since the first decade of the twentieth century, European motor vehicle production exceeded U.S. output. From that point on it was larger.[36]

While American producers were building big and high-powered cars at home, abroad their affiliates were frequently producing "European-style cars"—designed for drivers on narrow roads, who paid steep charges for gasoline, and who lived in countries with tax structures that penalized large units. When we talk about "European production," remember that includes the output of U.S. companies *in* Europe.

In the late 1960s, Japanese cars began to appear more frequently in world markets. Like the European cars, they were smaller, lighter, generally cheaper, and certainly more fuel-frugal than their American-made counterparts.

By 1970 German vehicle producers—still the largest exporters worldwide—held 24.3 percent of world motor vehicle exports compared with France's 17.6 percent, Japan's 12.5 percent, the U.K.'s 10 percent, and the U.S.'s 4.4 percent.[37] In 1971 and 1973, the United States devalued the dollar. European exports to the United States dropped. Japanese exports were not as affected.

In 1974 Japan replaced Germany as the world's largest motor vehicle exporter. Its motor vehicle exports captured 23.4 percent of the total world exports of motor vehicles, compared with France's 17.4 percent, Germany's 16.8 percent, the U.S.'s 7.3 percent (much of which went to Canada), and the U.K.'s 6.5 percent.[38]

In 1973–1974, OPEC pushed oil prices upward. In 1975 in the United States, the Energy Policy and Conservation Act (EPCA) provided for annual, mandatory mile-per-gallon standards for companies, with a fleet average of 27.5 miles per gallon to be reached by 1985. In the United States, gasoline prices climbed. While they remained substantially lower than such prices throughout Europe,[39] the rising gasoline prices, along with the car companies' responses to the EPCA requirements and the fuel-frugal Japanese and European imports, meant the American consumer not only rejected the "gas guzzler," but had viable options to replace such cars.

The mid- and late 1970s saw dramatic changes in the world automobile industry. In response to increased demand, lower tariffs in the industrial world, the falling dollar, the new worldwide automotive competition, and the new regulatory environment, the locales of production and the passenger car itself took on a new look. The British-made car lost out in world markets. When in 1973 Britain joined the European Common Market, its domestic automobile industry faltered under the intense competition from the Continent. Lower tariffs meant parts of cars could be produced in different countries. Economies of scale could be achieved. Cars were no longer "national" products. Trade in both parts and end products rose.

However, the reduced U.S. tariffs were offset by the falling dollar. For exporters to the United States, the devalued dollar was the virtual equivalent of a tariff. Volkswagen's U.S. sales plummeted. After several years of uncertainty, in 1976 Volkswagen decided to produce in the United States. In 1978 in the United States, General Motors built 5.3 million cars; Ford, 2.6 million; Chrysler, 1.1 million; American Motors, 164,000; Volkswagen, 40,000.[40] Volkswagen was "America's" fifth largest car maker and seemed likely to move quickly to fourth (or even third) place. It could not have accomplished this had it not had a full-fledged marketing organization in place when it started U.S. production.

In March-April, 1978, American Motors and Renault announced plans for joint distribution of Renault's Le Car in the United States and assembly of the medium-sized Renault in the United States. In the fall of 1979, Renault acquired a 5 percent interest

in American Motors (for $15 million); it planned to acquire a
22.5 percent stake. Full production of Renault cars in the United
States was scheduled for 1982.[41]

Japanese companies watched carefully the yen-dollar exchange
rates. During the 1960s, Japanese firms had developed products
suitable for the U.S. market and established extensive marketing
networks in the United States. By 1975, when Toyota assumed
first place among U.S. car imports, its retail sales were 328,918
and it had 975 dealers.[42] Toyota (and other Japanese companies
that had appointed dealers) opened service facilities and arranged
for parts inventories. The Japanese companies considered whether,
like Volkswagen, they too would have to assemble and to manufacture in the United States. The key consideration was could they
continue to sell in the United States without plants in this country?

Honda decided to assemble motorcycles in Ohio in 1977 and
suggested in time ("several years") it might assemble cars.[43] By
the fall of 1979, however, no Japanese automobiles were built in the
United States and the *Wall Street Journal* noted that the three
major importers of Japanese units (Toyota Motor Sales, U.S.A.;
Nissan, U.S.A.; and American Honda Motor Company) accounted
for about 80 percent of all foreign-made cars sold in this country.[44]

The Japanese success was extraordinary. Japan had become the
world's largest exporter of passenger cars. In 1977 Japan exported
almost 3 million passenger cars (2,958,879). France, exporting
slightly over 2 million (2,084,473), and Germany, just under 2
million (1,832,724), were clearly bested.[45] Japan did so well in
worldwide competition because of the factors that related to effective marketing: product (design and quality), dealer and service
organization, advertising, and price.

Attractive and quality Japanese cars fit well into the new environment of the mid-1970s. In the 1970s, worldwide government
regulators had become increasingly conscious of pollution, automotive safety, and energy conservation. Japanese cars had a head-
start on emission controls, early introduced safety measures and,
of course, had always been fuel-efficient.

The Japanese multinational corporations' establishment of a
marketing organization comparable to "domestic" networks in the

United States was instrumental in maintaining sales as the dollar/ yen rates deprived Japanese automobile manufacturers of any price advantage. In today's American market, the Japanese car competes as a differentiated product on the basis of design and performance, but not, I would suggest, on the basis of price. Worldwide, Japanese cars are appearing in markets once dominated by nationally- (or in the case of Europe, European-) produced products.

By the 1970s, the automobile industry had become truly a global one. By 1978 passenger cars were produced in twenty-two countries around the world. While the U.S. remained the country with the largest automobile output, U.S. passenger car production in 1978 accounted for little more than 29 percent of the world total.[46] According to data provided in *MVMA Motor Vehicle Facts and Figures '79*, by 1977 thirty-nine nations had more than one car per ten people.[47] Multinational corporations had penetrated markets on a grand scale. Not only U.S. and European firms competed, but Japanese multinational enterprises had assumed importance. The development of marketing organizations for the passenger car has been nothing short of formidable.

Notes

1. Allan Nevins and Frank Ernest Hill, *Ford: The Times, The Man, The Company* (New York: Scribner's, 1954).
2. D. W. Fryer, *World Economic Development* (New York: McGraw Hill, 1965), p. 459.
3. *Commerce and Navigation of the United States for 1909*, 173, pp. 493–494.
4. Mira Wilkins, "Crosscurrents: American Investments in Europe, European Investments in the United States," in Paul Uselding, ed., *Business and Economic History*, 2nd ser., VI, 1977, p. 25.
5. See Cyril Ehrlich, *The Piano, A History* (London: J. M. Dent & Sons, Ltd., 1976).
6. Daimler Manufacturing Company, *The American Mercedes* (Long Island City, 1906).
7. Nevins and Hill, *Ford*, op. cit.
8. Mira Wilkins and Frank Ernest Hill, *American Business Abroad: Ford on Six Continents* (Detroit: Wayne State University, 1974), pp.

1, 15, 20.

9. *Ibid.*, pp. 1, 21, 27, 28, 32, 41.

10. *Ibid.*, pp. 50, 51.

11. Mira Wilkins, *The Maturing of Multinational Enterprise: American Business Abroad from 1914 to 1970* (Cambridge, Mass.: Harvard University Press, 1974), pp. 72–75, deals briefly with the expansion of the U.S. companies abroad in the 1920s.

12. Wilkins and Hill, *American Business Abroad, op. cit.*, pp. 238–241.

13. *Ibid.*, p. 441.

14. There is a history of Volkswagen: Walter Henry Nelson, *Small Wonder* (Boston: Little, Brown and Co., 1970).

15. Based on figures in W. W. Rostow, *Stages of Economic Growth* (Cambridge, Eng.: Cambridge University Press, 1960), p. 171.

16. Patrick Fridenson, *Histoire de Usines Renault* (Paris: Editions du Seuil, 1972), I, pp. 144–145.

17. Data from Patrick Fridenson, Roy Church, and George Edward Domer, "The History of the American Austin and Bantam." *Automobile Quarterly*, XIV (1964), pp. 404–429.

18. Based on statistics presented in Mira Wilkins, "Multinational Automobile Enterprises and Regulation: An Historical Overview," in Douglas H. Ginsburg and William J. Abernathy, *Government, Technology, and the Future of the Automobile* (New York: McGraw-Hill, 1980), pp. 257–258.

19. Based on personal interview.

20. *MVMA Motor Vehicle Facts and Figures '79*, p. 20.

21. George Maxcy and Aubrey Silberston, *The Motor Industry* (London: George Allen & Unwin, 1959), pp. 17, 228.

22. See figures in Wilkins, "Multinational Automobile Enterprises," *op. cit.*

23. Maxcy and Silberston, *Motor Industry, op. cit.*, pp. 223, 227, 228.

24. Nelson, *Small Wonder, op. cit.*, p. 332.

25. *Ibid.*, pp. 140–147, 172, 174.

26. Lawrence J. White, *The Automobile Industry since 1945* (Cambridge, Mass.: Harvard University Press, 1971), p. 182.

27. Mira Wilkins, *Foreign Enterprise in Florida* (Gainesville: University Presses of Florida, 1979), p. 112.

28. Wilkins, "Multinational Automobile Enterprises," *op. cit.*

29. *Ibid.*

30. Wilkins, *Foreign Enterprise in Florida, op. cit.*, pp. 112–113.

31. Based on figures in Rostow, *Stages of Economic Growth, op. cit.*, p. 171.

32. *Toyota: The First Twenty Years in the U.S.A.* (Torrance, Calif.: Toyota Motor Sales, 1977), pp. 9, 131.

33. *Ibid.*, p. 25 ff.

34. Harbridge House, *The Imported Automobile Industry* (Boston: Harbridge House, 1976), p. 44.

35. In 1970 imports from other EEC nations into France were 16 percent (compared with 1 percent in 1958, the first year of the Common Market), into Italy, 28 percent (compared with 2 percent in 1958), into Germany, 25 percent (compared with 7 percent in 1958). See Louis T. Wells, Jr., "Automobiles" in Raymond Vernon, *Big Business and the State* (Cambridge, Mass.: Harvard University Press, 1974), p. 246.

36. Figures in *MVMA Facts and Figures*, p. 20.

37. *Ibid.*, p. 81.

38. *Ibid.*

39. *Ibid.*, p. 30.

40. *Ibid.*, p. 11.

41. *Wall Street Journal*, Apr. 3, 1978 and Oct. 17, 1979.

42. *Toyota, op. cit.*, p. 134.

43. *Miami Herald*, Oct. 12, 1977.

44. *Wall Street Journal*, Sept. 20, 1979.

45. *MVMA Fact and Figures*, p. 81.

46. *Ibid.*, p. 21.

47. *Ibid.*, pp. 34–37.

COMMENTS

1

Kin'ichiro Toba
Waseda University

Professor Wilkins' paper clearly shows how the automobile found its market first within its own country and then in the world, and also shows how important a role the modern American-type marketing system has played in the successful development of such companies as Ford and General Motors. In connection with the supremacy of the American marketing system, Professor Wilkins takes Volkswagen and Japanese car manufacturers (in particular Toyota) as examples that have achieved great success in the postwar world market by utilizing these systems.

It seems to me, however, that she puts too much stress on the role of the marketing system. It is true, of course, that the American-born marketing system has contributed greatly to the business success of the big automobile companies of today and that its importance and role will be great in future. However, market conditions for the automobile have been changing rapidly, especially since the 1970s. Now twenty-two countries around the world are producing passenger cars and thirty-nine nations have more than one car per ten people. In such a global market, cost problems will again become more important than marketing problems. Even within the field of marketing, such marketing methods as adjustment for local conditions in size and design will become more important than other factors. This is my first qualification.

A second qualification is that the recent success of Japanese car manufacturers in exporting to the U.S. and other countries is not only because of the successful introduction of the American-born marketing methods, but also due to the innovation of the mass production system. As Professor Yamazaki clearly points out in his paper, Toyota's new production system of multi-product and small volume was a revolutionary innovation in car production. The innovation was based on a new idea and well fitted for today's global market. This technology came from the idea that management should maintain a close relationship between mass production and mass distribution in order to adjust for a wide global market. I would say that the characteristic feature of American marketing methods is to try to follow production closely, but Toyota's idea was to keep harmony between mass production and mass distribution. Thus, the idea of marketing is changing its character in today's global market conditions.

My third qualification is concerned with Professor Vernon's product life cycle model. Around 1900, European technology in the car industry was superior to that of the United States and, therefore, the American attempt to export their cars to Europe failed. However, after the 1920s, American manufacturers succeeded in exporting, assembling and also producing their cars in Europe, and the supremacy of American car manufacturers in the world continued until well after the Second World War. This was because of the mass production and mass distribution systems that America had achieved in the 1920s. However, a big change occurred in the world car industry particularly after the 1960s, and the American share in the world market began to shrink. Why did this happen? The automobile is a "special" consumer durable item because of its high price, need for maintenance and supply of parts. This means that if the manufacturer wishes to sell in volume, it is necessary to combine both a mass-production technology and a mass distribution system.

The United States was the most favored country for developing the mass production and mass distribution systems because of its size and population, equal distribution of income and so on, and the manufacturer who combined both systems most efficiently could take the supreme position in the domestic and world markets. Compared with the United States, European countries had fewer advantages for developing such systems. It was only after the

establishment of the Common Market that European automobile
manufacturers gained an equal footing with the U.S. in terms
of the size of market.

Because of the favored social and economic conditions, the
automobile as a product had reached a state of maturity in the
United States by the 1950s. But since the 1960s, the technologies
of the automobile industry have been open to all car manufacturers
in the world. Now, as is seen in Professor Lim's paper, even such
semideveloped countries as Korea have started catching up. Her
car manufacturers may be able to develop and actively participate
in world competition in a short time, just as Japan did earlier. It
seems to me that Professor Vernon's product life cycle model is ap-
plicable to the situation of today's American automobile industry.

2

Akio Okochi
University of Tokyo

1) Professor Wilkins emphasizes the vital importance of
international markets to the growth of the automobile industry.
Reviewing the experiences of American and European automobile
companies' success and failure, she points out the historical tendency
of the industry to internationalize according to the following
pattern: (1) export of built-up cars;   (2) development of marketing organization abroad; and (3) establishment of manufacturing
facilities abroad. Thus in the long run, direct investment abroad
substituted for exports.

I agree with Professor Wilkins' view so far as this pattern is
illustrated by the historical evidence given in her paper. It seems
to me, however, that there remains room for further investigation,
if we understand this pattern as the stage theory of internationalization. It is true that export is always a prerequisite for direct investment. Export and investment are, however, not always in the

relation of the first stage and the last stage of development. Sometimes they stand together as alternatives of strategy. Once the manufacturer has succeeded in exporting a car, he will either want to export more or to manufacture abroad; to export or to invest is a matter of choice of strategy. If we find in this choice of strategy an irreversible tendency "from export to investment," the reason for such a change must be explained.

2) As to the success of Volkswagen in the U.S.A. after World War II, Professor Wilkins suggests three reasons: (1) H. Nordhoff was well aware of the American method of marketing, and he had developed a marketing organization in the U.S.A.; (2) American automobiles were not competitive with Volkswagen's because they were big and expensive; and (3) American automobile manufacturers ignored the segment of demand for smaller cars like those of Volkswagen. This is an attractive explanation of the success of Volkswagen in America. There remain, however, some questions. Why did American manufacturers, with all their marketing organizations, fail to see and respond to the demand for smaller cars? Professor Wilkins points out the need for specially designed cars in large markets. Did Volkswagen ever try marketing operations which included the development of new products (specially designed cars) to meet the needs of American drivers?

The Internationalization of Japanese Manufacturing Firms

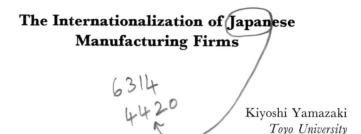

Kiyoshi Yamazaki
Toyo University

I.   Some Questions on Professor Raymond Vernon's Model

I am among those who appreciate the brilliant work and strong influence in the academic world of Professor Vernon's product life cycle model. Actually his life cycle model serves effectively as the starting basis for this paper which tries to present a model of internationalization, which may be suitable for Japanese manufacturing firms to adopt. While developing the model, however, I was seriously embarrassed by some questions which will be summarized below.

(1)   The meaning of "industrial innovation"

Can technological advantage be equated too closely with product innovation, as Vernon stressed in his model? I consider technological innovation to be something ambivalent in its nature and something which interacts with product *and* process. "The predominant mode of innovation shifts from radical product innovation to incremental innovation," William J. Abernathy writes in his book *Productivity Dilemma*, "and process innovation increases in relative importance to product innovation."[1]

This is deeply relevant to my proposition that Japanese competitiveness depends more upon process innovation as a "follower country" whereas the U.S. multinationals tend to keep their advantages more in product innovation. What I will refer to as an "advantage of the standardized technology" means such dependence on process innovation or improvement in the major Japanese manufacturing industries, which compete very well on the U.S. market.

Vernon characterized the situation as follows:

> As long as the Japanese used a bidding technology that was well
> known and widely dispersed in other countries, their bargaining
> position was relatively strong. Paradoxically, however, as nations
> approach the industrial innovation frontier, their bargaining position
> tends to weaken in certain respects; the technology they are reaching
> for is much more closely held. Except perhaps for the United
> States, there is no advanced nation in the world capable of generat-
> ing more than a fraction of the technological elements needed for
> a highly advanced society. As Japan approaches that frontier,
> therefore, her negotiating position in relation to U.S.-controlled
> enterprises could well decline.[2]

Vernon pointed out above the vulnerability inherent in Japanese
dependence on product innovation from foreign countries, but
his forecast indicates at the same time that he lacks any idea about
Japanese firms' very capable refinements of manufacturing technology achieved by their combined efforts.

(2)   Technological difference between Japan and the U.S.

Another aspect of the technological advantage to which Vernon
referred in the context of U.S. multinationals is relevant to the
existing U.S. technological system which is different from those of
Europe and Japan. While the former is based upon labor-saving technology, he claimed, the latter is based upon material-saving technology: "Whereas a global growth in the demand for high-income
and labor-saving products was reasonably sure," he argued, "one
could not be nearly so sanguine about the growth in demand for
material-saving and capital-conserving products."[3]

Recently even in the U.S., however, workers tend to dislike
working in the fully automated factories where work is so mo-
notonous and alienating, and they are increasingly coming to
require something more in their factories.

Furthermore, General Motors, for example, which had coherently
led the American automobile industry to make big cars for a long
time, has now decided to make their cars smaller and lighter, in
order to meet government standards for fuel economy to be attained
by 1985.

On the other hand, the Japanese manufacturing firms have

consistently bought the newest possible machinery to rationalize production in their factories and they have also learned many management skills from the U.S. Nevertheless their competitive success is perceived to derive more from their labor-saving-oriented attitude and cost consciousness in raising productivity as high as they can. The differences between the technological systems of Japan and the U.S. are therefore tending to decrease as the two attitudes converge.

(3)   Advantage of low-cost labor

Vernon further wrote:

> A serious projection of the future position of Japan involves numerous other elements, of course, one of these is whether Japan will appear as quite so much a threat to U.S.-controlled enterprises as she has in the past, capable of mobilizing low-cost labor to perform high-cost manufacturing tasks. Another is whether Japan will need increased export to the advanced countries in order to market home-produced goods of an increasingly sophisticated sort. If Japan's labor grows scarce and costly and if U.S.-based enterprises feel they have less to fear from the capacity of Japanese enterprises to draw on low-cost labor, one incentive for developing alliances with these potential rivals will be weakened.[4]

Contrary to his assumptions, however, the Japanese competitive position with respect to the U.S. and Europe has not only been firmly held but has even strengthened, though Japan has lost its advantage of low-cost labor and was forced to raise the yen exchange rate in 1971. That Japan has been able to keep her competitiveness, despite losing a so-called "comparative advantage" over other advanced countries, is then a matter worth discussing further, which is what I shall do in my report.

Vernon's proposition that "efforts by Europeans to establish their producing facilities in the United States, unaccompanied by any obvious technological advantage that could lubricate the transfer, are exceedingly hazardous"[5] is justified now that America has U.S.-made Volkswagens rolling from its Pennsylvania factory. It may not be necessary to repeat that the major Japanese manufacturers are now producing color TV sets across the Pacific Ocean without feeling much risk, after the U.S. restriction on imports.

If Vernon's proposition is right, then finding the exact nature of this "obvious technological advantage" that the Japanese manufacturers seem to have might be an urgent requirement.

II. Development of "Standard Technology": A "Follower's" Approach for Survival

The product life cycle model Professor Vernon developed for explaining the spread of U.S. multinationals is still useful in tracing the way Japanese manufacturing firms responded to the predominant U.S. technological advantages. It may be possible to superimpose the Japanese manufacturing firm on the Vernon model to give a "follower's" method of competing with the leading U.S. multinational firms.

The threat by U.S. multinationals to overwhelm Japanese industry forced the government to take a series of protective measures, from building tariff walls to subsidizing reconstruction of war-damaged industry.

On the other hand, firms had to acquire new products and new technologies in order to compete with rivals for survival. With heavy investment, however, the firms grew to enjoy a "comparative advantage" and an economy of scale sufficient to enable them to gain a fair amount of profits from export.

For example, protective measures offered by the government to the Japanese automobile industry can be enumerated as:

1) protective tariffs
2) excise tax favoring domestically-produced cars
3) import restrictions by means of foreign currency exchange Controls
4) restrictions on foreign capital
5) low-interest loans from government financial institutions
6) subsidies
7) special depreciation policies
8) exemption of import tax imposed upon machinery
9) preferential approval for import of foreign technology

A Japanese economist writes "whereas one may usually enumerate import restriction, productive tariffs, subsidies and the like as a

TABLE 1 Development of Japanese competitiveness in the product life cycle.

life cycle / Country Area	Introduction	Maturing	Standardizing	Globalism Nationalism ××××××××××
			GLOBAL STRATEGY	
U.S.A.	TECHNOLOGICAL ADVANTAGE (product) domestic investment → economy of scale innovation → export	increasing imports foreign investment	restrictive measures to imports ×××××	investment local production imports investment in the U.S.
Japan	government: ×××× tariffs protective policies for infant industry firm: import of technology	×××××××× restrictive policy on foreign capital domestic investment COMPARATIVE ADVANTAGE exports commercial investment to promote exports to U.S. market economy of scale	increasing exports TECHNOLOGICAL ADVANTAGE (process) investment in LDCs	investment in LDCs
LDCs		imports	COMPARATIVE ADVANTAGE local ×××× production ×× ×× production import-supplement industries	exports U.S. offshore export-promotive industries

means of protecting an infant industry, as a matter of fact, government policy concerning the automobile industry not only involved all these factors, but its perfection reached even to the body, parts and accessories, in addition to excise tax favoring domestically-produced cars, foreign currency restriction, special depreciation policy and so on."[6]

As the product was standardized and therefore the comparative advantage disappeared, firms had to make every effort to reduce costs and raise productivity to keep their competitive position. Special attention was paid to improving production technology and introducing process innovation in the factories as much as possible. This is what I call an "advantage of standardized technology" which enabled firms to maintain their competitiveness in the world market regardless of any comparative disadvantage. When the U.S. government introduced import restrictions against Japan, firms could successfully change their international strategy and, thanks to their technological advantages, produce in the United States.

The matrix I made from Vernon's product life cycle model generally indicates the way Japanese manufacturing firms responded to the behavior of U.S. multinationals and developments in Southeast Asia. In the case of the Japanese automobile industry, it may even be possible to apply this matrix to potential future investment and manufacturing in the United States, since they are, I feel, surely soon to go there.

III. Lessons from Abernathy's Model

I was profoundly interested in the general model William J. Abernathy developed to clarify the relationships between innovation and productivity in the process of technological progress in manufacturing firms. In particular, several points proposed in his model threw light on how my model could be developed in different ways:
(1) Approach[7]

His approach departs from several conventional views:

(a) his proposed model views productivity improvement as a phenomenon that has costs as well as benefits;

(b) his model departs from product life cycle studies and learning-curve studies, where either product or process may be of concern, but not both.

(2) Two types of innovation[8]

(a) product:

"Before a dominant design is achieved, product innovation is manifest in the introduction of radically different products. Subsequently, however, innovations act to improve an existing design and are necessarily more incremental but also more cumulative in effect."

(b) process:

"As a product becomes standardized, production volume rises, and cost becomes an increasingly important basis of competition. These concurrent changes stimulate process innovation through reduction in product variation, increased competitive pressures, and rising demand for greater output."

(c) interaction:

"The predominant type of innovation will shift from major to incremental and will result in an overall decrease in major innovation. The rate and importance of process innovation will also increase relative to product innovation."

(3) Fluid vs. Specific[9]

"In the first case, the product is standardized, change is incremental, production systems are rigid (specific) but efficient information about needed product features is relatively visible, and the economic impact of any improvement is large and immediate. In the second case, product design is subject to radical change, product characteristics are in flux, the emphasis of product innovation is on improved functional performance rather than cost reduction, production systems are flexible (fluid) but inefficient, and even major innovation has little immediate economic impact. These patterns are not independent of one another, however. It is apparent in the automobile industry and several other industries that products currently represented by the specific pattern were much more like the fluid one at the time of their origin."

(4) Shifting locus of process innovation[10]

"As a product unit evolves from an early fluid condition toward a more advanced stage of development, the originating source of major process innovation shifts outside the unit." An example is the machine-tool industry for the automobile firms.

(5)   Implication for management[11]

"It is not assumed that progression toward a more advanced state of development is always beneficial or inevitable. To the contrary, it may be argued that management can and should control both forward and reverse transition. If a typical path of transition can be described, then better judgment can be made about the advantages and disadvantages of reaching a new stage of development."

"Neither extreme state, Fluid or Specific, would be attractive to the firm or to the economy as a whole."

(6)   U.S. automobile industry, mature or not?[12]

"All the changes discussed might seem to imply that the automobile has matured as a product, but this is not the case."

(a)   "The automobile is not the relevant unit of analysis; the productive unit is a better focus. As long as new productive units are being added, or as long as existing ones are resisting extreme states of development, the car has not matured. There is every indication that new technologies are now being introduced, notably in electronics and engine controls."

(b)   "Maturity must be defined in relation to the market's preferences. If the product line matches market needs, the product would be mature. This is not the case presently in automobiles. Recent regulations and the consumer's interest in fuel economy have changed the competitive environment."

IV.   Corporate Characteristics of General Motors (GM)

(1)   In 1969, I wrote the following in my book "GM":

"In response to these challenges, what changes can be expected to take place during the 1970s in the United States' automobile industry? Of course, some assumptions may not be fulfilled, but one thing I can say is that Detroit will be forced to reexamine the concept of the car as a basic means of transportation and the government may have to intervene even in materials and designs of automobiles."

"In such a case, could GM respond with flexibility to the social changes, as it has so far? The entire structure of GM, which has been built on an alienation from the basic means of transportation for fifty years, will be exposed by severe trials during the 1970s. To put it more straightforwardly: as long as the existing principles of management are held and the structure of vanity persists, it is assumed that GM would not be able to adapt itself to such a situation and return to a basic means of transportation more appropriate for the coming age."[13]

(2) When I visited GM Overseas Operations (GMOO) in New York in 1971 and met the director in charge of forward planning, I was surprised to find that he could understand neither the definition of multinational enterprise which is generally well known, nor the meaning of what I had written in my book, "GM":

"It is observed that Ford shows a more positive attitude toward overseas operations (than GM). This may reflect an inferior position to GM in the domestic market but relative importance in foreign operations instead. For example, Ford established "Ford of Europe" in 1967, and strengthened the independence of its overseas operations. This suggests that Ford is one step ahead of GM in which GMOO in New York continues to hold the reins as far as its organization as a world enterprise is concerned.... In order to adapt its organization to cope with such a world enterprise as Ford has done, GM will need objective conditions and circumstances more critical and more emergent for its total management."[14]

(3) GM's strategy:

1) "Product design was conceived as a dynamic process that would lead to an ultimate target through incremental change."

2) "Market needs would be met through the product-line policy rather than independent designs."

3) "Radical product innovations were to be avoided. Sloan says it was 'not necessary to ... run the risk of untried experiment.' "[15]

(4) Toward global strategy and reorganization:

"GM starts from a position far behind Ford overseas. Estes is blunt about it: 'Our first objective (overseas) is to move ahead of our chief domestic competitor.' Not only did Ford beat GM overseas as regards time, but it was also way ahead of GM in internationalizing its overseas operations. GM was still Vauxhall in Britain, Opel in Germany and Holden in Australia when Ford was producing cars for all those markets, built from interchangeable parts."[16]

"GM lags well behind Ford outside the U.S., but after years of what amounts to benign neglect of its overseas operations, the company is gearing up to become a truly global entity. The integration began back in 1974, when Pete Estes became president and was given command of overseas operations. Last year, foreign and domestic operating staff were combined."[17]

V. Small Cars

(1)   Reluctance of GM to introduce small cars
"The Big Three have traditionally been unenthusiastic about small cars. Only American Motors has enthusiastically embraced the concept. The Big Three have seen them as less profitable items that would only steal sales and profits from the large, full-sized cars that Detroit considered standard. Furthermore, the attitude of the Big Three toward small cars may well have included recognition of their mutual interdependence. The production of a small car by a single producer might well have been worthwhile for that producer because it would mostly take sales from the others. But production of small cars by all three would mean that they would be jointly depriving themselves of sales. In the absence of external pressures, it is unlikely that the Big Three would have produced small cars."[18]

(2)   Changed attitude of GM towards small cars
Nevertheless, GM initiated the production of so-called "world-cars"—the Chevette—in the United States after 1975 as an aspect of its newly adopted global strategy. The Chevette was quite a new product, very different from the Vega which failed as a subcompact because of its insufficient conceptualization of small cars. The

Chevette was developed by the Opel staff and produced in Brazil, Japan and other countries. GM subsequently introduced in the spring of 1979 another kind of "world-car," known as the "X-car," and is now developing the "J-car" which could be called a real "world-car."

(3)   I consider the spread of small cars in the United States, from the standpoint of national history as a phenomenon that a return of the concept of the car as a basic means of privately owned transportation, like the Ford Model T.

(4)   I also view small cars as worldwide standard cars, symbolizing the third stage of development reached by the U.S. automobile industry after its two earlier stages, here summarized:

First stage:	Ford Model T, small car for world market, free competition,
	single product line
	technology: product and process innovation
Second stage:	GM cars, big car for U.S. market, domestic oligopoly,
	multiproduct line
	technology: few innovations
Third stage:	World-car, small car for world market, international competition among oligopolies,
	multiproduct line
	technology: product and process innovation

VI.   Japanese Auto Makers and Competition

Ironically, the protective policies of the Japanese government which had been extended beyond the limit of necessary protection delayed development of the oligopolistic system in the Japanese automobile industry, contrary to the intention of MITI to form a Big Two system.* It was due to these policies that the smaller producers, other than Toyota and Nissan, could not only

---

*   According to the director of technology of one of the top makers, the Japanese automobile industry had already reached an international level in the context of both economy of scale and performance of cars by around 1965, when it still enjoyed the government's protective policies.[19]

enter the industry without much difficulty, but could also survive
securely despite competition from the Big Two in the domestic
market.

As the Big Two pushed them hard with increased concentration
in the domestic market, there was no way for those smaller producers to escape other than to the export market, upon which they
largely came to depend.

In addition, the persistent concentration of GM on big cars
enabled Japanese auto makers easily to penetrate into the biggest
but most oligopolistic market in the world. Thus it can be said
that the Japanese auto makers, including the Big Two, were constantly under competitive pressures in both the domestic and
overseas markets, though the former became increasingly oligopolistic.

VII. Technology and Management

(1) Entrepreneurship

On August 15, 1945, the then president of Toyota Motors,
Kiichiro Toyoda (who died in 1952) stated to his employees,
"Catch up with the United States within three years, or the Jap-
anese automobile industry will fail to grow."[20]

Another time he said to his cousin, Eiji, the present president,
"It may be the best way that in such an integrated industry as the
automobile industry, each item of parts or components should be
delivered 'just in time' on the line for the assembly of cars."[21]

(2) The role of an engineer

The executive vice president of Toyota Motors, Taiichi Ohno,
who was among those employees deeply impressed by the words
of the late president just after the war, faced the challenge of
catching up with the United States and tackled it with a project
of process innovation quite different from the concept of the American production method. This was a production system of multi-
product and small volume, instead of single product and large
volume as practiced the United States. He successfully completed
his project of process innovation as well as a newly devised manage-

ment system to be adapted to the new technology; this is well known as the "kanban method."

A Japanese engineer like Ohno usually takes on three different roles during his career in his firm:

1)   as a member of the advisory staff for decisions made by the top management,

2)   as a researcher working on developmental aspects in the laboratory,

3)   as a production manager at the factory, to stay in touch with blue-collar workers.

The advisory role of staff engineers is most important when a decision must be taken concerning new technology or a new product to be selected. Their technological advice is often respected by the top management because of their access to abundant technological information. Their capability may make as great a contribution as government guidance in the import of foreign technologies in particular.

Another important role of engineers which characterizes the Japanese style of management is that they tend to dislike white-collar work at the headquarters and prefer to work with blue-collar workers at the factory. For example, Ohno confessed he cannot leave the operating works, even now that he is a member of top management.

One can find in Toyota's production methods a close relationship between technology and management. Furthermore, it is interesting to note that Toyota focuses on process innovation, whereas Honda and Mazda tend to run risks with product innovation such as development of the C.V.C.C. engine and rotary engine.

VIII.   Toward an International Oligopoly

In each of the three periods listed below, the U.S. automobile industry has had to respond to external factors conditioning each decade.

The powerful oligopoly long established in the U.S. automobile

	Product	Period	Investment abroad	External factors
1)	compact cars	late 1950s	in Europe	European cars
2)	subcompacts	late 1960s	in Japan	Japanese cars and VW
3)	world-cars	late 1970s	global	fuel economy Japanese cars

industry has in part gradually collapsed through the rounds of response to small foreign cars. In the first round the Big Three seemed successfully to drive out European small cars, except Volkswagen, and fortified their manufacturing bases in Europe to enlarge their small car lines.

In the second round, the Big Three responded to the invasion of Japanese small cars with the same strategy as in the previous round, that is, developing a smaller car, the subcompact car, and investing in Japan to make their bridgeheads for local production. This time, however, they failed not only to drive out Japanese small cars from the American continent, but to build fully-owned manufacturing subsidiaries in Japan. Furthermore, a new development of subcompacts, close to imports in size and performance, induced them to join in price competition with Japanese small cars, making their oligopolistic position somewhat vulnerable.

In the third round, the Big Three faced a more critical situation caused by the oil embargo and increased oil prices, in addition to the continued threat posed by Japanese small cars. These external pressures forced GM to change its fundamental policy which had been unshaken since the 1920s, and thus they had to introduce a new concept of small cars as "world-cars" and start to make all the lines from Chevrolet to Cadillac smaller and lighter.

In order to make smaller cars more profitable, however, they needed to change strategy from the domestic-oriented to the global-oriented and then make their foreign and domestic operations more closely integrated. Therefore, the domestic oligopoly on which they have so long been based seems to be dissolving itself into a global one which may create a new international division of labor within their worldwide networks.

NOTES

1. William J. Abernathy, *Productivity Dilemma* (Baltimore: The Johns Hopkins University Press, 1978), p. 71.
2. Raymond Vernon, *Sovereignty At Bay* (New York: Basic Books, Inc., 1971), p. 255.
3. *Ibid.*, p. 109.
4. *Ibid.*, p. 255.
5. *Ibid.*, p. 111.
6. Hiroya Ueno and Hiromichi Muto, "Automobile," in *Industrial Organization in Japan*, Hisao Kumagai ed. (Tokyo: Chuokoron-sha, 1973), p. 125.
7. Abernathy, *op. cit.*, p. 7.
8. *Ibid.*, p. 76.
9. *Ibid.*, p. 71.
10. *Ibid.*, p. 170.
11. *Ibid.*, p. 173.
12. *Ibid.*, pp. 166–167.
13. Kiyoshi Yamazaki, *G. M.* (Tokyo: Chuokoron-sha, 1969), p. 204.
14. *Ibid.*, p. 174.
15. Abernathy, *op. cit.*, pp. 34–35.
16. *Forbes*, April 2, 1979.
17. *Fortune*, May 7, 1979.
18. Lawrence J. White, "The Automobile Industry," in Walter Adams ed., *The Structure of American Industry*, fifth ed. (New York: Macmillan, 1977), pp. 193–194.
19. Ueno and Muto, *op. cit.*, p. 134.
20. Taiichi Ohno, *Toyota's Production Method* (Tokyo: Daiyamondo-sha, 1978), p. 7.
21. *Ibid.*, p. 137.

COMMENTS

* b·314
4420
japan

Mira Wilkins
Florida International University

It is with pleasure and admiration that I comment on Professor Yamazaki's paper. I too have puzzled over the issue of process versus product innovations in product cycle theory. I would like to push us back in time to the early twentieth century. The automobile was the *product* innovation. The European car was "handmade." When first place in automobile production shifted from Europe to the United States and when the United States became the true leader, the innovation was perhaps in product *concept*—the idea of a cheap car—but not in product *per se*. The product concept was achieved through the U.S. innovation in *process*—in the introduction of the assembly line and interchangeable parts. Americans imitated and innovated—just as Professor Yamazaki shows that the Japanese have done.

I have often felt that the insights on labor-saving versus material-saving technological innovations, while useful, may lead to over-simplifications. Clearly, the United States, once rich in raw materials, is so no longer. We are seeing many "material-saving" innovations. I find myself in full agreement with Professor Yamazaki's notion of convergence between U.S. and Japanese patterns of process and product innovations that are material-saving.

In the product cycle, as the product is made outside the country of origin, the reasons for such production vary. The reasons can be governmentally induced (including tariffs, subsidies, quotas on imports, etc.) and/or cost induced (including transportation, labor, other production, or *marketing and servicing* costs). I would argue that in the Japanese case, production was initially government induced. But as the industry developed, costs in general (*not* simply labor) became lower than in the United States and Europe. In the sequence, the Japanese could adopt, or adapt, the very latest technology. Moreover, Japanese cars became differentiated products. I will return to this in a moment.

I liked Professor Yamazaki's demonstration of how the Japanese industry developed under the umbrella of protective measures offered by the government. Clearly, the protection was far greater than that received by the infant U.S. industry many years earlier. Yet we should not forget that the U.S. industry was initially protected by a 45 percent tariff.

Is the Japanese advantage one of "standardized technology," which enables it to hold its competitiveness in world markets? Perhaps. I wonder, however, whether the advantage is also—or now perhaps primarily—related to the differentiated products.

How does the Japanese car compete in the United States and Europe? In the United States the initial competition—the early entry—was based on price, but price alone could not sell the car. The product had to be competitive in design and quality, as well as having a backup marketing and service organization.

Now, in the United States—at least in the eastern part of the United States—Japanese cars seem to have no price advantage. They sell because of their reputation as quality products. They are well advertised and effectively marketed.

I share with Professor Yamazaki the belief that it is vital to integrate product and process innovations in order to have an understanding of the development of the automobile industry.

I have long been disturbed by the facet of product cycle theory that relates to the definition "product." What is a product? A car, a car with an internal combustion engine run on gasoline, a custom-built car, a mass-produced car, a large car, a small car, a gas-guzzler, a fuel-economy car, a red car, a black car, a Ford, a Toyota, a Capri, a Corolla.

Abernathy follows Vernon in talking about a dominant design, a standardized product. I feel slightly uncomfortable with these terms. Moreover, how do we define incremental change; is the addition of automatic transmission incremental, of a clock accessory? What about a diesel engine as distinct from a gasoline-powered engine? The early cars were for an elite market; cars are now sold to a mass market. When does "standardization" occur?

Is the product designed for the elite market the same as the one designed for the mass market?

In the automobile industry, as mass production took place was there really a reduction in product variation? It depends again on what we mean by product. Clearly, we have more colors, more variety in accessories.

What was the major innovation in automobiles? The car itself (first perfected in Germany) or the mass-produced car (an American innovation)? Abernathy suggests that the U.S. automobile industry is *not* a mature one—because of new technologies and new opportunities to meet consumer demands. Major innovation remains possible.

In conclusion, I wish Professor Yamazaki would help us to understand how the Japanese automobile processes differ from those in the United States and Europe. Is the Japanese factory really multiproduct and small volume? Again, we're back to that awful word "product." What do we mean by multiproduct?

Can we generalize about the Japanese industry when Toyota focuses on process innovation, while Honda and Mazda emphasize "product" innovation (that is, experimental engines)?

What is the future of the Japanese automobile industry? Will Japanese companies invest in the United States? If they do so, will their process technology be substantially different from that of the U.S. companies or Volkswagen? Does Mr. Yamazaki suggest that by investing in the United States, Japanese companies can transfer to American shores a cost-reducing technology and management method that would mean Japanese companies producing in the United States would have *lower* costs than GM, Ford, Chrysler, or Volkswagen?

Professor Yamazaki's paper is a very stimulating one. It poses numerous important questions.

PART IV

INDUSTRIALIZATION AND EVOLUTION OF MARKETING

Development of Marketing in the Course of Industrialization in Korea

Jong Won Lim
Seoul National University

Introduction

What, how, and for whom should goods and services be produced? Differences in social value judgements will lead to different solutions in each society. Under a free economic system, a price mechanism is supposed to allocate scarce resources to each industry. Since Chamberline, non-price variables have exerted a strong impact on business activities. Especially in developing countries, the role of marketing has been reevaluated in its practical contribution to the economic growth and welfare of a society.[1] We can consider two kinds of business decisions: those to get rid of internal and external constraints, and those to direct the optimal level, mix, and allocation of available resources under given constraints. Marketing decisions involve the two kinds of decisions simultaneously. Therefore it is the perspective of this author that marketing can be an effective pathway to economic development.

In this paper it is intended to trace the changing recognition of marketing development along with the rapid process of economic growth in Korea. With this perspective it is fruitful to compare and analyze "marketing in the course of industrialization and internationalization."

The first part reviews the historical process of introducing modern marketing over the last seventeen years.[2] In Table 1, 674 articles are classified by period and subject. This analysis describes the changing topics and analytical techniques as well as the position of automobile marketing in the history of marketing in Korea.

TABLE 1 Changing Areas of Interest in Marketing Development over the last 17 years.

Classification of Marketing Development	The period of Introduction (1962–1966)	The period of Conceptualization (1967–1971)	The period of Marketing Development (1972–1976)	The period of New Marketing concept (1977–1978)	Total
Major product lines of analysis* / Information output & analytical process	medicine 4 agricultural & marine products 2 raw silk 1	medicine 13 clothes 14 food 6 autos 7 electrical appliances 6 agricultural & marine 27	medicine 19 clothes 13 daily products 10 electrical appliances 14 agricultural & marine 30	medicine 5 clothes 12 autos 5 agricultural & marine products 4	
I. Market Opportunity (target market, identify unmet needs, consumption pattern, market position)	3	86		10 (48%)	99
a. Image and behavioral studies		6	31	7	49
b. Market segmentation		4	8	1	13
c. Market share analysis			4	1	5
d. Sales trend analysis		2	1	2	5
Subtotal	3	98 (41%)	44 (14%)	21 (27%)	166
II. Marketing Resource Deployment					
a. Product studies		6	25	1	32
New product tests		3		1	4
Packaging tests		1			1
Design and style studies				1	1
Subtotal		10	25	3	38
b. Promotional studies	2	1	31	1	35
Media analysis		13		4	17
Media effectiveness		3			3
Message effectiveness		2		1	3
Sales promotion		18		5	23
Personal selling		4		2	6
Subtotal	2	41	31	13	87
c. Price studies product line price competitive price promotional pricing		5	8	1	14

d. Physical distribution; stock turnover, warehouse origin and destination, location, breadth and depth of stock assortment	1		14	2	17
e. Channel network analysis; channel conflict, vertical marketing system, dealer policy	1	31 (35%)	46 (14%)	9 (10%)	87
Subtotal	3	88 (37%)	124 (39%)	28 (35%)	243
III. State of Nature	2		21		23
a. Competition		2	12		14
b. Invention and change, technology transfer		2	10		12
c. Distribution stracture		16	10	5	31
d. Legal studies		8	3	2	13
e. Consumerism and ecological issues		5	13	3	21
Subtotal	2	33 (14%)	69 (21%)	10 (13%)	114
IV. Export Marketing	1	21 (8%)	82 (26%)	20 (25%)	124
Total	9	240	319	79	647

*   The number on the right side of each commodity describes the number of articles dealt with for that product.

The development of marketing is also constrained by the distribution structure in each country; changing environmental forces induce subsequent change in distribution structure. The second part examines these environmental forces and special features in designing a new distribution structure in order to keep pace with the economic growth.

The third part of this paper describes some of the major characteristics of automobile marketing over the last twenty years. Korea has been an attractive market for such motor companies as General Motors (GM) or Ford. However the local market is not big enough to develop its own industry. This is a dilemma that might be solved by the application of modern marketing. It is a question of how the three domestic motor companies can survive and grow in the future.

The fourth part summarizes the major contents of this paper as a conclusion.

I. The Historical Process of Introducing Modern Marketing over the Last Seventeen Years

The development of marketing can be traced by looking back upon the changing pattern of consumption. Among those factors that have influenced the consumption pattern are the Korean War and the Korean government's series of five-year economic development programs since 1962. Following the Korean War in 1950 the continuous overflow of U.S.-made or Japanese-made goods was strong enough to change the way of life into two types of market behavior; the rich were anxious to use the blackmarket, the poor were striving to survive in daily life. During the war, most of the productive facilities were destroyed. From 1953 to 1961 the Korean economy experienced all the disadvantages of a dual economy as well as social and political turmoil. Where domestic producers could not find an effective demand, there was no ground for marketing development.

After the military revolution in 1961, the Korean economy began to mobilize towards economic progress. Therefore, it seems natural to categorize the past period by a series of five-year economic development programs.

In Table 1, the study of marketing over the last seventeen years is classified by period, information output, product and analytical process.[3]

The first five-year period (1962–1966) can be explained as the period of introduction. During this period several marketing textbooks were published. Major commodities used as the subjects of marketing analyses included medicine, agricultural and marine products, and raw silk. The research approach in those days was just conceptual, dealing with no specific marketing techniques.

It was the successful completion of the first five-year project that stimulated the application of marketing theories to real world problems for the period from 1967 to 1971. Therefore this period can be classified as the period of conceptualization and application. Professional journals in business management and marketing have been published since 1967. As the quality of life began to be elevated by rising incomes, there was an increased demand for basic drugs, clothes, and food. Those who had rapidly gained wealth during the early industrialization began to be sensitive to different models of automobiles.

The product lines of marketing concern widened even more broadly in the first five-year period. They covered medicines, clothes, automobiles, electrical appliances, insurance, hotels and tourism. About 40 percent of the selected articles dealt with evaluating marketing opportunities for new products. Manufacturers of consumer goods became conscious of promotional problems and channel design but they paid little attention to pricing and product studies. The general level of price and/or quality was greatly inferior to those of foreign products. The real problems for the local manufacturers were the lack of technology and the small local demand that could not guarantee an economy of scale. While large manufacturers tried to find their own channel networks, government planners also recognized the emergence of a distribution bottleneck.

There was a five-year plan for the modernization of the distribution structure which started in 1969 and ended in 1973. The essence of this plan included the introduction of a chain store operation in the retail and wholesale sector. But it was not very successful.

There was also a great demand for foreign exchange currency to carry out the five-year economic development programs. As the bottom of the third column in Table 1 indicates, many studies had been centered on export marketing. Most of these research projects were funded by the government sector. Therefore the scope of these projects naturally covered only the general analysis of demand in each country.

The third five-year period (1972–1976) can be characterized as the period of development. During this period there was much concern about the marketing environment such as competition, invention and technological transfer, ecological issues and distri-

(17)
TABLE 2   R & D Expenditure.

Year	1967		1971		1977	
Category	Total	Company	Total	Company	Total	Company
R & D*	48	7	107	13	1,083	417
% of GNP	0.38		0.34		0.71	
Gov.: Company	86:14		88:12		62.38	

* unit: $20,000
Source: *Science and Technology Annual*, Ministry of Science and Technology,
          Rep. of Korea, 1977 and 1978.

TABLE 3   International Comparison of R & D Expenditures in 1977.

Country Category	Korea	Japan	U.S.A.	West Germany
R & D**	2.16	120	429	117
Gov.:Company	62:38	27:73	50:50	48:52
% of GNP	0.71	1.70	2.29	2.30

** unit: $20,000
Source: *Science and Technology Annual* (Korea, 1978), *Handbook of Science and
          Technology* (Japan, 1979).

bution structure. Behavioral studies were introduced to evaluate marketing opportunities. The major areas of focus were around export marketing, distribution structure and individual channel networks, and product studies. But price studies and legal studies were still the two neglected areas of marketing in this period. The major product lines of marketing analysis in Table 1 reflect those industries which had realized the need for the application of modern marketing techniques.

If industry management does not realize the urgent need to apply marketing concepts to their business, modern marketing cannot be easily introduced in that industry. Among those factors that influence the formation of new marketing concepts are the transition from sellers' market to buyers' market, the need to secure a certain market position, the need to study the consumer behavior of the target market, and the development of new products to satisfy unmet consumer needs.[4] These factors are the core elements of the "new marketing concept." Modern marketing should incorporate the operation of the new marketing concept. In this respect, technological development and research and development (R & D) expenditure may be used as an indicator for the evaluation of modern marketing development in each industry. Therefore, inferring from Table 1, modern marketing has not yet been developed in such industries as cameras, automobiles, aircraft, computers and atomic plants. Table 2 compares R & D expenditures by absolute amount, percentage of GNP, and government versus private company.[5] In 1977, the R & D expenditure was ten times that of 1967. It also shows that private companies too had increased their portion of R & D expenditure upon realizing the importance of new technological development.

Table 3 indicates that R & D activities of private companies in Korea are still far behind those of Japan, the U.S.A. and West Germany.

It is possible to derive the following inference from the above three tables. Some private companies in such industries as medicine, agricultural and marine products, electrical appliances, textiles, and automobiles had recognized the sales concept of pushing their products into markets at a high price. Since 1972, the importance of the new marketing concept has been realized in several basic commodities (textiles, electric appliances, medicines, etc.). If we examine the size and trend of R & D expenditures, which is the core of the new marketing concept, the major product lines of modern marketing analyses are still too limited in Korea. It is necessary for both government and private sectors to expand R & D expenditures, for modern marketing through R & D will direct a better way of resource allocation, and thereby increase the quality of life in developing countries.

II. Emergence of a Distribution Bottleneck

Despite rapid economic development during the last seventeen years, the distribution structure was not able to absorb increasing economic activities. As an attempt to change the traditional market structure, the Korea Marketing Association (K.M.A.) was established in August 1969. K.M.A. has carried out a series of studies and recommendations on how to improve marketing systems in Korea. During the period between 1970 and 1978, K.M.A. engaged in more than forty research projects. Among them was the five-year plan (1969–1973) for the improvement of marketing systems.

1. Characteristics of Traditional Marketing Institutions

The most visible point from Table 4 is the extremely small size of a large number of individual retail units in the structure of marketing institutions for the years of 1968, 1971 and 1976. More than 98 percent of wholesaling was operated by individual owner-ship, but, during the period from 1971 to 1976, corporate forms of retailers increased by 9 percent. In an effort to introduce new innovative retail institutions, the Korean government pro-vided various financial incentives for the super-chain organization of mass merchandising companies.[6] More than 98 percent of retail store units employed less than five persons. The percentage of retail stores whose sales were more than $100,000 had increased from 0.08 percent in 1968 and 1971 to 1.9 percent in 1976.[7] This growth reflected the successful operation of large retail institutions such as department stores and super-chain stores.

The second problem was the lack of well established trade practices between channel members and customers. There was much haggling over prices. Retailers used to push away low-quality products selling at a high price. Retailers and/or wholesalers would engage in cornering and hoarding in order to manipulate the market price.[8]

The third problem was the ease with which many intermediaries in the channel network had transferred distribution costs.

The fourth problem was the conflict among landowners, building owners and merchants. Since most of the merchants did not have enough money to buy their own store building, they had no interest in doing a better business. Increased sales might induce increased rent, and finally the landowner would take over the successful business. It is clearly indicated in Tables 4 and 5 that channel structure was very stable over the last ten years; so was the con-sumption pattern of all families in cities (Table 6). From these

TABLE 4   Structure of Marketing Institutions: 1968, 1971 and 1976.

Types of M. Institution	Establishment (% of total)			Private management (% of total)			No. of stores employing fewer than (% of total)			No. (and %) of stores with annual sales greater than $100,000		
Year	1968	71	76	68	71	76	68	71	76	68	71	76
Wholesaler	4.8	4.9	4.9	99.68	99.81	98.95	80.3	81.8	77.6	542 (4.1)	1300 (7.9)	6314 (31.4)
Retailer	95.2	95.1	95.1	95.82	98.28	87.38	98.7	98.2	98.2	214 (0.08)	289 (0.08)	6939 (1.9)

Source: Adjusted by this author from the tables in "Dynamic Changes of Korean Marketing Structure" by Kim, W. S., *The Korean Business Journal* (December 1978), pp. 52–101.

TABLE 5   Structure of Retail Stores: 1968, 1971 and 1976 (% of total).

	1968	1971	1976
Food Stores	48.9	50.4	50.5
Textile and Clothing Stores	20.1	20.3	15.3
Drug Stores	7.3	6.4	4.9
Others	23.1	22.9	29.3
	100.0	100.0	100.0

Source: Adjusted by this author from the table in "Dynamic Changes of Korean Marketing Structure" by Kim, W. S., *The Korean Business Journal* (December 1978), p. 75.

TABLE 6   Monthly Consumption Expenditure of All Families in Cities (% of total).

	1967	1971	1976
I. Food and beverages	44.2	41.0	43.0
1. Cereals	20.2	17.7	19.5
2. Meat, fish, milk & eggs	7.2	8.6	7.8
3. Vegetables, seaweed & fruit	8.6	6.8	6.3
4. Condiments	8.2	3.3	3.7
5. Others		4.6	5.7
II. Housing	18.4	18.8	18.0
III. Fuel and lighting	5.8	5.4	4.8
IV. Clothing	10.3	9.4	9.0
V. Miscellaneous	21.3	25.4	25.2
	100.0	100.0	100.0

Source: *Economic Statistical Yearbook*, Economic Planning Board, 1968 and 1978.

inferences, we can assume that a traditional distribution structure cannot easily be changed in a short period.

2. Environmental Changes

Along with the rapid economic growth, there has been a visible change in the marketing environment. Efficient methods of transportation such as subways and the highway network have had a significant influence on urban migration, trade area, hierarchy of market structure, and formation of suburban apartment complexes.[9] While exporting industries have introduced new products in local

TABLE 7   Changing Contribution of Distribution Industry to GNP.

	1966	1967	1968	1969	1970	1971	1972	1973	1974	1975	1976	1977
						Industry						
Distribu- tion	18.5%	20.3%	21.4%	31.5%	22.4%	23.4%	24.2%	25.2%	24.5%	24.1%	23.6%	23.7%
Manufac- turing	14.7%	16.8%	18.9%	19.9%	21.7%	23.3%	23.9%	28.3%	30.5%	31.7%	34.7%	35.2%

Source: *Economic Statistical Yearbook*, Bank of Korea. Adjusted by this author from the yearbooks for the period.

markets, there has also been an influx of foreign goods because of the
substantial reduction of tariff barriers. It is these environmental
changes that have fostered the attractive growth rate of several
department stores in central places and some other super-chain
organizations of mass merchandising retail institutions. These
institutions are expected to play an innovative role in the distribution industry.

3. Challenging Job: The Desire to Introduce Retail Revolution in Korea

The Korean government realized the growing problems in the
efficient flow of goods and services from producers to consumers
or users. The changing contribution of the distribution sector to
the GNP indicates that some positive measures should have been
effectively taken since 1972 (Table 7). During the third economic
planning period (1972–1976), about $140 million was spent to
modernize channel institutions. Some of the issues included a franchise organization of small retailers, dealers' help, government
financing for the establishment of warehouses and freight terminals,
and modernization of market facilities.

The Korean economy has experienced a drastic inflation rate
which has been one of the major public concerns for the viability
of sustained economic growth. As a last resort to eliminate cost-
push pressure, economic planners have turned their attention to
renovating the distribution structure. The impact of complex
channel systems on the market structure can be explained by
examining the simple diagram presented by Forrester.[10] In Fig. 1,
Forrester had simplified distribution structure as a channel network
of producer-wholesale-retailer chains. If there is a sudden 10 percent increase in retail sales, there begins a much bigger fluctuation
of orders from retailers and wholesalers. The point is that it takes
fifty-two weeks before the fluctuation is stabilized, the result of which
causes increased distribution costs. If a number of small retailers and
wholesalers were intermingled, we could expect amplifying waves
of inventory fluctuation, which, in turn, would affect the cost
burden to consumers.

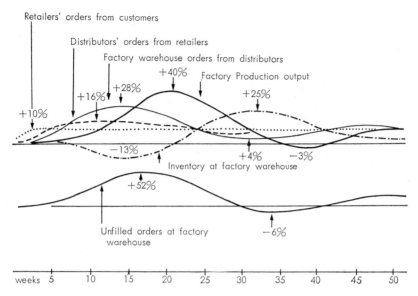

FIG. 1   Response of production-distribution system to a sudden 10% increase
in retail sales.

Source: Forrester, J. W., "Industrial Dynamics," *Harvard Business Review*
(July August 1958), p. 43.

Consumerism as a social force has always cried out against the
price manipulation of middlemen.

4. The Role of Government in Retail Innovation in Korea

In a free economic system the creative vitality of entrepreneurs has
been one of the major driving forces in economic growth. However
businessmen may not have enough capital and technology to carry
out innovative ventures in developing countries. The government may lead the van in building a new retail industry, but the
scope and nature of government activities should be limited to
a certain degree so that the creative vitality of entrepreneurship
will be stimulated.

A government-driven economy may cause serious problems.
Businessmen may depend too much on government incentives such
as tax benefits and financial assistance. These incentives, which

may induce corruption and waste of the government budget, are detrimental to productive business activities. The following guidelines can be suggested to reorganize the traditional distribution structure in Korea. (1) The government may have to build a more efficient marketing information system for the flow of transportation, inventory control, market information, and market financing. (2) The government should rearrange the marketing laws so that they induce well-established trade practices to protect consumers. (3) The government should take all positive efforts to derive price competition. (4) Market institutions should be geographically rearranged for different ranges of goods. An efficient hierarchy of market institutions should reduce urban migration and unnecessary traffic flow.

5. Future Direction of the Retail Revolution in Korea

Several hypotheses have been proposed to explain institutional change in the retail industry: cycle theories (wheel of retailing, accordion theory), dialectical process, vacuum theory, and the crisis-change model.[11] The recent development of super-chain stores in Korea may be explained by the vacuum theory.

Big business firms in Korea have not actively engaged in distribution. Neither manufacturers nor retailers have been able to find any way in which they could carry out the various needed marketing functions.[12] However, manufacturers are now anxious to find efficient channel types as an alternative means of cost reduction, early collection of sales revenue, and maintenance of market position.

While entrepreneurs neglect marketing opportunities in retailing, consumers in urban areas want to find a new marketing institution to secure quality products at a reasonable price. These economically-minded shoppers are willing to sustain such inconvenience as additional travel in order to buy at a discounted price. There is a growing tendency for cooperative associations to become involved in the market place. This tendency may provide attractive marketing opportunities for innovative retailers. Consumer markets have also been segmented as a result of rising incomes.

It is difficult to predict which types of retail institutions will dominate the consumer market in the next decade. But those successful may be characterized by the following: wholesalers or retailers with limited marketing functions, low-cost mass merchandising approach, franchise organization of channel institutions, nonstore retailing, and warehouse operating principles.

III. Development of Modern Marketing in the Automobile Industry

1. The Dawning Period (1962-1966)

The Korean War completely destroyed most productive facilities. By 1962 there were many cars available which had been heavily used during the war. Garage technicians became skillful in remodeling the used parts. The foundation of today's auto industry in Korea can be traced back to the protection law of the automobile industry in 1962. Neither government nor business could afford to build an automobile plant at that time, but under the veil of capital formation, the government allowed one motor company to begin importing small Japanese cars. This was the beginning of local demand for automobile parts, a good sign for parts manufacturers. Since the supply of cars fell far short of the demand, marketing was neglected in these days.

2. The Formative Period of the Automobile Industry (1967-1971)

In 1967, several motor companies such as Ford, Fiat and Toyota began to assemble small cars. The major competitive weapon was not price but engineering qualities suitable to local conditions. The level of demand was much greater than that of supply. Order lead time was on average up to six months. Local prices of small cars were two or three times higher than those in the international market. During this period, both motor companies and parts suppliers had accumulated capital and a certain level of technology. The government had even set a regulative quota in order to discourage the increasing demand for cars. There were no distinctive marketing efforts on the part of motor companies. Taxes and fees covered almost 40 percent of the final price that consumers had to

TABLE 8 Historical Progress of Developing Modern Marketing in the Automobile Industry.

	The Dawning Period (1962–1966)	The Formative Period (1967–1971)	The Localization Period (1972–1976)	The Market Development Period (1977–Present)
I. Environmental Forces				
A. Gov. Policies				
1. Automobile industry	Protection law for auto industry (62.5)	—	Presidential message for the promotion of auto industry (73.9)	Suggestions for mass production
2. Technology development	—	—	Selection of affiliated firms for parts production (75.1)	8–10% of tax allowance for R & D Reserve fund for R & D
3. Tax benefits and financing to create local demand	—	Regulative quota for passenger cars for private use	Replacement fund of worn-out cars and buses for business	Accelerated depreciation for plant and machinery. Passenger cars for business should be replaced within three years.
4. Others				
B. Development of auto industry and competitive structure	Remodeling worn-out cars used in Korean War. Domestic cars were produced.	Several motor companies were established. They assembled Fords, Toyotas, and Fiats.	Hyun Dai Motor introduced its own model, Pony, successfully. General Motors Korea introduced several GM models. Kia motor also successfully introduced small cars.	The major motor companies have enjoyed substantial growth.
C. Road situation in meters (the length of road over no. of passenger cars)	$\frac{27{,}169{,}111}{30{,}814} = 881.71$ (1962)	$\frac{34{,}799{,}454}{60{,}697} = 573.33$ (1967)	$\frac{42{,}867{,}617}{150{,}035} = 215.72$ (1972)	$\frac{45{,}974{,}718}{343{,}836} = 133.65$ (1978)
II. Marketing Resource Deployment				
A. Product-Market Components: Brand No. of cars sold Market share (%)				

	68	69	70	71	72	73	74	75	76	77	78
1. Hyundai	—	Cortina, Ford 20M			Cortina, Ford 20M,			Pony			Mark IV
		5,589	2,910	2,001	2,705	4,880	5,844	4,875	14,048	26,952	56,067
		30.4%	20.8%	19.2%	32.8%	39.1%	39.1%	28.0%	57.0%	62.2%	65.5%
2. Saehan (G.M.K.)	—				Rekord, Chev.1700, Camina					Camina, Gemini, Rekord	
					810	7,143	1,580	2,685	3,629	4,508	11,813
					9.8%	57.3%	21.2%	15.4%	14.7%	10.4%	13.8%
3. Kia	—						Brisa I, Brisa II			Brisa I, Brisa II	
							21	9,874	6,975	10,249	16,539
							0.3%	56.6%	28.3%	23.7%	19.3%
4. Asia*	—		Fiat 124		Fiat 124						
			1,122	2,545	1,981	444					
			8.1	24.3	24.0	3.6					
5. Shin Jin (G.M.K.)**	—	Corona, Crown									
		12,816	9,936	5,899	2,752	2					
		69.6%	71.1%	56.5%	39.4%						
Total no. of small cars sold in Korea		18,405	13,968	10,445	8,248	12,469	7,445	17,434	24,602	43,323	85,601

B. Price Components: Retail prices have been maintained at the same level all over the country. The changing components of price terms were not traced in this table over the last 17 years.

	Base price	taxes	fees	total price	% of taxes & fees to total price
1. Typical price structure as of Sept. 23, 1979					
Pony 1238 cc standard	$3,834	$1,142	$1,233	$6,209	38.3%
Gemini 1492 cc DLX	$4,495	$1,340	$1,728	$7,563	40.6%
Brisa 1272 cc K303	$4,201	$1,252	$1,252	$6,705	37.3%

2. Changing ratio of basic price and taxes to per capita GNP for small cars from 1974 to 1978:

year	74	75	76	77	78
ratio	12.0	8.0	6.0	5.0	4.5

*   Asia Motor was affiliated with Kia Motor Co.

**   Shin Jin Motor was affiliated with Saehan Motor Co.

***   Data in this table are approximate.

bear. Price levels were also regulated by the government. Since consumers were waiting in line, motor companies did not have to put much emphasis on marketing activities.

3. The Localization Period (1972–1976)

The core of marketing includes consumer satisfaction and consumer welfare. Automobile models developed in foreign countries did not exactly fit the local conditions. The survival and growth of a motor company depended on the engineering quality of its cars in this period. It was Hyundai Motor Company that realized the importance of its own model; the "Pony" was the successful crystallization of Hyundai's marketing concept. Shin Jin (GMK)-Saehan (GMK) Motor had enjoyed more than 50 percent of the market share up to 1973. The Chevy 1700, the small car model selected by G.M.K., was not at all successful compared to other models such as the Cortina, Pony, and Brisa. G.M.K. has consistently been the most active in sales efforts of all motor companies, but, at least in the small car market in Korea, it has been proven that an aggressive sales concept cannot beat an honest marketing concept.

4. The Market Development Period (1977–Present)

Since 1975, the productive capacities of the three major motor companies have substantially increased to cover the local market. There must be a certain level of demand in order for these plants to remain in full operation. The total volume of small car sales increased sharply from 7,445 in 1974 to 85,601 in 1978 but it is questionable whether such accelerated growth can continue in the decade ahead. It is possible to deduce the kinds of traffic problems in urban areas (Table 8). If we count *all* types of cars on the road, the length of road per car is less than 133.65 m. Considering the soaring gas prices, high rates of taxes and fees, and other maintenance expenses the saturation level of the domestic market may not be far away. If domestic industry sales are growing 30 percent yearly, what kinds of marketing strategies are most appropriate for the three motor companies? Which model of small cars will dominate the local market in the near future? What is the size and trend of the domestic market for small cars in the future? These are some of the questions that each motor company is facing.

5. Marketing Practices of the Auto Industry in Korea

As stated earlier, motor companies do not have to make additional efforts in marketing. It may take another generation for the Korean motor companies to use marketing strategies such as those adopted by the famous motor companies in the world. In this section, current marketing practice is briefly described. A detailed analysis of marketing efforts has not yet been published.

Product studies:

It is not easy to develop a new model which is uniquely fitted to the local market; therefore, product managers are primarily concerned with functional or stylistic modifications of existing models.

Market studies:

There have been few attempts to apply consumer behavior models to find determinant attributes and evaluative criteria in the target market. Each company has used market segmentation techniques for the determination of sales branches and sales planning.

Channel studies:

Three types of distribution channels have been adopted:

(a)   manufacturer—sales branch—consumers
(b)   manufacturer—sales agent—consumers
(c)   combination of the above two types

Most of the marketing functions are performed by manufacturers. The major job of a sales agent is negotiating with customers. Since such agents are selected from large garages, they are interested in securing repair work. The requirements which must be met by garages are so rigorous that facilities alone cost at least $200,000.

Price studies:

Demand has been much larger than supply. The automobile market is also characterized by an oligopolistic structure. The government has engaged in coordinating the market price based on full-cost pricing. Therefore motor companies have adopted skimming policies, target pricing and going-rate pricing. The local price is usually twice the price set in the international market. The major factors that are considered in pricing are production

TABLE 9   Historical Trend of Advertising Message Contents (1967–1979).

Year	Brand	\multicolumn{23}{c}{Attributes stressed in advertisements}
------	-------	1	2	3	4	5	6	7	8	9	10	11	12	13	14	15	16	17	18	19	20	21	22	23
		1	2	3	4	5	6	7	8	9	10	11	12	13	14	15	16	17	18	19	20	21	22	23
67	Corona																O							
68	Publica																							
69	Cortina	O					O	O				O		O										O
70	Fiat				O							O			O	O								
70	Ford-20M	O			O					O				O										
71	Corona 1600			O											O									
71	New Cortina			O											O	O								
73	Rekord			O	O								O					O						
73	Chevy 1700															O	O		O					
75	Rekord Royal		O		O	O						O	O											
76	Camina				O				O						O	O	O	O			O			
76	Pony															O	O							
76	Brisa																							
79	Gemini			O	O											O								
79	Granada	O						O		O				O	O	O				O	O			
Total frequency of each attribute over 15 models		1	2	1	3	7		2	1	3			2	5	2	3	5	8		1	3	2		1

I. Comfort and convenience
1. Heater
2. Ventilation
3. Air conditioner
4. Roominess
5. Seat
6. Instrument legibility
7. Ash tray accessibility
8. Door handle operation
9. Visibility
10. Ease of getting in and out
11. Luggage capacity
II. Operation
12. Transmission
13. Brakes
14. Ease of handling

15. Freedom from breakdowns
16. Durability
III. Performance
17. Drivability
18. Acceleration from standstill
19. Passing acceleration
20. Starting ease
21. Riding quality
22. Handling ease
23. Highway stability
24. Gasoline economy
IV. Styling
25. Overall exterior appearance
26. Front-end appearance
27. Side appearance
28. Wheel appearance

(see key below for list of attributes by number)																													Total No. of Mentions
24	25	26	27	28	29	30	31	32	33	34	35	36	37	38	39	40	41	42	43	44	45	46	47	48	49	50	51	52	
O	O																									O	O		2
																											O		1
							O					O														O		O	7
		O			O																				O	O	O		12
		O													O			O		O								O	5
		O							O																			O	1
O																												O	9
O	O					O																O				O			3
O																										O			4
		O								O	O			O		O	O					O							3
O										O	O	O													O	O			2
O	O																												4
																													1
																										O	O		5
								O											O									O	2
6	7				1	2	2	4	1			2			2		1	1		1		3		1	7	4	6		

29. Rear-end appearance
30. Grill appearance
31. Bumper appearance
32. Tail light appearance
33. Overall interior styling
34. Instrument panel styling
35. Steering wheel styling
36. Appearance of seats
37. Upholstery appearance
V. Workmanship
38. Body workmanship
39. Exterior moulding fit
40. Fit of doors

41. Paint finish
42. Quality of chrome trim
43. Window operation
44. Freedom from leaks
45. Overall quietness
46. Level of engine noise
VI. Others
47. Prestige of car
48. Warranty coverage
49. Future resale value
50. After-sales service & parts
51. Order lead time
52. Safety features

Source: Reynolds, F. E. and Wells, W., *Consumer Behavior* (New York: McGraw-Hill, 1977), p. 226.

costs, returns on investment, financial ability of consumers, and pricing practices of other companies. Since the channel structure is integrated by manufacturers, the distribution cost is almost negligible in pricing.

Promotion studies:

Personal selling is widely used by each company. District sales managers evaluate their salesmen on the criteria of job performance, sales planning, customer education, and training. Manufacturers have adopted various measures for sales promotion. Table 9 describes the historical trend of advertising message content in daily newspapers for the period from 1967 to 1978. For each of the five newspapers (two business papers and three leading papers in Seoul), five weeks per year were randomly selected for analyzing such advertisements. Among the attributes mentioned more than four times were seat comfort, brakes, durability, drivability, gas economy, overall appearance, price, after-sales service and parts, and safety.

The following attributes were not mentioned at all: instrument legibility, ease of getting in and out, luggage capacity, acceleration from standstill, handling ease, appearance of front, side, seat, and wheel, styling of instrument panel, steering wheel, body workmanship, moulding fit, paint finish, freedom from leaks, level of noise and warranty coverage.

Summary

Marketing discipline can contribute to the economic growth and welfare of a society. Marketing decisions also direct the flow of scarce resources. In this paper development of marketing in general has been traced by reviewing the available literature along with the series of five-year economic plans. This historical analysis was designed to learn the following:

(1)   What were the major product lines of marketing studies in each period? Was there any relation between these products and the stages of economic growth?

(2)   What kinds of marketing techniques have been introduced?

(3)   Which marketing activities have received most attention from the researchers?

(4)   What are the major environmental forces that direct and constrain marketing activities?

(5)   What is the role and position of automobile marketing in Korea?

From the above analysis, distribution structure and channel institutions are noted as the emerging bottlenecks in economic progress. Therefore the second part of this paper has focused on the previous studies of channel structures. The future direction of the retail revolution was also described in the latter section of part two. The third part offered a brief history of the automobile industry and its development of marketing. The automobile industry has been protected by government policies. Demand has always been greater than supply. Motor companies do not have to make additional efforts in marketing.

Table 8 describes the major changes in the automobile industry over the last seventeen years. The crux of marketing success in the Korean automobile industry seems to have been the engineering quality of cars and their adaptability to unique local conditions. An aggressive sales concept cannot beat an honest marketing concept.

Since 1975, productive capacities have been substantially increased. Motor companies have realized the need to secure a certain level of demand in order to enjoy economy of scale. Some positive measures must be taken by these companies if they are to survive and grow in the future.

NOTES

1.   Drucker, P. F., "Marketing and Economic Development." *Journal of Marketing* (January 1958), pp. 252–259.
2.   These articles consist of all the M. B. A. theses, and some other articles in marketing from the *Korean Business Journal* and the *Practice of Management* (1967–1978).
3.   This classification scheme is adjusted from the following reference. Fisk, F., "The Functions of Marketing Research," in *Handbook of*

Marketing Research, F. Ferber, ed. (New York: McGraw-Hill, 1974), pp. 1, 19–20.

4. King, R. L., "The Marketing Concept," in *Science in Marketing,* G. Schwartz, ed. (New York: John Wiley & Sons, Inc., 1965), pp. 81–85.

5. Hong, J. I., "Promotion of R & D Expenditure for Innovation," an unpublished paper presented at Advanced Management Program at Seoul National University in August, 1979.

6. Minister of Commerce and Industry, "Financial Assistance for the Modernization of Distribution Structure." *Notice No. 79–16 and No. 79–18* (May 1979).

7. Kim, W. S., "Dynamic Change of Korean Market Structure (1968–1976)." *The Korean Business Journal* (December 1978), pp. 52–101.

8. The Korean Economic Research Center, *Direction of Implementing Marketing Modernization* (Seoul: The Chamber of Commerce and Industry, 1978), pp. 64–65.

9. Oh, S. L., "Effects of Express Highway on Wholesale Markets for Perishable Agri-Marine Products." *The Korean Business Journal* (June 1976), pp. 121–133.

10. Forrester, J. W., "Industrial Dynamics." *Harvard Business Review* (July–August 1958), pp. 37–66.

11. Stern, L. W. and El-Ansary, A. I., *Marketing Channels* (Englewood Cliffs, N. J.: Prentice-Hall, 1977), pp. 240–251.

12. The major reasons can be explained by the following factors: lack of capital and managerial ability, limited variety of product lines, and too many "corner stores," most of which are owned and operated by family members.

SOURCES CONSULTED

Books

Bartel, R., *The History of Marketing Thought,* 2nd ed. (Columbus, Ohio: Grid Inc., 1976).

Ferber, R. ed., *Handbook of Marketing Research* (New York: McGraw-Hill Book Co., 1974).

Goble, R. L. and Shaw, R. T., *Controversy and Dialogue in Marketing* (Englewood Cliffs, N. J.: Prentice-Hall, 1975).

Kim, D. K., *Theory of Modern Channel Institutions* (Seoul: Bak Young Sa, 1974).

The Korean Economic Research Center, *A Study on Supermarket Chain Organization in Korea* (Seoul: Korea Chamber of Commerce and Industry, 1977).

Oh, S. L. et al., *Promotion of Modernization for Distribution Structure* (Seoul: Korea Chamber of Commerce and Industry, 1978).

Oh, S. L. et al., *Research Report on the Improvement of Distribution Structure*, Planning and Coordination Dept. of the Prime Minister, Rep. of Korea, 1974.

Pashigian, B. P., *The Distribution of Automobiles, An Economic Analysis of the Franchise System* (Englewood Cliffs, N. J.: Prentice-Hall, 1961).

Reynolds, F. E. and Wells, W., *Consumer Behavior* (New York: McGraw-Hill, 1977).

Journal Articles

Drucker, P. F., "Marketing and Economic Development." *Journal of Marketing* (January 1958): 252–259.

Kim, W. S., "Dynamic Changes of Korean Marketing Structure (1968–1976)." *The Korean Business Journal* (December 1978): 52–101.

———, "A study on the Measurement of Marketing Productivity." *The Korean Business Journal* (December 1974): 1–88.

Lee, J. Y., "New Seoul Cooperative Chain Store." *The Korean Business Journal* (August 1970): 104–138.

Oh, S. L., "The Role of Government in Korean Marketing." *The Korean Business Journal* (March 1968): 1–211.

———, "Effects of Highway on Wholesale Markets for Perishable Agri-Marine Products." *The Korean Business Journal* (June 1976): 1–24.

———, "Direction of Modernization of Retailers and Retail Markets in Korea." *The Korean Business Journal* (March 1969): 1–72.

———, "Establishment and Improvement of Chain Store Operations in Korea." *The Korean Business Journal* (September 1975): 1–12.

———, "A study on the Marketing System in Korea." *The Korean Business Journal* (March 1976): 1–44.

———, "Agricultural Produce Marketing Center of National Agricultural Cooperative Federation: Its Problems and Solutions." *The Korean Business Journal* (September 1976): 1–26.

Unpublished Papers

Chun, S. J., "A Study on Automobile Marketing," M.B.A. thesis presented at Graduate School of Business, Korea University, 1976.

Lee, H. S., "A Study on Purchase Decision Processes: Behavioral Analysis

of Taxi Buyers," M.B.A. thesis presented at Graduate School, Seoul
National University, 1978.

Han, I. S., "A Study on Personal Selling in Automobile Marketing,"
M.B.A. thesis presented at Graduate School, Seoul National University,
1972.

Park, J. W., "A Study on Installment Financing for Automobile Sales in
Korea," M.B.A. thesis presented at Graduate School of Business and
Public Administration, Sung Kyun Gwan University, 1974.

COMMENTS

Matao Miyamoto
Osaka University

To begin with, I would like to express my gratitude to Professor Lim for giving us valuable information about the history and present state of the Korean distribution structure and automobile industry. I, myself, as a Japanese historian who knows little about the Korean economy, have learned much of our neighboring country from his paper. My first impression of Professor Lim's paper is that this is a well-organized, well-prepared and well-presented paper, using modern and scientific marketing methods.

Professor Lim's paper is composed of three chapters and a summary. I would like to raise five questions: one on the first chapter, three on second and the remaining one on the third. My questions concentrate mainly on the traditional distribution structure in Korea, because I have studied that of Japan.

1) In the first chapter, Professor Lim analyzes the process of marketing development, by examining the changing topics, analytical techniques and major product lines reviewed in 674 articles on marketing science published in Korea. From his analysis I have learned the process by which modern marketing was introduced into the Korean academic world. I believe that he assumed changing interests in the academic circle itself reflect to some extent changing attitudes on marketing issues in the real business world. Although I do not disagree with this assumption, it is unlikely that the interests of the academic world coincide perfectly with those of businessmen. I suppose there are gaps (lead or lag) between the two. I would like to ask Professor Lim to what extent the scholarly works have been influenced by the needs of Korean businessmen, and what

effects these scholarly works have had on the business world.
I would appreciate it if he would explain these relationships between the academic and business worlds, giving some examples.

2)   My second question is related to his second chapter. Professor
Lim argues that in the evolution of distribution in Korea, the
traditional distribution structure has emerged as the bottleneck and
therefore the reorganization of this structure has become an increasingly urgent problem. My question is concerned with the
transformation of the Korean retail system which will occur in
the near future.

When we look back on the distribution revolution in the United
States, we can find that it took a long time; chain stores were developed in the 1920s; these were followed by supermarkets and
then by discount stores. The process was relatively gradual and
sequential. On the other hand, as stated in Professor Maeda's
paper in this book, in Japan chain stores, supermarkets and discount
stores emerged almost simultaneously during the postwar period of
economic growth and in many cases actually combined operations.
Japan's distribution revolution took place so rapidly that friction
between new and traditional distribution institutions arose and
traditional merchants' problems in adjusting to new market conditions became serious. In response to the emergence of new commercial activities, scholars have often seen the traditional distribution
structure as useless and have condemned, for example, the continued existence of the wholesaler. I wonder if the same retailing
revolution—concurrent emergence of chain stores, supermarkets
and discount stores—is not also occurring in Korea, and if problems
similar to those encountered in Japan have not arisen. I would
like to ask Professor Lim for his opinion in this regard.

3)   My third question concerns the nature of the traditional
distribution structure in Korea, and how this has affected the
distribution revolution there. It is often mentioned that in Japan
one of the major obstacles to changing the traditional structure
has been the financing power of wholesale merchants. These
merchants have traditionally helped small producers with advanced
payments and the putting-out system, and have offered retailers
deferred payment plans. To the extent that small retailers and pro-

ducers continue to rely on wholesalers for financing, it is extremely difficult to reorganize the complex distribution structure, and in fact it may be undesirable to do so. I would like to ask Professor Lim to compare Korea's case with that of Japan, and to tell us to what degree it differs.

4) I have learned from this paper that small-scale retailers and complex channels of distribution are the characteristic features of the traditional distribution structure in Korea. The same is true of Japan where, the distribution revolution notwithstanding, small-scale wholesalers and retailers have actually increased in number in the last twenty years. What has happened in Japan is that in the course of the distribution revolution individual stores have not necessarily increased in size, but the firms which own them have. These firms have created chains, some of them strictly voluntary, which enabled them to reduce stock purchasing costs through economies of scale. In this sense, I think it is true that managerial changes may be more important than increasing the size of individual stores or shortening distribution channels. I would like to ask Professor Lim for his opinion in this regard.

5) My fifth question concerns his third chapter, on the development of modern marketing in the automobile industry. Professor Lim pointed out that the development of the Korean automobile industry can be divided into four periods: the dawning period from 1962 to 1966, the formative period from 1967 to 1971, the localization period from 1972 to 1976, and from 1977 to the present. I have learned from his paper that in the first two periods, imported cars from Japan and foreign countries such as Ford, Fiat and Toyota produced by Korean assembly factories played a role in the expansion of the Korean domestic market. If so, what kinds of influence did these cars have on the subsequent development of automobile marketing techniques in Korea, especially on the channel of distribution and on the managerial techniques of dealers? Are there any vestiges of these influences in the latter two periods? I would appreciate it greatly if Professor Lim would give us further explanation on this.

p. 235; Comments

2

* 6330
  5310   Korea
  S.

Kenjiro Ishikawa
Doshisha University

On pages 246 and 247 of his paper, Professor Lim refers to Forrester's diagram and states that "the complex channel system on the market structure . . . causes increased distribution costs." This is true, but the process can also be seen as follows.

To the extent that channel systems become more complex, information with regard to products becomes varied and more available, and both suppliers and consumers can use this increased wealth of information to select their products more carefully. In this way, suppliers can reduce their market risk and consumers can obtain things which they really want. If suppliers simplify channel systems simply in order to cut distribution costs, the amount of information available is reduced and less precise and risk increases accordingly. On the other hand, consumers will accept cost burdens as long as these are perceived as necessary to obtain or receive more precise information on products. In other words, the channel system must be complex to a certain extent for suppliers to produce goods which can actually be sold and for consumers to obtain things they really want.

I would like to ask Professor Lim whether he agrees with this. I think it is at least necessary for us to consider both the advantage (reduced risk) and disadvantage (increased cost) of the complex channel system. Finally, with regard to Korea, I would like to ask whether one of the problems in Korea is one of information flow rather than of complexity of the channel system.

The Evolution of Retailing
Industries in Japan

6333

Kazutoshi Maeda
Komazawa University

I. The Changing Pattern of Japan's Distribution Structure

This paper examines the development of retailing industries in Japan's modernization and industrialization. The retailers cater directly to the consumer at the end of distribution channels, carry out the distribution function that combines production with consumption, and establish the distribution structures. As a result, to study the development of the retailer with this function involves tracing the history of marketing in each country.

The distribution structures are regulated by economic, social and cultural conditions and take a different pattern in every country and in each period. As is widely known, the following are the distinguishing characteristics of the Japanese distribution structure. First, the Japanese distribution structure consists of a large number of smaller establishments whose productivity is rather low. However, a disproportionate share of the total sales is concentrated among a small number of large-scale establishments in the structure. Secondly, the distribution channels are highly complex and circuitous. In addition, traditional trade practices, which have become rather more complicated, still exist in the contemporary distribution structure.[1] These features had a formative role in the industrialization of Japan and laid deep roots before World War II. Although the Japanese distribution structure has changed with rapid economic growth during the postwar decades, it basically retains its prewar features.

The wholesalers (*tonya*) in Japan had dominated the distribution system for many years since they established their position

265

in the Tokugawa era. The opening of the treaty ports in 1859 and
the subsequent reforms by the Meiji government affected the
trading organization, but did not change it in substance. The
traditional distribution structure also survived, in spite of rapid
industrialization, because of the government policy of stressing
capital goods and because of the differential structure in Japanese
industry. As a consequence, the traditional distribution system
dominated many industries. Some manufacturers in the modern
industrial sector, however, reorganized their traditional distribution system and created their own marketing channels. In the
Taisho era, the modern distribution channels were well established
among some manufacturing industries, such as beer, foreign liquor,
confectioneries, cosmetics, chemical seasoning, electric appliances,
paper (Western style), wheat flour and sugar. A few manufacturers
producing confectioneries and cosmetics, in particular, included
the retailers in their sales organization. In most cases, however,
the intensification of marketing channels stopped at the wholesale
level. Some manufacturers among these new consumer industries
are generally known as marketing-oriented firms.

The traditional distribution system suspended its functions
during the period of the controlled economy—from World War II
to some time after the war. For that reason, they could not meet
the changing conditions in the postwar period.

Japan has, during the postwar decades, achieved rapid economic
growth and has been undergoing remarkable social changes. The
time of a mass consumption society has arrived. In the early 1950s
manufacturing industries made intensive commitments to new
capital investment. The innovative investments stimulated the
very rapid growth of industries, particularly those producing
consumer durables. Dynamic investment in the private sector also
resulted in further growth in output. Thus, the Japanese economy
reached its prewar level in the early 1950s and thereafter the
country's GNP increased rapidly. Between the mid-1950s and the
mid-1960s income level doubled and showed a tendency to stand-
ardize. As the standard of living rose, consumption patterns and
modes of living altered. In the late 1950s Japan had thus entered
into a mass consumption society.

As the environment of distribution changed, large-scale manu-facturing firms began to reorganize their own sales organizations from the mid-1950s onwards. The existing distribution systems changed as a result. Changes in the distribution system were notable in the consumer industries, because the marketing-oriented manu-facturing firms were increasing. The consumer industries most innovative in their approach to marketing were electric home appliances, automobiles, synthetic fibers, pharmaceuticals, cosmet-ics, cameras, and processed foods. Some large-scale manufacturing firms of producers' goods such as steel, paper and the like also actively performed marketing functions.

Thus, the traditional distribution system dominated by the wholesalers over many years changed fundamentally. The producers took the place of the wholesalers who had dominated distribution channels, and the result was the emergence of a manufacturer-dominated distribution system with vertical integration.

The development of distribution systems in postwar Japan was as follows. In the early 1950s most manufacturing firms set up their marketing channels dependent on the existing trading organization. However, some manufacturers of electric home appliances estab-lished their own sales subsidiaries about this time. In and after the mid-1950s large-scale manufacturing firms systematized cooperative wholesalers and retailers, giving them various kinds of assistance. A few of the more innovative firms attempted to go one step more and organize consumers.

The trend to systematize the distribution channels was particu-larly notable in such industries as automobiles, electric home appliances, cosmetics and cameras, where producers' control over the channels of distribution was increasing. In the electric home appliance industry, in particular, the systematization of distri-bution channels did not stop at the wholesale level, but reached the retail level. Around 1960 some firms in such industries as home appliances and cosmetics had organized the consumers with intent to avoid price cutting and to expand the market. In the mid-1960s manufacturers tightened their control over marketing channels. For instance, manufacturers of such products as household soap, toothpaste and drugs tightened the systematization by means of the resale price maintenance system. Producers in the home appliances industry established many sales subsidiaries on a territorial basis and controlled them rather tightly.

The distribution structure changed with the development of retailing industries. Since the early 1900s, when department stores came into existence, the Japanese retailing structures had consisted of a small number of department stores together with a large number of small-scale independent retailers. However, as the new type of large-scale retailing institutions emerged during the mid-1950s, signs of change appeared in the retailing structure. During the 1960s new retailing institutions developed considerably, putting pressure on the existing institutions.

The traditional distribution structure was thus forced to change under pressure from both manufacturing and retailing sides. During the 1960s, as a result, the distribution revolution (*ryūtsū kakumei*) began and it is still continuing now.

It was the wholesaling sector that was most affected by this distribution revolution. Although it is premodern in that it is a structure consisting of a large number of small-scale establishments and multiple levels, the number of wholesalers is still increasing. It was said that the changes in the wholesaling structure would become clear in the late 1970s.[2] Of course, some wholesalers adapted quickly to the new environment. The trading firms whose role had been expected to decline promoted the policy of vertical integration in phases of domestic trade and began strongly to influence the formation of new distribution systems. Some progressive wholesalers have also attempted to organize voluntary chains and to develop original product lines as well as private brand merchandise.

The primary factors regulating the development of the distribution sector are the structure of production, the level of economic development, and such social conditions as the level and distribution of income, the growth and movement of population, the lifestyle and the technologies of communication. Legislation, industrial policy and cultural patterns are also influential; and the development of the distribution sector strongly depends on the place of entrepreneurship in the economic, social and cultural environment of any given country.

The above historical examination of the Japanese distribution structure has shown the rapid changes it experienced in the postwar decades. The recent retailing sector, in particular, has changed most drastically and has strongly affected the entire distribution structure. However, the structural features of the old Japanese retailing sector, consisting of a large number of small, inefficient retail outlets, still exist.

There were more than 1.61 million retail establishments in Japan in 1976. Their sales figures amounted to an annual total of about ¥55 trillion; they had slightly less than 5.6 million employees. Their sales floor space was 77 million square meters. Here we should note that 95.9 percent of all retail establishments were small shops with nine employees or less. Retailers with two employees or less, in particular, still accounted for 61.9 percent of all retail establishments (compared with 70 percent in 1958). But their annual sales in 1974 was only 15.1 percent of the total sales volume. On the other hand retail establishments with 100 employees or more represented 0.1 percent of all retailers, and were responsible for 15.6 percent of the total sales volume.[3]

The Japanese retailing sector lagged far behind the manufacturing sector in its modernization. In spite of rapid economic growth, retailing forms did not develop by stages in prewar Japan because the capacity of the distribution network to change was limited. But the conditions that limited development changed substantially after the war, and the entire distribution structure began to respond to them. In the retailing sectors, such new large-scale retailing institutions as supermarket chains, installment-plan department store chains and speciality store chains emerged and grew.

Changes in the retailing sector did not necessarily occur suddenly in the postwar period. Although they had a certain limit, as social and cultural conditions changed gradually with industrialization, the challenge to break with convention was faced continually by the existing retailers. Consequently, the department stores were established in the 1900s, and such new retailing institutions as installment-plan stores and chain stores appeared between the 1920s and 1930s. Some private railroad firms also set up the unique retailing institution known as the terminal station department store, and consumer cooperatives also went into retailing. Although none of them attained full growth except the terminal station department store, they had the potential to develop as retailing industries in the postwar period. I would like to examine the changing pattern of retailing institutions in the following section.

II. The Age of Department Stores and Small-Scale Independent Retailers

During the first decade of the Meiji era not a few old-fashioned merchants went bankrupt because of a slump in domestic trade. In such cities as Tokyo and Yokohama the newly-risen merchants emerged in their place. From the late 1870s the domestic market grew and the distribution of merchandise rose in line with the expansion of production and foreign trade, the growth of the infrastructure of transportation and communication, and the changes of lifestyle attendant upon Westernization. Retail activities consequently showed a buoyancy and the number of retail establishments increased. In 1885 there were over one million,[4] a large number of which were in such categories as confectioneries, grain, alcoholic beverages, dry goods and green groceries or fruit, kitchenware and notions.[5] The number of merchants dealing in Western-style articles (hats, umbrellas and clothing) also increased rapidly. In the early 1870s most had combined wholesaling and retailing businesses, but later they specialized gradually in one or the other.[6]

The types of retailers began to differentiate as the number of establishments increased. In big cities and in the early period, general stores grew gradually into stores dealing only in a single line of merchandise. Some among the latter became large-scale speciality stores. In the course of time, they also formed a shopping street, thoroughly planned versions of which appeared in big cities. The first modern one was the Ginza, completed in 1878 as part of the government policy toward modernization. It comprised representatives of the progressive merchants and has since been a model for shopping streets.[7]

A collective form of retailing called "*Kan Koba*" appeared. It was a kind of leased department store where the owner of a building leased space under one roof to various independent retailers. It was originally established as a public institution by Tokyo Prefecture in 1878.[8] After that, such stores were established successively by private, progressive people in such cities as Osaka, Yokohama, Fukuoka, Sapporo and Shizuoka between the early 1880s and the 1900s. It attained the highest stage of prosperity in Tokyo between the late 1880s and the 1900s, and there were twenty-seven establishments in 1902. It influenced the modernization of retailing by means of an acceptance of one-price policy and open display, employment of saleswomen, introduction of company organization and so on.[9] However, it declined from the late 1890s because of excessive competition among joined retailers, or because of a lack of able managers and funds.

The first type of large-scale retailing institution was the department store. It was the most significant institutional innovation in the prewar retailing sector. Soon after the coming of the new century the old, famous, dry-goods stores in such big cities as Tokyo, Osaka and Kyoto—for example, Mitsukoshi, Shirokiya (Tokyu), Daimaru, Takashimaya, Matsuzakaya and Matsuya— converted themselves into department stores. Within a short period of time they introduced a company organization, expanded their lines of merchandise, improved their displays, introduced rudimentary sales promotion and consequently developed into modern department stores. Thereafter the change to department stores extended to dry-goods stores in such provincial cities as Sapporo, Kagoshima, Okayama, Sendai and so on.

As stated above, most of the prominent central department stores in Japan developed from dry goods stores. Most of them, furthermore, had been founded in the Tokugawa era. In particular, Mitsukoshi, one of the leading department stores in Japan, originated in Mitsui's Echigoya. As is well known, Echigoya, in 1683, introduced the innovative methods of small profits and quick returns based on a policy of "cash-pay, low prices, no mark-ups."

It is important to note that some of the innovative business practices occurred in this period.[10]

Between the end of the Tokugawa era and the early Meiji era many long-established merchants went into a slump, while dry goods stores of some merchants gradually changed their traditional business operations in and after the late 1880s. They were the first to deal in Western clothes, and from the late 1890s they improved their sales methods and changed from traditional business organizations and practices.

The entrepreneur who first established the department store in Japan was Ōsuke Hibi, Mitsukoshi's founder. He was a graduate of Keio Gijuku and was one of those college graduates whom Hikijirō Nakamigawa, the leader of Mitsui in the 1890s, systematically employed at that time. Though most of these graduates went into the modern industrial sectors, Hibi endeavored to set up a modern enterprise in the retailing sector and ran Mitsukoshi on the one-man/one-business principle. Hibi's ideas on department store management owed much to Harrods of London. However, the traditional spirit of small profits and quick returns lay at the root of his ideas and it was his business policy that department stores offer good articles, carry out honest advertising and satisfy their customers first of all.[11]

Mitsukoshi broadened its range of merchandise after its foundation in 1903, and consequently it dealt in various articles—cosmetics, hats, children's clothing, bags, footwear, Western umbrellas, boots and shoes, combs and ornamental hairpins—until 1907. Mitsukoshi also reopened its tailor's shop and established a restaurant and photo studio. When a Renaissance building of three stories was completed in 1908, it dealt in precious metals, tobacco and stationery. Then Mitsukoshi began to handle foreign liquor and groceries when a new five-story building with escalators, air conditioning and a sprinkler system was completed in 1914. Mitsukoshi thus completed all the essential features of the modern department store.[12]

The other stores in metropolitan areas followed Mitsukoshi with the extension of buildings and the broadening of product lines. Although their buildings were commonly of three stories in the early days, they became five-story ones between the end of the Meiji era and the beginning of the Taisho era. It was in and after the 1920s that buildings of seven stories first appeared. The department stores established their base, as they spread from big cities to provincial cities between the end of the Meiji era and throughout the Taisho era, with such features as the introduction of advanced display, the enforcement of cash-pay and one-price policy, and the offer of total shopping comfort.

The genesis and growth of department stores are related to the rise of the urban market. Urbanization in Japan began in the middle period of the Meiji era and continued into World War I. Of the nation's entire population, the percentage in areas with 10,000 or more increased from 11 percent in 1879 to 18 percent in 1898, 25 percent in 1908 and 32 percent in 1918. During this period the number of cities increased remarkably; in particular, big cities with populations of more than 100,000 increased from six in 1891 to sixteen in 1920.[13] It is important also to note that the populations of Tokyo and Osaka doubled during this period. The concentration of people in cities made for a broader and deeper market than in rural areas.

Although the traditional dry goods store, the predecessor of the department store, had social prestige and accumulated funds, it had reached its limits. As a result, some progressive stores grew to be department stores with the absorption of foreign know-how and talent. However, conservative family ownership and other traditional factors persisted in the management of the original department stores. For instance, with regard to types of customers handled by each department store, Mitsukoshi's were people of property and peers descended from court nobles, Daimaru's were ordinary people downtown, and Takashimaya's were the aristocracy.[14] Their customers were mainly the upper and upper-middle classes. However, as social changes became clear in the turning-point period of World War I, department stores directed their efforts toward a more general clientele.

It was due to price rises during World War I that department stores changed their image. They broadened their appeal, expanded varieties of everyday necessities and attached importance to discount sales. For example, Mitsukoshi sold, at a discount, dry goods, miscellaneous goods and groceries in 1919, and built a discount sale corner in 1922. It was in this period that department stores began to sell at a discount a series of articles with famous brand names, while also strengthening dependence on household items.

Conditions in retailing changed rapidly between the late Taisho era and the early Showa era. In Tokyo, particularly, the serious Kanto earthquake in 1923 spurred such changes. As a result, department stores broadened their appeal further with the selling of miscellaneous goods, the expansion of branch networks and the abolition of a requirement that customers remove their shoes when entering the store. During this period they altered their multistory buildings and eliminated any reference to their draper's shop (*go-fukuten*) origin from their name. And all through the depression at the beginning of the Showa era they competed with each other in the construction of branch stores: for example, Mitsukoshi had ten branches in 1933. At the same time, some department stores moved to Ginza, Shinjuku and elsewhere as these areas grew. These moves were to profoundly affect these stores' later development.

The social changes between the late Taisho era and the early Showa era not only made the existing department stores change their business policy but also created a new type of department store. It was "the terminal station department store" that was owned and managed by private railroad firms in such metropolitan areas as Tokyo and Osaka. It was Ichizo Kobayashi—the founder of Hankyu Corporation—who developed this new idea. He was a creative entrepreneur who set up, for the development of railroad firms, such related businesses as housing land development, recreation areas and department stores.

Kobayashi sensitively responded to changes in urban living and the rise of the middle classes and introduced new practices in the railroad business. He built a market dealing in groceries and miscellaneous goods under the firm's direct management in the Hankyu Building in 1925. In 1929 he opened Hankyu Department Stores. This Hankyu Hyakkaten directed its appeal to the new middle classes living along railway lines and, unlike the traditional department stores gave priority to restaurants, groceries and miscellaneous goods.[15] The "terminal station department stores" also emerged in Tokyo, and in 1934 Tokyo Yokohama Electric Railway (a forerunner of Tokyu Corporation) built the Toyoko Department Store (a forerunner of Tokyu Department Store); the other railroad firms followed suit.

The number of department stores had increased rapidly by the mid-1930s with new ones being built in metropolitan areas and provincial cities to join those which had developed from dry goods stores. Department store companies increased from 8 in 1921 to 14 in 1925, to 21 in 1928 and to 41 in 1933.[16] When the Japan Department Store Trade Association (*Nihon Hyakkaten Shogyo Kumiai*) was organized in 1933, it had 36 members who qualified by having at least 3,300 square meters of sales space in the six largest cities, and a minimum of 1,650 square meters in provincial cities.[17] Then, when the Japan Department Store Association (*Nihon Hyakkaten Kumiai*) reorganized in conformity with the 1937 Department Store Law, its qualified members (stores with at least 3,000 square meters of sales space in the six largest cities, and with a minimum of 1,500 square meters in places other than those cities) numbered 87, and they represented a total of 151 establishments.[18]

As the number of department stores increased, the competition among department stores in metropolitan areas intensified with the operation of special discount sales and other services. In each department store, therefore, expenses and fixed assets increased, and ultimately profits decreased. In addition, the antagonism of smaller-scale retailers toward department stores which had existed since the end of the Taisho era became even stronger in this period. The anti-department store movement intensified during the depression period in early Showa, extended from metropolitan areas to provincial cities and became a social and political issue. The Japan Department Store Association announced a policy of strict self-control of department store practices and finally the department stores were forced to conform to the Department Store Law enacted in 1937.

It is not clear how strong the influence of department stores in the entire retail sector was. In Tokyo there were 58,812 retail establishments in 1931. Their sales figures amounted to ¥657

million. Small-scale retailers accounted for 98.1 percent of all retail outlets and 53.3 percent of total retail sales. By contrast, the
department stores, consisting of only eight establishments, accounted
for 33.2 percent of total retail sales.[19] In addition the department
stores in Tokyo City in 1934 accounted for 24 percent of total retail
sales.[20]

The prewar structure of the Japanese retail sector consisted of a
large number of small retail outlets on the one hand and a small
number of large-scale department stores on the other. However,
there were signs of change. As social and economic conditions
changed from the middle of the Taisho era, public and private
retail markets were set up and consumer cooperatives began retailing operations; also such new types of retailing institutions as
installment stores and chain stores appeared. Installment stores and
chain stores in particular represented changes that would fully
develop in the postwar retailing industry.

In the prewar period, also, a small number of firms or entrepreneurs were concerned about the adoption of a system of chain
stores that was developing in the United States of America. A few
firms in the consumer industry had already promoted the chain
system to tighten their control of marketing channels in the 1920s.
They did not establish a firm basis at that time, although some
manufacturers, wholesalers and retailers began to introduce the
chain system. Takashimaya, a department store, began to operate
variety stores, meeting with considerable success. From 1930,
Takashimaya developed chains in such cities as Tokyo, Osaka and
Kyoto, and had 51 stores in 1932. But Takashimaya abandoned
this policy in accordance with the Japan Department Store Association's announcement of self-control. It then set up a subsidiary
in 1938 and enlarged the chains. It grew rapidly and had 106 stores,
2,172 employees and sales floor space of 38,989 square meters by
1941.[21] In the early Showa period some voluntary and cooperative
chains appeared. Although development here was limited, they
represented a new movement of small retailers to counter the
department stores during the depression. It is interesting to note
that Ito-Yokado, a typical mass merchandiser, participated in the
formation of cooperative chains in this period.[22]

Stores which sold on the installment plan also groped for a new direction. The modern installment system was introduced by Singer, one of the makers of sewing machines in the United States of America, which moved into the Japanese market in the early 1900s. Subsequently, these measures were adopted by manufacturers of such durable consumer goods as cash registers and musical instruments. But Japan already had an installment system which had been introduced in the Tokugawa era; this expanded from the Meiji era on and installment-plan stores were set up in such cities as Tokyo and Osaka between the end of the Meiji era and the early Taisho era. They dealt mainly in furniture and clothing, and some of them introduced multistore operations. Although they were not highly regarded by most people in the prewar period, some of them continued to modernize, eliminating traditional methods in the process. Marui, the leading installment-plan department store chain, was the innovator here.[23]

The sales of department stores reached a peak in 1934, but as the economy became more and more controlled, retailers found it impossible to operate freely. Thus, such new types of retailing institutions as chain stores and installment stores could not grow, although they had been established. It is, however, noteworthy that some of the existing mass merchandisers were founded between the end of the Taisho era and the opening years of the Showa period.

III. The Growth of New Retailing Institutions and the Change of Traditional Retailing Institutions

In the early 1950s, when the Japanese economy again reached its prewar level, free operations resumed in the retailing sector. Department stores took the lead and new retailing institutions that were mass-merchandise-oriented and chain-operated emerged from the 1960s onward; these were supermarkets, speciality stores and installment-plan department stores.

The most important and immediate force prompting the emergence of new large-scale retailing institutions in Japan was the rapid change in the retail environment. The dynamic growth of the postwar Japanese economy created a new society, different from that before the war. Japan's gross national product increased rapidly, and between the early 1950s and the early 1970s the annual real growth rate averaged around 10 percent.[24] In comparison with an annual average real growth rate in the prewar period of around 3 percent, postwar economic growth was remarkable.[25]

This rapid economic growth brought about structural changes in the Japanese economy. A particularly noteworthy phase was the development of the consumer durables industry and the entry of large-scale firms into this field. As the manufacturing industries grew, so too did the pace of urbanization. In 1955 over 50 percent of Japan's entire population of 93 million lived in cities, and in 1975 the urban population accounted for 75 percent of the entire population of 111 million. Furthermore, the concentration of population in big cities and their satellite towns is very high in Japan. In 1975 two out of every ten people lived in cities of one million or more, and four out of ten lived in cities of 250,000 or more.[26]

The standard of living rose and the mode of living changed with the rapid economic growth, the evolution of heavy and chemical industries, and the trend to urbanization. Per capita income increased from ¥81,797 in 1955 to ¥265,951 in 1965 and to ¥1,148,034 in 1975. In this same period, real private consumption expenditure also rose from ¥120,319 to ¥242,485 to ¥449,341. Japan also equalized the national income distribution. Changes in the mode of living appeared as a decrease in Engel's coefficient on the one hand, and an increase in expenditure on such things as culture and entertainment on the other. In the late 1960s the percentage increase of the latter rose considerably and the mode of living was diversified.[27] Westernized lifestyles permeated both cities and rural areas, which meant changes in the Japanese value system. In addition to these basic factors, changes in the labor market, popularization of higher education, internationalization and the development of a mass media greatly changed the retail environment.

The Japanese retailing structure had the following features in the mid-1960s, as compared with the United States and Britain. First, the relative importance of chain stores was less than that of department stores in the large-scale retailing sector. Second, small-scale retail outlets accounted for a higher proportion of total retail establishments. Their organization was low, and they showed a trend to increase in contrast with a decrease in other countries.[28] Yet the Japanese retailing structure changed with the growth of new large-scale retailing institutions that emerged because of the social changes from the late 1950s onward. The Japanese retailing sector, as a result, diversified into department stores, supermarket chains, speciality stores, installment-plan department stores and independent retailers (some organized by voluntary chains). In addition, consumer and agricultural cooperatives entered into the mass merchandising field.

It was the department stores and supermarket chains that carried out the leading role in the postwar retailing sector. In the 1970s supermarket chains replaced department stores as the leaders in the retailing sector. Supermarkets based on the self-service and chain-store systems have grown, stressing high volume, low margin, high turnover and limited service. The number of self-service stores increased rapidly from 492 in 1958 to 1,337 in 1960, 4,790 in 1966, 9,403 in 1970, 10,635 in 1972, 12,034 in 1974 and 14,543 in 1976. By 1972 self-service stores accounted for 8.7 percent of the total retail sales, exceeding the share of department stores (8.4 percent).[29] There were, in 1960, only 19 retailing firms whose annual sales volume exceeded ¥6 billion; all of them were department stores. However, by 1970 the number of retailing firms with this same annual sales volume reached 101. Among these firms were 47 department stores, 38 supermarkets, 4 installment-plan department stores and 12 speciality stores.[30] Thus, in a decade or so the emerging large-scale retailing institutions had become a dominant force in the Japanese retailing sector. The following is a review of the postwar evolution of Japanese retailing industries with emphasis on department stores and supermarket chains.

The department stores reached their prewar level in the early 1950s.[31] Thereafter, they rapidly expanded their sales volume and accounted for nearly 10 percent of the total retail sales by around 1960. Department stores during this period tended increasingly to be located in subcenters of large cities and at terminal stations of railroad lines, and an increasing number were local department stores. In terms of merchandise, groceries and household articles increased, while clothing decreased in contrast with the prewar period.[32] During the 1950s the department stores grew with their popularization. As a result, a second Department Store Law was enacted in 1956 as the department stores began to have a strong influence on small retailers. It regulated their operations and placed some restrictions on their future growth.

A typical example that shows the growth of department stores in the 1950s is Isetan. It moved from Kanda to Shinjuku in 1937 and grew rapidly, taking advantage of the geographic shift of population. With the development of Shinjuku as the subcenter of Tokyo, the firm took the one-store principle and developed an aggressive merchandising strategy. It took the initiative in exploiting the youth market, aiming its appeal at the young as well as making efforts to develop original product lines and provide parking facilities. At the same time, the firm insisted on cash transactions.[33]

As department stores grew, innovative retailers appeared who introduced and put into practice new retailing know-how from the United States. The first innovation that they carried out was the adoption of self-service selling techniques. They intended to achieve a large sales volume by reducing prices and stressing large volume, self-service purchasing. The first store operating on a self-service basis was Kinokuniya, which opened at Aoyama in Tokyo in 1953. Although self-service spread to a variety of retailers, it was necessary to adopt modern business administrative systems for the promotion of lower prices and bigger volume of sales.

Between the late 1950s and the early 1960s a definite movement toward the establishment of a new type of large-scale retailing institution based on self-service and chain-store systems began. At the same time, a group of innovative marketers and a few department stores managed by private railroad firms quickly emerged and created a new type of retailing institution. The former include Daiei, Okadaya (a forerunner of Jusco), Izumiya, Ito-Yokado, Nichii, who are the representative supermarket chains at present, while the latter are Toyoko Store (a forerunner of Tokyu) and Seiyu stores. In this period some big trading firms and local department stores also entered into this field.

The greatest innovation in the postwar retailing sector was the emergence of supermarket chains. They succeeded as price-appeal retailers and grew to be full-scale mass merchandisers. Daiei is a typical case: it began in 1957 when Isao Nakauchi, a wholesaler dealing in pharmaceuticals, opened the store, selling such merchandise as cosmetics, canned and bottled groceries and relishes. From 1958 on Daiei began to set up chains and broaden its lines of merchandise, establishing discount retailing to compete with the existing distribution organizations. By 1962 Daiei had six stores with an annual sales volume of ¥10 billion, 12,000 employees, and sales space of 11,550 square meters. The firm set up its head office at Nishinomiya in 1963 and laid the groundwork for future rapid growth.[34]

The number of supermarkets increased rapidly in the late 1950s, but many went bankrupt during the 1965 recession. They experienced another period of rapid growth with the development of the chain-store system during the late 1960s. Branch stores in particular increased rapidly and at the same time grew larger to provide for the influx of foreign capital into the Japanese market with the liberalization of capital transactions. Also, in addition to such lines of merchandise as processed foodstuffs, perishable foods and clothing, they began to carry durable goods at the end of the 1960s. Thus, supermarket chains had taken a firm hold in the Japanese retailing sector by 1970.

Japanese supermarket chains can be categorized into three major types by the different composition of their merchandise. The first type is those that sell mainly food and related products. The second is made up of those whose principal merchandise is clothing and related products. The third consists of those that have well-balanced lines of merchandise, including clothing, cosmetics, household items, and home appliances. The supermarket chains of the third type, or general merchandise stores, achieved a notable growth. Although they are called "super chains" in Japan, this unique type of retailer emerged because supermarkets, chain stores and discount stores that had grown stage by stage in the United States were introduced in Japan at the same time and on a wide basis.[35]

Supermarket chains competed intensely in the 1970s, and as a result, mergers and affiliations began to occur among them.

The first large merger was the establishment of Jusco in 1968 through the combination of three regional chains. Furthermore, not only mergers and affiliations among supermarket chains but also a variety of affiliations between supermarket chains and big trading companies began. Also, from the mid-1970s prominent supermarket chains actively spread to provincial cities and moved towards a formation of networks of national chains. This reflected the fact that metropolitan and provincial markets were becoming the same in character.

As a result of the mergers, the trend toward concentration among larger supermarket chains grew. Supermarket chains then changed their policies and strategies. In terms of the composition of merchandise, the range of clothing, durable consumer goods and leisure articles increased as the stores grew larger. Stores also began to diversify into such retailing industries as speciality stores and convenience stores, into such fields as shopping center development and real estate, and into such leisure-related industries as restaurants and amusement centers.

Supermarket chains continued to struggle with large manufacturers over the price-setting process, and as supermarket chains expanded their lines of merchandise, the tension between them and manufacturers increased. Supermarket chains experienced difficulty at the beginning in buying large manufacturers' products. However, when they had reached the point at which the large manufacturers could not ignore their sales, supermarket chains acted with considerable freedom with regard to price setting. Furthermore, some of them introduced private brands thus increasing their absolute trading volume. When supermarket chains worked with large manufacturers, however, for the development of private brand merchandise, they were given a certain criterion for floor price by the manufacturers. Although supermarket chains also adopted a "dual brand" policy where merchandise bore both the manufacturers' and the retailers' brand names, it was considered a kind of compromise. Some of them began to go a step further by advancing into manufacturing in order to break down this limitation. Nevertheless, it can generally be said that large manufacturers still have the initiative in price setting.

Two types of large-scale retailing institutions, chain-operated, installment-plan department stores and speciality stores, grew with the supermarket chains. The installment-plan department store is a unique retailing institution that specializes in installment credit sales. There are four leading companies in this field. In the prewar period when consumer financing was rudimentary and consumer use of future payment systems was not common, a considerable number of stores were already selling merchandise on installment credit. Some of them set up a new type of installment-plan department store. These grew with the adoption of the chain-store system, the advance into the youth market, and the application of merchandising strategy and advertising adapted to the rising middle class.

A variety of speciality stores also grew to become large-scale retailing institutions with the adoption of the chain-store system. Among them are retailers dealing in a vast volume of standard items and in quality articles or fashionable goods. The former includes electric home appliances, books and pharmaceuticals and the latter includes clothing, boots and shoes. Chains of speciality stores also emerged and grew in such fields as furniture, cameras, watches, precious metals, jewels and glasses.

Department stores, which depended on traditional methods of operation, were slow to respond to the changing environment. As a result, they could not but stand on the defensive with the rapid growth of the mass merchandiser. Major department stores, however, aggressively adopted new policies and strategies to meet the changing conditions. On the one hand, they entered into supermarket operations by setting up subsidiaries, and built permanent self-service corners in their stores on the other. From the mid-1960s they began to expand and improve their main stores, and at the same time shifted to multistore operations by setting up branch stores in suburban areas and provincial cities. They formed cooperative buying groups and worked to develop high-quality, original merchandise lines and also to sell under private brand names. Furthermore, they actively promoted diversification in line with the development of shopping centers, the formation of speciality store chains, the adoption of selling through catalogues by close ties with foreign retailers, and the entry into real estate and leisure-related industries.

As a result of the adoption of these policies, department stores have enjoyed steady development. Their relative importance in the Japanese retailing sector has nevertheless been declining. Although most large department stores entered into supermarket operations by 1970, almost all of them except some "terminal station department stores" could neither adopt new selling and management techniques nor succeed in such operations. Local department stores with fewer managerial resources, in particular, faced a crisis as large department stores, supermarket chains and other mass merchandisers expanded their networks.

New factors worked against the growth of large-scale retailing institutions. One of these was the rise of cooperative department stores, cooperative supermarkets, and voluntary chains organized by small and medium-sized retailers. Another was the introduction of supermarkets operated by consumer and agricultural cooperatives, and franchised chains in the 1970s.

A movement to organize small retailers into cooperatives began through the policy of the Ministry of International Trade and Industry (MITI) in the early 1960s. From the mid-1960s, MITI took particular interest in the development of voluntary chains. In 1970 there were 64 wholesaler-sponsored chains and 55 retailer-sponsored chains (cooperative chains) that belonged to the Japanese Voluntary Chain Association, the national association of voluntary chains; in 1975, there were 62 wholesaler-sponsored chains and 75 retailer-sponsored chains.[36] The latter increased rapidly during this period. Voluntary chains had a total sales volume of some ¥1,000 billion, which accounted for about 10 percent of the total retail sales. There were six voluntary chains whose annual total sales exceeded ¥600 billion.[37] They had, however, some unsettled problems related to a limited managerial ability to take advantage of economies of scale.

Consumer cooperatives accounted for about one percent of the total retail sales by 1970. One of them, the Nada Kobe supermarket chain, comprised fifty-five stores, and its total annual sales were around ¥123 billion. Consumer cooperatives became especially active through the 1970s rise of consumerism, but were subsequently regulated by the Consumer Cooperative Act.[38]

Agricultural cooperatives also entered into supermarket operations to supply a variety of items to farming households. In particular, they have set up full-scale supermarket chains (Co-ops) in various places since 1973. These operations are regulated by the Agricultural Cooperatives Law.[39]

The franchise system was introduced by firms in various fields in the 1960s and has spread rapidly since the end of that decade. It has been estimated that franchise businesses had over 100 individuals with around 15,000 franchise shops and that their total sales volume exceeded ¥100 billion in 1972.[40] The main sectors to adopt the franchise system were restaurants and groceries. In 1976 there were 301 people with 35,475 franchise shops, with sales of ¥1,800 billion.[41] About half of these were restaurants, while clothing stores, supermarkets and convenience stores were also relatively numerous. The franchise system that was introduced into Japan was based on the American model, but modified to give more emphasis to traditional personal relations than to contractual relations.[42]

The Japanese retailing industry diversified considerably and changed structurally in the 1970s. The most fundamental change was the growth of supermarket chains, which were supported by the growing middle class. Initially the government did not regulate their development because of the need for modernizing the distribution sector and for strengthening its international competitive ability, but as their influence on other retailers increased some form of regulation was demanded by small retailers and department stores. The department stores pointed out that although they were of similar scale supermarkets avoided the regulations of the Department Store Law by setting up different corporations on every floor. The Large Scale Retailer Act was thus enacted in 1973 to protect small retailers and consumers and to promote the modernization of the distribution sector. It closed all loopholes so that every large-scale retailer became subject to regulation, also alleviating problems arising from conflicts of interest.

As a result of this Act, the Japanese retailing industry entered a

new phase in which competition among large-scale retailing institutions increased and multiform types of retailing institutions
emerged.

Conclusion

Needless to say, the development of retailing is strongly influenced
by the economic, social and cultural environment and the growth
of the Japanese retailing industry has, therefore, followed the
changing pattern of development of its economy and society. The
Japanese retailing industry started to modernize at the time of the
Meiji Restoration (1868) using the distribution system built in the
Tokugawa era as its basis. Although modernization was slow in
the prewar period, there were many attempts at innovation. While
the industry did not grow rapidly or change structurally until
the postwar period, especially after the 1960s, its ability to adapt
itself had already been shown in the prewar period. It is important
to note that throughout the history of Japanese retailing many
innovations were made by existing retailers, because government
policy was primarily geared towards assisting large-scale manufacturing industries and until recently paid no attention to the
distribution sector. Of course, there were some social policies to
help small merchants.

The new types and techniques that emerged in the Japanese
retailing sector were almost all introduced with foreign, particularly
American, models as their basis. However, if foreign techniques and
institutions could be introduced successfully to a sector powerfully
affected by cultural conditions, the process implies not a simple
imitation, but an adaptation to the new environment. Japanese
retailers were quite successful in modifying foreign techniques and
institutions. Department stores which emerged in the early 1900s
have grown into representative retailing institutions in the cities
and are institutions offering not only shopping comfort but also
cultural facilities. Japanese supermarket chains, which grew rapidly
in the postwar period, took up and reworked different types and
techniques of retailing introduced from foreign countries and,
after an experimental period of trial and error, established themselves.

Modernization in the postwar retailing industry has advanced with the growth of large-scale retailing institutions based on mass production in manufacturing and an orientation towards mass demand and materialistic consumption by consumers.[43] Although larger retailers and more multiform types of retailing emerged through the distribution revolution, the structural characteristics of Japanese society certainly affected their development, as well as that of other retailers.

The growth of new types of large-scale retailing institutions gave rise to severe competition not only among the same type but also among different types of retailers. As a result, individual characteristics became blurred and the operations of the large-scale retailing firms tended to resemble each other. Although they have expanded and adapted themselves to social changes, the conflict between large-scale retailers and large oligopolistic manufacturers over distribution initiative has yet to be solved.

NOTES

1. M. Y. Yoshino, *The Japanese Marketing System: Adaptations and Innovation* (Cambrige, Mass.: The MIT Press, 1971), pp. 10–22.
2. Koji Asada, "Wagakuni oroshisho no kozo to tokucho [Structures and Features of the Japanese Wholesalers]," in: Shoji Murata (ed.), *Nihon no ryutsu kozu* (The Composition of Japan's Distribution Structures) (Tokyo: Zeimu keiri kyokai, 1978), p. 79.
3. Tsusho sangyo sho, ed., *Waga kuni no shogyo, 1977* (Japan's Commerce, 1977) (Tokyo: The Ministry of International Trade and Industry, 1978), pp. 3–18.
4. Tokei kyoku, ed., *Nihon teikoku tokei nenkan, dai 5 kai* (The Japan Imperial Statistical Yearbook, Vol. 5) (Tokyo: Statistics Bureau, 1887).
5. Kazuo Yamaguchi, *Meiji zenki keizai no bunseki* (Analysis of Economy in the Early Meiji Era) (Tokyo: University of Tokyo Press, 1963), pp. 46–47.
6. Nihon kourigyo keiei-shi henshu iinkai, ed., *Nihon kourigyo keiei-shi* (History of the Japan's Retailing Business) (Tokyo: Kokai keiei shido kyokai, 1967), p. 48.
7. *Ibid.*, pp. 52–54.
8. Setsuzan Tani, ed., *Saikin shoko-shi* (History of Recent Industry and

Commerce) (Tokyo: Hochi sha, 1918), pp. 171–172.

9. Chuo-ku, ed., *Chuo-ku-shi* (History of Chuo Ward) (Tokyo: Chuo-ku, 1958), vol. 1, pp. 599–600.

10. Takao Tsuchiya, *Nihon keiei rinen-shi* (History of Japanese Managerial Thought) (Tokyo: Nihon keizai shinbun sha, 1964), p. 170.

11. Hochi sha, ed., *Meiji shoko-shi* (History of Industry and Commerce in the Meiji era) (Tokyo: Shobun do, 1910), pp. 247–252.

12. Junjiro Takahashi, *Mitsukoshi 300-nen no keiei senryaku* (Mitsukoshi's Strategy in the Past Three Hundred Years) (Tokyo: Sankei shinbun sha, 1972), pp. 93–94.

13. Yoshiro Nasu, "Dokusenshihon no shinten to kokuminseikatsu [The Evolution of Monopoly Capital and the People's Livelihood]," in: Shiro Konishi et al., eds., *Seikatsu-shi* (History of Livelihood) (Tokyo: Yamakawa shuppan sha, 1969), vol. 3, p. 246.

14. Hachisaburo Tsukamoto, *Hyakkaten omoide hanashi* (Reminiscences of Department Stores) (Tokyo: Hyakkaten omoidehanashi kanko-kai, 1950), pp. 39–40.

15. Hidemasa Morikawa et al., *Nihon no kigyoka* (3) (Entrepreneurs in Japan, vol. 3) (Tokyo: Yuhikaku, 1978), pp. 113–116.

16. Tokei kyoku, ed., *op. cit.*, vols. 42, 49, 54 (1924, 1930, 1935).

17. Nihon hyakkaten kyokai, *Nihon hyakkaten kyokai 10 nen-shi* (A Ten-year History of the Japan Department Store Association) (Tokyo: The Japan Department Store Association, 1959), p. 7.

18. *Ibid.*, p. 15.

19. Kinichiro Toba, *Nihon no ryutsu kakushin* (The Distribution Revolution in Japan) (Tokyo: Nihon keizai shinbun sha, 1979), p. 100.

20. Yukichi Mizuno, *Hyakkaten ron* (A Theory of Department Stores) (Tokyo: Nihon hyoron sha, 1937), p. 39.

21. Takashimaya Co., Ltd., *Takashimaya 135 nen-shi* (One-hundred-and-thirty-five-year Company History of Takashimaya) (Osaka: Takashimaya Co., Ltd., 1968), pp. 258–259.

22. Nihon kourigyo keiei-shi henshu iinkai, ed., *op. cit.*, pp. 185–193.

23. *Ibid.*, pp. 130–136.

24. Takafusa Nakamura, *Nihon keizai* (Japan's Economy) (Tokyo: University of Tokyo Press, 1978), p. 174.

25. *Ibid.*, p. 17.

26. Toba, *op. cit.*, pp. 111–113.

27. Nakamura, *op. cit.*, p. 210.

28. Keizai shingikai ryutsu kenkyu iinkai, *Korekara no ryutsu* (The Future of Distribution) (Tokyo: Nihon keizai shinbun sha, 1972), p. 68.

29. Tsusho sangyo sho, ed., *op. cit.*, 1965, 1967, 1969, 1971, 1973, 1975, 1977 (1965, 1968, 1970, 1972, 1974, 1976, 1978).
30. Hajime Sato, *Nihon no ryutsukiko* (The Japanese Distribution Structure) (Tokyo: Yuhikaku, 1974), pp. 195–196.
31. Nihon hyakkaten kyokai, *op. cit.*, p. 365.
32. *Ibid.*, p. 367.
33. Takao Tsuchiya, *Nidai kosuge tanji* (A Biography of Tanji Kosuge, Jr. (Nidai)) (Tokyo: Isetan Co., Ltd.) vol. 2, pp. 199–209.
34. Kinichiro Toba, ed., *Ryutsukakumei 20-nen no shomei* (Demonstration of the Distribution Revolution in the Past Twenty Years) (Tokyo: Kokusai shogyo shuppan, 1977), pp. 24–67.
35. Sato, *op. cit.*, pp. 197–198.
36. Takao Iwasawa, "Borantari chein (Voluntary Chains)," in: Murata, ed., *op. cit.*, p. 169.
37. Nihon keizai shinbun sha, ed., *Ryutsu keiei no tebiki, 1978* (A Guide to the Economy of Distribution, 1978) (Tokyo: Nihon keizai shinbun sha, 1977), p. 104.
38. Toichiro Miyakawa et al., *Shin ryutsu sangyo* (New Distribution Industries) (Tokyo: Toyo keizai shinpo sha, 1972), pp. 126–134.
39. *Ibid.*, pp. 134–139.
40. Nihon keizai shinbun sha, ed., *op. cit.*, 1974 (1973), p. 168.
41. Ken Yamazaki, "Furanchaizu chein (Franchise Chains)," in: Murata, ed., *op. cit.*, p. 200.
42. Thomas Sakamoto, *Furanchaizu chein* (Franchise Chain) (Tokyo: Nihon keizai shinbun sha, 1973), p. 199.
43. Cf. Yoshino, *op. cit.*, pp. 78–81.

REFERENCES

M. Y. Yoshino, *The Japanese Marketing System: Adataptions and Innovation* (Cambridge, Mass.: The MIT Press, 1971).
Kinichiro Toba, *Nihon no ryutsu kakushin* (The Distribution Revolution in Japan) (Tokyo: Nihon keizai shinbun sha, 1979).
Hajime Sato, *Nihon no ryutsukiko* (The Japanese Distribution Structure) (Tokyo: Yuhikaku, 1974).
Johannes Hirschmeier and Tsunehiko Yui, *The Development of Japanese Business 1600–1973* (London: George Allen & Unwin Ltd., 1975).
Kazutoshi Maeda, "Maketingu [Marketing]," in: Keiichiro Nakagawa, ed., *Nihonteki keiei* (Japanese Management) (Tokyo: Nihon keizai shinbun sha, 1977), pp. 159–183.

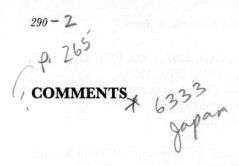

COMPONENTS

Jong Won Lim
Seoul National University

Professor Maeda describes very clearly the historical processes of retail evolution in the Japanese distribution structure over the last hundred years.

He traces the three different types of power loci which designed new channel networks in order to overcome the inherent weaknesses of traditional channels. Large-scale manufacturing firms have integrated their channel members to obtain systemic economies since the 1950s. Innovative retailers were another power locus to set up modern enterprises in the retail sector. They operationalized the marketing concept in retail activities by introducing innovative methods of offering good products at low prices. These innovators developed department stores, discount houses, supermarket chains, and several types of mass merchandising institutions which have utilized multistore/multiplex marketing strategies. Contractual vertical marketing systems have appeared in response to the above two patterns of channel organization. They include wholesaler-sponsored voluntary groups, retailer-sponsored cooperative groups, franchise systems, and consumer cooperatives.

If the policy of cash payment, low prices, and no mark-ups was the major concept of innovative retailers, the retail revolution could be explained by the wheel of retailing hypotheses. In terms of width of product line, the accordion hypothesis also provides a powerful model to describe institutional changes in retail industries.

The author examines how each retail institution interacts and changes with respect to its changing environment, such as new urban formation along with rapid economic growth, the movement of population, distribution of income, changing lifestyle, and technology of communication. It is indicated that retailers have been capable of adapting creatively to a changing environment over the last hundred years of retail evolution.

However, there seems to be a vacuum in the modern retailers' coverage of the market. Why should there exist such characteristics as complicated trade practices and complex and circuitous channel structures? A number of small retail establishments may reflect the intensive distribution networks for convenience goods. Is there any systemwide orientation or inclusive goal among these establishments? If the Japanese retailing sector lagged far behind the manufacturing sector in its modernization, as mentioned by the author, the dysfunctional effects of these independently owned and managed establishments might well be analyzed in more detail.

In his historical analysis of retail evolution, the author also explains the changing emphasis on the functions of retailing over the last hundred years for each different type of retail institution. The paper briefly describes several methods of pricing, merchandising, advertising and service practiced by successful retail institutions.

In the course of retail evolution, there must have been various kinds of channel conflict among channel members. The existence of conflict is both dysfunctional and functional in achieving systemic economies of a distribution structure. The author mentions such specific areas as entrepreneurship among retailers and several laws (Department Store Laws and the Large Scale Retailers Act) passed to resolve or regulate conflict arising between different types of retail institutions.

Further analysis on the following questions might also have offered a valuable perspective on the underlying processes of the evolution of the Japanese retail industries. What have been the major sources of conflict between traditional retailers and modern retail institutions? What are the nature and scope of the laws in retail revolution? Is it possible to derive any strategies of conflict management from the practices of the leading retail institutions?

It may, however, be beyond the scope of the paper to discuss the changing hierarchical structure of market institutions, the efficiency of the retail sector, the concentration of economic power, competitiveness, and retailing as part of a channel structure. Retailing is nowadays regarded as an important function of urban

formation. Some of the complex traffic flows and urban migrations
are generated by the spatial locations of different market institutions. Theories of urban market development would have to include
an analysis of retailing in central city environments. Some of the
leading authors in this area include W. Applebaum, P.D. Converse,
D. L. Thompson, D. L. Huff, and J. B. Mason. Future research
on these perspectives may be very useful in evaluating retailing in
various urban situations.

Nevertheless, Professor Maeda's paper efficiently provides readers
with valuable insights into the future of the Japanese retail industries.

SUMMARY OF CONCLUDING DISCUSSION

53/10
6/30 N A

Koichi Shimokawa

In opening the final discussion, Koichi Shimokawa, the project leader, raised a number of discussion points based on the suggestions of the conference participants. The various papers in the conference had highlighted the historical trends and special features of the automobile industry in several countries, with special reference to the development of retailing and marketing in industrialized countries. The discussion focused on the following points:

1) What are the unique features of automobile marketing and its historical development, compared with other products?

2) Which characteristics of automobile marketing can be considered general and which are unique to a particular country? How can the differences be accounted for?

   a) How do the different channels of automobile distribution practiced by, e.g. Volkswagen, Benz or Toyota, compare with the U.S. system?

   b) Was the U.S. franchise system introduced directly into each country or was it modified, and if so, how?

   c) What differences were there in the operational process of the franchise system (e.g. used car policy, rebate, discount, dealer help, and so on) and why?

   d) What were the special characteristics of the dealer in each country? If there were dealer or repair workshop organizations or associations, what were their regulations and bargaining power?

3) How was commerce traditionally carried out in each country? How did this affect the distribution structure and introduction of modern marketing techniques?

4)   What were the historical developmental and changing patterns of the automobile market in each country?
  a)   What is the definition of a mature market? What are its
       criteria: a mass market for popular cars, the rate of car
       ownership, personal income level and car price, replace-
       ment demand, demand for a second or third car?
  b)   How does the rural vs. urban market dichotomy affect
       marketing policy in each country? What are the effects of
       perceived income level, status or occupational group and so
       forth?
  c)   How is the mature market cycle of a particular country
       affected by international considerations?
5)   What is the impact of changing technology, customers'
requirements and automobile category on a car's life cycle?
6)   What are the different attitudes and techniques of a tech-
nological-and production-oriented entrepreneur, as compared
with a marketing-oriented entrepreneur: e.g. Ford vs. General
Motors, Austin vs. Morris, Citroën vs. Renault? How do they
view each other?

Shimokawa's paper described U.S. automobile marketing, using
Sloan's General Motors' case as a typical example in the 1920s.
He described modern marketing as a systematized integration
of marketing techniques, the most important being sales forecasting
and production schedule. This model was transferred or introduced into other countries, but as each country, whether industrialized or relatively undeveloped, had its own characteristic distribution and retailing structure, it thus developed its unique pattern,
passing through different stages according to its different situation,
government policy, customers' requirements and so on. The problems faced in the attempt to internationalize U.S. automobile
marketing and modify it for each country were reviewed in an
international comparison.

After posing the six primary questions which had emerged from
the conference, Shimokawa opened the final discussion by showing
a chart contrasting traditional commerce and modern marketing
from a general standpoint. He showed that in traditional commerce there are a large number of small firms and a correspondingly

CHART   **Simple description of Traditional Commerce vs. Modern Marketing**

Coordinating flow of material/Risk-taking on sales activity	
Traditional Commerce	Modern Marketing

—Domestic Situation—

Traditional Commerce	Modern Marketing
○ Objective Structure	○ Direct or Conscious Activity
○ Large Number of Small Firms	○ Big Manufacturers or Mass Retailers
○ Distribution Outlet (Complicated)	○ Channel (Simple)
Wholesalers ⎰Collection of Goods, (Middle- ⎪Classification, men) ⎱Evaluation, Stock, ⎪Financing, ⎪Distri- ⎩bution ⎰Physical ⎱Ownership	Selected or Organized Channel —Dealer Diminishing or Eliminating Middlemen
Specialization in Each Commodity Item Separation of Vertical Steps Dispersion of Risk-taking	Two Ways— ⎰German Way ⎪(Cartel) ⎱American Way ⎩(Marketing)
○ Large Number of Small Retailers	○ Small Number of Big Manufacturers or Mass Retailers
○ Scattered Consumers Division of High-class and Popular Market	○ Mass Market ⎰Comparative Homogenous ⎱ Market ⎩Popular Market

—International Situation—

Traditional Commerce	Modern Marketing
○ Higher Proportion Relatively Large Firms, Greater Sophistication	○ Multinational Enterprise Overseas Agent Overseas Sales Branch
○ Trading Firm ⎰Specialization ⎱General	Overseas Manufacturing Plant
○ Merchant Bank	○ Organized International Money
○ International Distribution Structure	Market, and International Financial Institution
○ World Trade Market under Invisible Hand	○ Logistics Planning (Worldwide)
Worldwide Scattered and Specialized Market	○ World Trade Market Under Visible Hand
Market Barrier due to Traditional Cultural Background	Worldwide Mass Market Worldwide Market Segmentation Worldwide Product Life Cycle Transfer of Lifestyle

large number of small retailers, serving a scattered market; thus the function of the wholesaler (middleman) tends to be very important. However, in modern marketing a limited number of big manufacturers, distributors and retailers serve a comparatively homogeneous mass market, and the role of the middleman tends to diminish. The channels of distribution are therefore simplified and the typical selected or organized channel is the dealer.

He stressed that although in the historical development of automobile marketing the wholesaler as such is eliminated, the function remains, to be taken over by the maker and/or the dealer. How is this function to be divided and who should take the risks associated with wholesaling? The maker cannot wholly abolish the dealer as some sort of buffer is needed to share the distribution risk. Shimokawa raised these questions and then showed that the franchise system created the conditions for some sort of compromise by installing distributors with the characteristics of independent business entities, which are nevertheless controlled to some degree by the maker and maker's standards.

Focusing on Shimokawa's chart, Professor Wilkins then pointed out that it concentrated on the domestic conditions of commerce and modern marketing, and suggested that it ought to be extended to cover the international situation, where a complete transformation from traditional commerce to modern marketing has not yet occurred. She gave the example of multinational enterprises which continue to have their overseas agents or sales branch, even when they build a manufacturing plant in the recipient country.

Professor Church emphasized that each country has its different definition of market structure and also argued that it was necessary to consider the high-class and popular car markets separately as they have very different characteristics. Wilkins added that traditional commerce tended to correspond to the high-class luxury market, while mass marketing techniques corresponded to the popular market.

Professor Fridenson argued that in France commerce and marketing have tended to develop in parallel and that from the beginning there have been many types of car distribution systems incorporating a direct distribution channel and using wholesalers. He emphasized that this was similar to the practices in Germany and quite different from those in the United States.

Referring to commerce and marketing in Korea, Professor Lim emphasized the importance of Shimokawa's third discussion point for industrializing countries. He showed that in Korea traditional commerce and modern marketing techniques coexisted, partly because the government had encouraged big distribution institutions in and around the cities to serve the growing urban society, while managing to prevent any major conflict with the small retail sector which continued to use traditional techniques. So far, this coexistence has been successful, but Lim also pointed out that retailing productivity in the distribution sector was increasingly becoming a problem in the industrialization of less developed countries such as Korea.

Thus it was shown that the different historical and national conditions influenced the relationship between traditional commerce and modern marketing in each country, and that this in turn affected the development of automobile marketing, as an example of typical modern marketing techniques.

The discussion then turned to consider the unique features of automobile marketing. Many people emphasized the important role of maintenance and after-sales service. Professor Blaich explained that one reason why the prewar motorcycle dealers in Germany had had difficulty organizing after-sales service was that their product was technologically complicated. In the early stages of organizing a dealer network, therefore, the motorcycle manufacturers often cooperated with agricultural machine or tractor dealers, establishing a mutually profitable business relationship with them, as shown in Professor Livesay's paper. Blaich went on to suggest that part of Volkswagen's postwar success could be attributed to the importance it attached to maintenance and after-sales service, and that even in recent times Japanese auto makers in Germany asked the tractor dealers for assistance in after-sales service.

Supplementing Blaich's remarks, Professor Udagawa mentioned a case in prewar Japan when imported cars from Western countries were at first distributed by *Shōsha* (general trading companies), but as they couldn't give after-sales service they eventually had to give up importing cars altogether. *Shōsha* were then replaced by independent, specialized import-car dealers such as Yanase and Nihonjidōsha, which could and did give after-sales service. Professor Daito supported Udagawa's contention that *Shōsha* had been able to give good market information but had failed because of the inability to give after-sales service to car buyers. Adding a British perspective, Church told how in the early days when imported cars were being introduced in the U.K. the British importers built a local plant to provide quick after-sales service. Professor Livesay then pointed out that the Japanese agricultural machine manufacturer, Kubota, has been selling its tractors in the U.S.A. for some time through local American auto dealers. Finally, Lim summarized the above discussion and emphasized the changing role of the dealer in the maker-dealer relationship, especially in the sphere of expensive maintenance activity.

Shimokawa suggested that they should look at the special features of the dealer's role in each country. To illustrate his point, he showed that the relationship between dealer and repair shop differed greatly between Japan and the United States. In the U.S. the dealer and repair shop function independently towards the auto maker and the extent of their activities is prescribed by law. In Japan, however, there is a close relationship between auto maker, dealer and repair shop. All of the dealers and almost all of the repair shops are organized by a particular auto maker's group. This kind of interdependent relationship is found not only in the maintenance field, but in sales financing as well.

Responding to Shimokawa's suggestion, most of the participants then examined and explained the maker-dealer-repair shop relationship in their countries. Livesay stated that in the U.S. the automobile has historically been indispensable for popular transportation and that maintenance and repair servicing has therefore been indispensable to the sales function. He claimed that the exclusive franchise system arose out of the need for a reliable system of after-sales service, but that when legal regulations prohibited the exclusive franchise, the repair shop emerged independently to fill the gap.

Fridenson argued that in France a distinction has to be made between domestic and import-car dealers: the import-car dealer has not generally provided after-sales service, while the domestic makers have supplied the dealers with trained mechanics to give maintenance and repair servicing. In addition, the automobile is not so indispensable to the French as it is to the Americans, and therefore most French dealers run a rental car service to supplement their sales function. Church said that the relationship between dealer and repair shop in Britain closely resembles that in France, but without any rental service by dealers. He also mentioned that there are several types of dealership in Britain, ranging from exclusive franchise to dealers which act as agents for several different manufacturers' vehicles.

Lim told the conference that Korean dealers lack a specific franchise system because they do not yet have a contract system. Accordingly, the main revenue for Korean dealers comes from maintenance and repair servicing, because commission on the sale of new cars is so low. Thus there is a very close relationship between dealer and repair shop.

Blaich commented that in Germany the auto maker has full control over the dealer's maintenance and repair service, even fixing the price the dealer may ask for servicing. The dealer retains only the right to set the price of used cars.

Professor Maeda questioned Fridenson about the retailer's service function in France, asking if a retailer who handles about 30 percent of the sales volume of a particular manufacturer has a service function or not. Fridenson replied that in this case the service function would belong to the manufacturer's branch or subsidiary dealer. Relating to this, Professor Nakagawa and Professor Okochi made comparisons with the electrical appliance retail situation. Nakagawa stressed that in Japan there is a powerful exclusive franchise system joining electrical appliance marketing and repair servicing, similar to that found in automobile marketing. Okochi pointed out that this role of the exclusive franchise in electrical appliance marketing has been decreasing as big supermarkets and discount houses become increasingly important. Wilkins contrasted this with American and British practice, where there is no exclusive franchise on electrical appliances.

After discussing some of the special features of the automobile

dealer system, Wilkins raised questions about the levels of auto
sales financing in different countries. She argued that in the U.S.
and Japan auto sales financing has historically been high, whereas
in France it has been low. She asked for information of sales financing in Germany and for a description of its specific features in Japan.
Blaich explained that in Germany the big banks had historically
played a major role in financing consumers through their credit
services, so that when Opel (GM) tried to institute sales financing
it came up against the strong opposition of the big banks. Shimokawa explained two of the special features of sales financing in Japan,
also emphasizing that developments were dependent upon the
particular conditions pertaining at a particular time. After the
war, especially in the period from 1950 to 1965, the Japanese auto
manufacturers and motor sales companies had to provide sales credit
services themselves, because the Japanese banks did not consider
loans for automobiles as a financing priority. (Recently, however,
the Japanese banks have been making credit loans available to car
dealers and buyers, and it remains to be seen how this will affect
sales financing by dealers.) Secondly, he explained the function of
the motor sales company, which combines the functions of sales
financing with wholesaler. Auto manufacturers without an attached
motor sales company, such as Nissan, have themselves taken on
these dual functions. Thus sales financing has been a very important
component of the maker-dealer relationship. Concerning this, he
also highlighted the informal but very close relationship which
arises through the maker's sales financing function and the dealer's
stock control. In Japan, the auto franchise agreement was almost
the same as GM's 1925 agreement, but its usual operation is considerably different; for example, in the Japanese franchise agreement
there is no detailed legal description about dealer stock, but the
maker and dealer always consult each other about trends and
forecasts for the market, especially in the short run. If there is a
tendency, for example, for the dealer to overstock, then the maker
and dealer will negotiate to redress the balance. Therefore, although
the Japanese franchise agreement may appear to be fairly loosely
defined in terms of legal obligation, in practice the relationship
between maker and dealer is enforced by custom and personal
relations, which in Japan are well defined and morally binding.

Professor Yuzawa then developed the discussion along another plane by reiterating Livesay's hypothesis that the franchise system, which had been developed specifically to fit the U.S. situation, selected a "face" or mode of operations suitable to each country; he asked how the appropriate face was selected and what its features were in each case. Addressing this question, Church summarized the European experience, where the American franchise system either adapted itself to cultural differences or failed. Ford in Britain first failed because it tried to impose the American system directly, without modifications, whereas VW's Nordhoff, when he was manager of Opel, was successful because he didn't try to introduce GM's franchise system directly, but recognized its limitations where the German market was concerned. Blaich, Fridenson and Lim all made contributions which supported Church's thesis.

The final discussion concerned the definition of a mature market. Church stated that his concept of a mature market was related to his definition of demand. He defined separately initial demand and mature demand, and agreed with Professor Yamazaki that different modes of innovation corresponded to each. Product innovation corresponded to initial demand and process innovation to mature demand. Where product innovation becomes diffused, as in auto standardization, it is replaced by process innovation. The intersection of the two types of innovation corresponds to the point of interception of mature demand and initial demand. He further argued that market maturity must be defined for each product and can be evaluated using income and price elasticity of demand. Wilkins pointed out that with respect to developing product improvement and standardization, an international mature market is already arising.

Lim explained his concept of the mature market by referring to his table describing a product life cycle model from the international point of view. The participants at the conference were not able to come to complete agreement on a definition of the mature market, although the very interesting discussion confirmed where the problems lie.

Although limitations of time meant that the conference was not able to clarify and thrash out all the points raised in the papers and discussions, many important aspects of marketing history, especially

in the automobile industry, were explored and the varying stand-
points contributed to a very stimulating and fruitful conference.

INDEX